READING AND WRITING DURING THE DISSOLUTION

In the years from 1534 when Henry VIII became head of the English church until the end of Mary Tudor's reign in 1558, the forms of English religious life evolved quickly and in complex ways. At the heart of these changes stood the country's professed religious men and women, whose institutional homes were closed between 1535 and 1540. Records of their reading and writing offer a remarkable view of these turbulent times. The responses to religious change of friars, anchorites, monks, and nuns from London and the surrounding regions are shown through chronicles, devotional texts, and letters. What becomes apparent is the variety of positions that English religious men and women took up at the Reformation and the accommodations that they reached, both spiritual and practical. Of particular interest are the extraordinary letters of Margaret Vernon, head of four nunneries and personal friend of Thomas Cromwell.

MARY C. ERLER is a professor in the English department at Fordham University, New York, and is the author of *Women, Reading, and Piety in Late Medieval England* (Cambridge, 2002).

Frontispiece: From *Memoirs of the Antiquities of Great Britain*, 1723.

READING AND WRITING DURING THE DISSOLUTION

Monks, Friars, and Nuns 1530–1558

MARY C. ERLER

CAMBRIDGE
UNIVERSITY PRESS

CAMBRIDGE
UNIVERSITY PRESS

University Printing House, Cambridge CB2 8BS, United Kingdom

Cambridge University Press is part of the University of Cambridge.

It furthers the University's mission by disseminating knowledge in the pursuit of education, learning and research at the highest international levels of excellence.

www.cambridge.org
Information on this title: www.cambridge.org/9781316601938

© Mary C. Erler 2013

First published 2013
First paperback edition 2015

A catalogue record for this publication is available from the British Library

Library of Congress Cataloguing in Publication data
Erler, Mary Carpenter.
Reading and writing during the dissolution : monks, friars, and nuns 1530–1558 / Mary C. Erler.
pages cm
Includes bibliographical references and index.
ISBN 978-1-107-03979-7
1. England–Church history–16th century.   2. Henry VIII, King of England, 1491–1547.   3. Mary I, Queen of England, 1516–1558.   4. Books and reading–England–History–16th century.   5. Christian literature, English–Sources.   I. Title.
BR756.E75 2013
271.00942′09031–dc23
2013000792

ISBN 978-1-107-03979-7 Hardback
ISBN 978-1-316-60193-8 Paperback

Additional resources for this publication at www.cambridge.org/Erler

Time with its Iron Teeth devours all,
And Time will come when ye last Trump shall call.
That erring Man shall know, & stand the Test
Of what Religions in this World were best.
Memoirs of the Antiquities of Great Britain, 1723

Contents

Illustrations

Acknowledgments

Some of the material in Chapter 1, on Simon Appulby, appeared previously in "A London Anchorite, Simon Appulby: His *Fruyte of Redempcyon* and Its Milieu," *Viator* 29 (1998), 227–39. An earlier version of Chapter 5 was published as "The Effects of Exile on English Monastic Spirituality: William Peryn's *Spirituall Exercyses*," *Journal of Medieval and Early Modern Studies* 42.3 (2012), 519–37.

I am grateful for particular suggestions and for long-term support to a number of friends: Nancy Bradley Warren, David Wallace and Rita Copeland, Sheila Lindenbaum, Martin Chase, SJ, and Maryanne Kowaleski. Fordham University has generously provided research support of several kinds.

In the sixteenth-century material quoted, spelling has been modernized except for surnames of individuals and for titles of published works, which retain their original forms.

Abbreviations

AC	J. A. and J. Venn, *Alumni Cantabrigienses: A Biographical List of All Known Students, Graduates and Holders of Office at the University of Cambridge from the Earliest Times to 1900, Part I (to 1751)*, 4 vols., Cambridge, 1922–27
Bindoff, *House of Commons*	S. T. Bindoff, *The House of Commons 1509–1558*, 3 vols., London, 1982
BL	British Library
BRUC	A. B. Emden, *A Biographical Register of the University of Cambridge to 1500*, Cambridge, 1963
BRUO	A. B. Emden, *A Biographical Register of the University of Oxford to A.D. 1500*, 3 vols., Oxford, 1957, 1958, 1959
BRUO 1501–1540	A. B. Emden, *A Biographical Register of the University of Oxford A.D. 1501 to 1540*, Oxford, 1974
Cook, *Letters*	G. H. Cook (ed.), *Letters to Cromwell and Others on the Suppression of the Monasteries*, London, 1965
CP	G. E. C. (ed.), *The Complete Peerage*, 13 vols. in 14, London, 1910–49
CPL	William Henry Bliss *et al.* (eds.), *Calendar of Entries in the Papal Registers Relating to Great Britain and Ireland: Papal Letters*, 12 vols., London, 1893–1933
CPMR	Philip E. Jones (ed.), *Calendar of Plea and Memoranda Rolls Preserved among the Archives of the Corporation of the City of London at the Guildhall A.D. 1458–1482*, 6 vols., Cambridge, 1961
CUL	Cambridge University Library
Dugdale, *Monasticon*	William Dugdale, *Monasticon Anglicanum*, 8 vols., London, 1817–30

EEBO	Early English Books Online: http://eebo.chad-wyck.com/home
EETS	Early English Text Society
Ellis	Henry Ellis (ed.), *Original Letters Illustrative of English History*, 3rd ser. 4 vols., London, 1846
Green, *Letters*	Mary Anne Everett Wood Green (ed.), *Letters of Royal and Illustrious Ladies of Great Britain*, 3 vols., London, 1846
ISTC	Incunabula Short Title Catalogue: www.bl.uk/catalogues/istc/index.html
JEH	*Journal of Ecclesiastical History*
Kingsford, *Stow*	C. L. Kingsford (ed.), *John Stow's Survey of London*, 2 vols., London, 1972
L&MCC	C. J. Kitching (ed.), *London and Middlesex Chantry Certificate, 1548*, London Record Society 16, London, 1986
LMA	London Metropolitan Archive
LP	J. S. Brewer *et al.* (eds.), *Letters and Papers, Foreign and Domestic, of the Reign of Henry VIII*, 22 vols. in 38, London, 1862–1932
ODNB	*Oxford Dictionary of National Biography*, Oxford University Press: www.oxforddnb.com
PCC	Prerogative Court of Canterbury
Smith, *Heads*	David M. Smith (ed.), *Heads of Religious Houses England and Wales, Vol. III: 1377–1540*, Cambridge, 2009
STC	*A Short-Title Catalogue of Books Printed in England, Scotland & Ireland and of English Books Printed Abroad 1475–1640*, A. W. Pollard and G. R. Redgrave, 2nd edn. rev. and enlarged, W. A. Jackson, F. S. Ferguson, K. F. Pantzer, 3 vols., London, 1976–91
TNA	The National Archives
TRP	Paul L. Hughes and James F. Larkin (eds.), *Tudor Royal Proclamations*, 3 vols., New Haven and London, 1964–69
VCH	*Victoria History of the Counties of England*
Wright, *Suppression*	Thomas Wright (ed.), *Three Chapters of Letters Relating to the Suppression of Monasteries*, Camden Society 26, London, 1843

Introduction

"My dere doghter Venus," quod Saturne,
"My cours, that hath so wyde for to turne,
Hath more power than wot any man ...
Myn is the ruine of the hye halles,
The falling of the toures and of the walles ..."
Chaucer, "Knight's Tale," ll. 2453–55, 2463–64

From 1534, when the Act of Supremacy was passed and Henry VIII became head of the English Church, until the end of Mary's reign in 1558 – approximately a quarter-century – the forms of English religious life evolved in newly complex directions. The frequency with which religious and social positions shifted, the fleeting duration of these positions, the resultant somewhat unfocused nature of personal belief, and the conflicts between friends and family have been widely noticed. In the comprehensiveness of these changes, it may have seemed to many that the planetary power of Saturn, with its destructive and sinister aspect, was in the ascendant.

The complexity of England's religious situation has made these years intriguing ones for modern scholars. It has stimulated efforts to trace a process of cultural accommodation widely agreed to be subtle, partial, gradual, and often surprising. Ethan Shagan, for instance, has called the Reformation "a piecemeal process in which politics and spiritual change are irrevocably intertwined" and speaks of "the majority who never wholly accepted nor wholly opposed the reformation."[1] At the heart of these changes stood the country's professed religious, male and female, all of whose institutional homes had been closed during the five years between 1535 and 1540. Their responses to religious change might be counted as fluid as those of their lay counterparts. For them, too, in Peter Marshall's words, "formations of religious identity ... were fundamentally dialectical

[1] Ethan H. Shagan, *Popular Politics and the English Reformation* (Cambridge, 2003), p. 7.

processes."[2] One way of assessing the complexity of this time is to look at their situation, and particularly at their writing and reading.

The starting point of this book has been bibliographical. All of the chapters but one began as bibliographical problems, but I have regularly thought of bibliography as a way of exploring lives – and so in what follows, bibliography finds itself in the service of biography. Both these disciplines, in turn, make their contribution to the social and religious history of a period narrowly outlined but satisfying to examine because of the rich diversity of the material it displays. If it is impossible to delimit a characteristic stance for an English religious in this quarter-century, the accounts that follow are broadly enough based to claim what might be called the authority of the vignette. The religious persons viewed here come from London and the regions and from various kinds of religious life: a friar, an anchorite, a monk, and several nuns. Indeed, the intentional pursuit of both men's and women's reading and writing broadens the sense at least of the rather different practical choices available to male and female ex-religious – if it does not differentiate them theologically.

Several written genres have been used: a chronicle, devotional texts, letters. The results are diverse and one of the results of this investigation is to show the variety of stances that English religious espoused at the Reformation and the accommodations that they evolved. Examining their writing and reading under Henry VIII, Edward VI, and Mary provides a vivid sense of the diverse alternatives that monks and nuns shared with their lay brethren during this complex time. Sometimes it is possible to see in the reading and writing of these years hints as to a future direction. Equally compelling, however, is a simple apprehension of the intellectual and social complexity produced by religious change for those most formally affiliated with the institutional church.

Some traces remain of religious men's and women's reading in the years just before the dissolution of the monasteries; reading that now might seem questioning, if not controversial. The variety of positions so characteristic of life in the 1530s and after was present as well during the years immediately preceding the dissolution. Famously, the last abbess of Denny, Elizabeth Throckmorton, in 1528 asked the wealthy London merchant Humphrey Monmouth for a copy of William Tyndale's translation

---

[2] Quoted in Ethan H. Shagan (ed.), *Catholics and the "Protestant Nation": Religious Politics and Identity in Early Modern England* (Manchester, 2005), p. 42.

of Erasmus's *Enchiridion*, which he provided. Monmouth asserted that this best-selling work, which condemned the greed and corruption of the Church and called for a reformed religious life, was orthodox enough, seeing that it was owned by John Fisher and read by Syon's confessor-general.[3] Similarly, in 1525 Syon received sixty copies of the *Ymage of Loue*, an attempt from within the church to re-think the use of images, written by Observant Franciscan friar John Ryckes. Like Erasmus's work, it inveighed against external forms and emphasized the centrality of scripture – though it cautioned "we may not leave off the honourable and devout customs and holy ordinances of the church" [E 3v].[4] Both these examples of reading might be understood as springing from a wish to participate in the period's re-examination of spiritual life. In the criticism of both authors, Erasmus and Ryckes, cultural matters – "observances" – loom as large as theological or religious ones; or, perhaps more accurately, cultural matters like images or processions are seen to reflect a larger position in need of refreshment.

The cultural changes that accompanied religious shifts are visible throughout this book, but are nowhere more arresting than in the life and writing of Simon Appulby, London's last anchorite and the subject of the book's first chapter. Appulby was the author/translator of *Fruyte of Redempcyon*, a series of meditations on Christ's Passion that he first published in 1514 and 1517. The book carries an endorsement by Bishop of London Richard Fitzjames and hence recalls a parallel effort just a hundred years earlier when, in 1410, Nicholas Love received the formal approval of Thomas Arundel, Archbishop of Canterbury, for the transmission of his similar meditative work, *The Myrrour of the Blessed Life of Jesus Chryst*. Both Appulby's book and Love's book were successful attempts to bring scripturally based devotion to a wide audience. Arundel's sponsorship of Love's work is generally seen as an effort to mobilize the Church's traditional educative resources against the threat of Lollardy in the early fifteenth century, and at the opening of the sixteenth century Lollardy was again (or still) a matter of concern for the London episcopate. Drawing upon Bishop Fitzjames's register and notes from his lost court book, Susan Brigden cites the testimony of about forty City Lollards who were detected

---

[3] John Strype, *Ecclesiastical Memorials Relating Chiefly to Religion, and the Reformation of It, and the Emergencies of the Church of England, under King Henry VIII, King Edward VI and Queen Mary I*, 6 vols. (Oxford, 1822), I, pt. 2, no. 89.

[4] The text of *Ymage of Loue* is printed as Appendix A and discussed by E. Ruth Harvey in T. M. C. Lawler, G. Marc'hadour, and R. C. Marius (eds.), *The Complete Works of St. Thomas More* (New York and London, 1981), VI, pt. 2.

The Lollards are still very active while Fruyte is written

and who abjured between 1510 and 1518 – the years when *Fruyte* was first published.[5]

Appulby's book had a second flourishing as well: three editions appeared in 1530, 1531, and 1532, and since 1530 marks the accession of John Stokesley as Bishop of London another episcopal initiative seems likely, especially since Stokesley was a notable conservative. Erudite, scholastic (he deeply admired Duns Scotus), and severe in his pursuit of heretics, Stokesley explicitly opposed lay access to scripture in English. It thus seems likely that the five editions of Appulby's *Fruyte of Redempcyon* were part of a mustering of traditional resources in order to bring scripture in supervised form to an ever-widening audience, an audience that the technology of printing could increase still further. *Fruyte of Redempcyon* represented orthodoxy's best efforts in the years just before the Reformation, the kind of initiative that had achieved remarkable success in the past.

But Appulby died in 1537, in the midst of the five-year period when England's religious houses were being closed one by one. Though he was a priest, Appulby's affiliation was not with a religious house but with the poor London parish where he lived and served: All Hallows London Wall. Like the monasteries and friaries that passed into secular use, Appulby's living space, the anchorhold on the city wall, became a piece of secular patronage and about a year after his death was given to a member of the Mayor of London's staff.

Appulby's realization that both his vocation and its shelter might not endure is clear in his will, which leaves the books and vestments in his anchorhold to his successor. The will adds, however, that if a successor is not appointed in a year and a day, the items shall be disposed by the anchorite's executor. Appulby's London neighborhood itself had been subject to massive alteration: the local priory that held the advowson of Appulby's anchorhold, Holy Trinity, was the first religious institution in the country to close, in 1532. This experience of change might be thought to identify Appulby as a backward-looking figure, as his historic vocation of anchoritism could no longer be sustained. His *Fruyte of Redempcyon*, offering a traditional mediated approach to scripture as productive of an affective relation to Christ, now seemed culturally out of favor as well. Yet an intense meditative focus on the Passion would be an element in the developing Ignatian spirituality of the next decade, the 1540s – an element that would continue to influence the spirituality of English men and women in the next century.

---

[5] Susan Brigden, *London and the Reformation* (Oxford, 1989), p. 87.

Her examples highlight the fact that not all of the clergy would feel the same.

Appulby's sympathies seem to have lain entirely with traditional beliefs and structures, but for others, loyalties were divided. The degree to which English religious were sympathetic to reform is so large a subject that scholars have found it difficult to do more than gesture toward individual cases. Certainly the letters these religious sent to Thomas Cromwell, effectively their overseer during the 1530s, contain several powerful conservative statements on the value of institutional religious life. John Shepey, Abbot of Faversham, Kent, explains that if an abbot's duties be considered to consist of property supervision, his age might disqualify him but "if the chief office and profession of an abbot be (as I have ever taken it)" to live chaste and solitary, to serve God quietly, to relieve the poor and have a vigilant eye to the good order and rule of a house, he is "as well able yet now to supply and continue these parts as ever I was."[6] Shepey is defending his decision to continue in place, though advanced in years, but his statement serves as a broader apologia for the system of which he was a part. In a much humbler vein, Jane Messyndyne, Prioress of Legbourne, wrote Cromwell: "Ye shall hear no complaints against us neither in our living nor hospitality keeping."[7]

But such unequivocal expressions occur side by side with more compromised statements and we might wonder about the effect of these powerful changes on the final years of conventual life, given the possibility – indeed the documented reality – of conflict within individual houses. Such conflict is particularly visible at the moment of the successful administration of the Act of Supremacy in late 1534 and early 1535 to most of the country's religious communities.[8] It was a notable achievement: with whatever reservations, individually or collectively, professed religious en masse had now formally agreed that the king was the head of the Church.[9] At the London Greenwich Observant house, the friars were unwilling to entertain a collective decision. Urged by Cromwell's visitors to leave their answer on the supremacy to the senior members of the house, they refused. "The convent stiffly affirmed that where the matter concerned particularly [individually] every one of their souls, they would answer particularly [individually] every man for him self."[10]

---

[6] Wright, *Suppression*, p. 104.   [7] Wright, *Suppression*, pp. 116–17.

[8] G. R. Elton, *Policy and Police: The Enforcement of the Reformation in the Age of Thomas Cromwell* (Cambridge, 1972), counts 168 institutions, "abbeys, priories, hospitals, cathedral chapters and colleges," that gave their assent. "The number does not exhaust that of all such bodies in the realm, but it is much more likely that some documents are lost than that anyone was left out."

[9] Peter Marshall has a thoughtful discussion of conformity and equivocation around this moment in *Religious Identities in Henry VIII's England* (Aldershot, 2006), pp. 217ff.

[10] Wright, *Suppression*, p. 42.

This happened in June 1534; on October 25 an imprisoned Franciscan, Frances Lybert, wrote to a friend asking for news of his fellow grey friars in London and the Greenwich Observants, marveling to hear that some had sworn to the supremacy. Lybert was wrong about the Observants, but his reflections on the dilemma that all English religious faced are at once judicious and generous. At the same time, in their inability to predict even a personal course of action, they have a baffled quality that many religious must have shared. "Notwithstanding, if they think that God is pleased with [their submission], their conscience discharged, the world edified, and any profit may come of it, we desire to have a more perfect knowledge and then we shall do as God shall inspire us – either suffer pain still or else go at liberty as they do."[11]

Such insistence on personal judgment meant that many houses suffered division. Richard Mounslow, the last Benedictine abbot of Winchcombe, Gloucestershire, had to cope with a member of his house who wrote a treatise against "the usurped power of the Bishop of Rome" that he sent Cromwell, and Mounslow's own letters to Cromwell make it clear that he had other monks whose disobedience was the result of conflicting religious positions.[12] Peter Cunich has recently noted that even at Syon, perhaps England's most conservative house, we can see

> evidence of an almost total breakdown in regular discipline among the brothers from about 1534 ... That so many of the brothers could have rebelled against the authority of their ailing Confessor-General [that is, in order to oppose the royal supremacy] in such an observant and well-disciplined community [shows] just how divisive the succession and supremacy policies were for religious communities around the country.[13]

The book's second chapter is set in a milieu that makes these tensions particularly visible. Historian A. G. Dickens called the friars "the most deeply divided section of the regular clergy" at the dissolution,[14] and the well-known letter of Thomas Chapman, warden (head) of the London Greyfriars, in which he assured Cromwell that he and his house were eager to relinquish their habits, has made that assessment seem a perceptive one.

The religious position of the anonymous member of that house who wrote the *Greyfriars Chronicle* is less clear. The chronicle comprises a series

---

[11] *LP*, VII, no. 1307.   [12] *LP*, IX, nos. 314, 321, 322, 934.
[13] Peter Cunich, "The Brothers of Syon, 1420–1695," in E. A. Jones and Alexandra Walsham (eds.), *Syon Abbey and Its Books, Reading, Writing, and Religion c. 1400–1700* (Woodbridge, 2010), p. 69.
[14] A. G. Dickens, *Thomas Cromwell and the English Reformation* (New York, 1959), p. 136.

of jottings recording events in the capital between 1539 and 1554. At the closure of their house, twenty-five men signed the surrender document; for about half of this number, some trace of their later life survives in the historical record. Most of the dozen continued to live in London and several secured clerical positions, even – somewhat surprisingly – as rectors of London parishes. Three of them might be considered candidates for authorship of the chronicle: John Richardson (†1560), John Baker (†1570), and Albert Coleman (†1572). Hence this chapter constitutes a study of what can be recovered from a particular community after its demise. The exploration can be only a tentative one, since half the house remains untraced; nonetheless it is to some extent a narrative of clerical continuity. Coleman's situation is particularly intriguing. After the dissolution, he was employed as a London parish clerk, although in 1548 he had been described as relatively unlearned. Yet his 1572 will leaves books (mostly unspecified), and his overseer and protector was Lord Chidiock Paulet, a recusant younger son of the Marquis of Winchester.

The manuscript containing the *Greyfriars Chronicle* was recognized early for its value and before the end of the century it began its passage through the hands of several notable collectors and historians: John Stow, Robert Cotton, William Camden, William Dugdale. More speculative is the possibility of earlier ownership by Dugdale's father John, himself an antiquary and historian, and the further possibility that former friar Albert Coleman transmitted the book to Dugdale *père*.

The *Chronicle*'s account of the twenty years in London just after the closing of its author's house might be read either as carefully neutral or at some points genuinely disengaged from the incidents it records. The execution of the Carthusians, or of Thomas More and John Fisher, are not condemned, merely noted. Though he describes "speaking against the sacrament" as "shameful," about 1534, the year of the Act of Supremacy, the author says "this year was the bishop of Rome's power put down." Political treason, however, regularly draws condemnation. The chronicler – who has been called "London's last Franciscan" – combines traditional belief in the eucharist, contempt for the papacy, anxiety at the pace of cultural change, and a profound personal loyalty to a series of rapidly changing rulers: Henry, Edward, Mary. The religious and political complexity of this troubled period is its author's central subject.

In the manuscript, the chronicle is preceded by narratives of general Franciscan history and a valuable listing of the burials in London's huge Greyfriars church. The author's own contribution to these materials, his mid-century London narrative, together with his addition of a regnal

roll-chronicle at the very end of the manuscript, allows us to see him as a
very late practitioner of the long monastic tradition of chronicle history
writing. Particularly revealing are the text's responses to the loss of familiar
cultural patterns.

This topic resurfaces in the third chapter, which is based on the administrative relation between three female heads of houses and Thomas
Cromwell. As in the *Greyfriars Chronicle*, one of the subjects is the evolution of new social structures after the disappearance of enduring institutional forms; here the subject is female community. Cromwell's far-flung
network of clientage extended not only to court and country but to
the religious institutions as well. Several male heads of houses maintained personal ties with him and this was true of female superiors also:
Katherine Bulkeley, Abbess of Godstow, Oxfordshire, was a recipient of
Cromwell's patronage in the mid-1530s, and her six surviving letters to
her sponsor reveal a relationship that was at times cheerfully informal.
Like two other female appointees about this time, Morpheta Kingsmill,
Abbess of Wherwell, Hampshire, and Joan Fane, Franciscan prioress of Dartford, Kent, Bulkeley had a brother who was connected with
Cromwell. These female appointments of the mid-1530s should probably
be considered supplementary favors, the primary recipient being the male
family member.

Like others in their families, Bulkeley, Kingsmill, and Fane might all
be thought to hold reforming beliefs in varying degrees. These are clear
in Bulkeley's often-reprinted letter, not unlike that of Chapman, the
Greyfriars warden, assuring Cromwell of her house's freedom from superstitious practices. She subsequently retired to a life with her family in
Cheshire and the statement of belief in her will is a reforming one. The
positions of the other two are less thoroughly documented. Though one
of Kingsmill's letters to Cromwell survives, it is her will that has made
her a figure of interest. The will, which leaves bequests to seven of her
nuns, has suggested the existence of a post-dissolution female living community. The ardently Protestant activities of Kingsmill's brother, however,
together with the abbess's apparently neutral mention in her will of the
husband of one of her former nuns, seems to rule out the possibility of
a renewed collective religious life structured along earlier lines. Unlike
the Hampshire abbey of St. Mary Winchester only twenty miles away,
where the nuns lived near one another in the cathedral close and continued as late as 1551, a dozen years after the dissolution, to wear their
habits in public, Wherwell's continued existence (if indeed that is how the
will bequests to former nuns should be interpreted) did not constitute a

witness to traditional religious belief, but may instead represent a successful economic accommodation.

Joan Fane is the only one of these nuns whose position is revealed through her reading. Her ownership of a printed copy of reformer Robert Crowley's 1550 edition of *Piers Plowman* has been recently discovered. Tellingly, Fane was not part of Dartford's attempts to continue religious life after the house's closure, as her nuns experimented with various forms of community, first in Kent and, after 1558, in the Low Countries. In particular, the prioress's absence from any of the small living groups recorded in rural Kent probably indicates some division in the house. Her connection with Crowley's work was probably made through Elizabeth Fane, wife of the prioress's brother Sir Ralph. Elizabeth was a patron of Crowley who had in 1550 published her poems (now lost) and in 1551 dedicated his own poem "Pleasure and Pain" to her. Lady Fane also supported various imprisoned and later martyred controversialists, including John Bradford, Thomas Rose, John Philpot, and Nicholas Ridley. Prison letters exchanged between several of these men and Lady Fane survive, and the young Anne Cooke, likewise a partisan of religious reform, dedicated to "Lady F" her first work, a translation of the Italian sermons of reformer Bernardino Ochino. Given these connections, it seems likely that Joan Fane got her copy of *Piers* from her sister-in-law or her sister's printer friend, and that both women understood the poem as expressing criticism of the institutional church, particularly in its wealth. The man to whom Fane left her book, William More, was certainly sympathetic to this perspective; an important local official and Member of Parliament for Surrey, he was identified in the first parliament of Mary's reign as a favorer of "true religion," that is, reform.

This relationship between the three religious superiors and the ecclesiastical institution that they served is clearest in the case of Katherine Bulkeley, though it is likely that Joan Fane too had reforming sympathies. The subject of the fourth chapter, Margaret Vernon, was probably also inclined to reform, if only because of what we can see of her long and close friendship with Thomas Cromwell. Intimate, chatty, thoroughly personal, her twenty-one letters provide rare evidence of a sustained connection between this female administrator and her famous sponsor, a connection that may have been based on shared religious perspectives and that included other members of Cromwell's circle.

The earliest mention of Vernon has been thought to come from two years of accounts that give her name as prioress of the nunnery of St. Mary de Pré, near St. Albans, Hertfordshire. The accounts run from Michaelmas

1513 to Michaelmas 1515. David M. Smith in his magisterial catalog of
heads of religious houses asked whether this could be the later superior of
Little Marlow, Buckinghamshire, and of Malling, Kent, but indexed her
as two different persons. The discovery, however, of a previously unnoticed
record of a royal pardon extended to Margaret Vernon, prioress, and the
convent of Sopwell, Hertfordshire, on November 20, 1509, makes it likely
that the Sopwell and the Pré prioresses are the same woman, given the
physical closeness of the two Hertfordshire houses, either near or in St.
Albans, and the dependence of both upon the great Benedictine abbey in
that city.

Margaret Vernon in fact had an administrative career unparalleled by
any other English nun, as head of four houses: Sopwell, St. Mary de Pré,
Little Marlow, and finally Malling. Her relationship with Cromwell began
in the 1520s before the minister's remarkable rise, when he was still in
Cardinal Wolsey's employ and was serving, it seems, as Vernon's financial
advisor while she was head of Little Marlow. Her letters show that she
was negotiating at this time to become prioress of the London house of
St. Helen's Bishopsgate, that she had received an assurance on this matter from Wolsey, and that Cromwell was acting as her agent. Though
this negotiation eventually proved unsuccessful, Cromwell entrusted his
only son Gregory to her care at Little Marlow for Gregory's first schooling, and her three letters about this matter outline a position that might
be described as that of family friend. Subsequently, in 1536 when Little
Marlow was closed, she sent Cromwell a letter remarkable for its undis-
guised anxiety, a letter that implores him to let her know what will happen to her.

Three months later Vernon had become abbess of the Kentish house of
Malling, an appointment for which Cromwell had been heavily pressured
by four or five of his other friends and connections. The conclusion of
her story as Malling was dissolved in 1538 is as remarkable as the rest: in a
most unusual initiative she asked Cromwell for permission to sell one of
the house's manors in order to provide payments for herself and her sisters.
Except perhaps for the invocation of the Holy Spirit, which may suggest
a reforming habit of language, her letters do not reveal her beliefs, but her
several casual mentions of Cromwell's intimates, all of whom shared his
interest in reform, suggest that she too knew these men and found their
perspectives congenial. Her remarkable rise had several elements: the personal sympathy that encouraged Cromwell to entrust his only son to her
and the openness to reform that facilitated his sponsorship of her made
possible her long administrative career.

These four heads of female houses all came from the reforming end of the spectrum and their responses to change were perhaps more open than we might have expected. But the coercive force of religious reform was great enough that the conservative segments of the religious community were likewise affected and even religious exile had its effective rewards, as the book's fifth chapter suggests. In 1555 William Peryn, a Dominican friar and an Oxford graduate, published a book titled *Spirituall Exercyses* and dedicated it to two English nuns whom he had come to know abroad, in Louvain. Peryn, a notable conservative preacher, had left England for religious reasons, probably in 1534. The two women represented a pre-Reformation spiritual elite: Katherine Palmer was later to be Abbess of Syon, the Brigittine house in exile, and Dorothy Clement was a Poor Clare, the daughter of Thomas More's protégé John Clement and More's adopted daughter, Margaret Giggs Clement.

The book transmitted to these English nuns the latest currents in continental spirituality. It was a translation and expansion of a work by Nicholas van Ess, who had been a close friend of the first German Jesuit, Peter Canisius, and had made the Ignatian spiritual exercises in 1543. He had a cell at St. Barbara's, the Cologne Carthusian house that published the work of Ruysbroeck, Suso, and Tauler and that sponsored the life and writing of the contemporary beguine mystic, Marie d'Oisterwijk. He had reformed several religious foundations, including Marie's beguine house at Diest, near Louvain. While van Ess's book was influenced both by Ignatius's method and by his Christocentric spirituality, in addition he drew heavily on the work of the Flemish mystic, Hendrik Herp (†1478). Peryn's *Spirituall Exercyses* contained his own translation of a part of a text by this important Dutch writer, the *Mirror of Perfection* (*Een Spieghel der Volcomenheit*), treating the most advanced level of contemplative life, what Herp called "superessential" union with God. *Spirituall Exercyses* thus provided a synthesis of new Ignatian spirituality and still-powerful Flemish mysticism influenced by the Devotio Moderna. Its influences were Jesuit, Flemish, female-oriented, mystical. This was what Peryn's translation brought into English for his two friends, and his book illustrates the fruitful possibilities of diaspora.

Peryn returned to England under Mary: the preface to his book is dated the last of December 1555, though the book did not appear until 1557. He was named head of the reconstituted Blackfriars – with Syon and Dartford, one of the six religious houses re-established in Mary's reign – but he died in 1558, just at the moment when Elizabeth's accession closed the Dominican house once again (and when Peryn's Dominican sisters from Dartford, along with Syon nuns, left England for a communal life on the continent).

While the approach of Peryn's *Spirituall Exercyses* might well have become even more popular had Mary Tudor lived, its synthesis, created for Englishwomen in exile, remained influential in England. *Spirituall Exercyses* was read by the Yorkshire martyr Margaret Clitheroe (†1588) and was recommended by the seventeenth-century mystic, Benedictine Augustine Baker, who was responsible for the spiritual direction of other exiled English nuns about a century later at Cambrai.

Continuity is illustrated again, this time at home in England, in this book's final chapter. Surprisingly, Richard Whitford, the man who has been called the most popular religious writer of the first half of the sixteenth century, continued to write and publish after the 1539 dissolution of his longtime home, Syon Abbey. In 1541, two years after Syon's closure and the year before his own death, Whitford issued a compilation of four texts, work very much of a piece with the humanist interests of his earlier career and with his long-continued role of spiritual director. Three pieces were translations from the Fathers: Cyprian, Isidore, and John Chrysostom. Two came from an early period of Whitford's life; two were probably more recent, from the 1530s. As with the author of the *Greyfriars Chronicle*, Whitford's loyalty to the monarch was strong, even after the effective conclusion of English monastic life. In condemning Martin Luther, Whitford's preface invokes Henry VIII approvingly; the king had "by his noble work condemned [Luther] for a heretic."

Such loyalty was perhaps more common than we might think. Indeed, it has been pointed out that obedience to princes was a firmly held obligation, while the papacy was notably corrupt, justifying the application of the duty of obedience to the king rather than the pope.[15] Despite the closure of his abbey, Whitford clearly felt that he still had an audience – and in this he was supported by his longtime printers. In fact, he was probably still enjoying some reduced form of community, since he mentions suggestions made by a brother regarding the book's contents. Though the thrust of Whitford's work in 1541 is not explicitly reforming, the author is here involved with something like the remarkable contemporary effort made by the Cologne Carthusian house of St. Barbara to combat heresy through a campaign of spiritual renewal, supported by printing. The German Carthusians, whose publications Syon knew, were explicit in their determination to oppose heterodoxy by means of a broad educative effort,

---

[15] Lucy E. C. Wooding, *Rethinking Catholicism in Reformation England* (Oxford, 2000), p. 6.

one that would bring spiritual texts the widest possible access. Because of the great popularity of his works in the 1530s – four editions of what has been called his "collected works" were published – Whitford was perhaps the man best suited to participate in a similar attempt in England.

The years from 1530 to 1558 were so intensely disruptive that the English religious, male and female, who lived through them might be thought to have been left behind as remnants of a cast-off system. This perspective, of course, is shaped by our knowledge of the evolution of religious history and of the outcome of the struggle between positions that then may have seemed more evenly balanced than they do now. If a common pattern emerges in these narratives, however, it is the understanding that finality is everywhere only apparent, and is necessarily partial. As in Chaucer's *Knight's Tale* Saturn's destructive power, so crushingly demonstrated in Arcite's death, is elided or circumvented through the ambiguous concluding marriage of Palamon and Emily, something similar might be thought to happen in the accounts of the ten persons that follow. Some can be clearly seen as hoping and even working for change of a reforming kind – Thomas Chapman, Katherine Bulkeley, Joan Fane, probably Margaret Vernon. Even those, however, whose beliefs lay closer to a traditional definition – Simon Appulby, the Greyfriars chronicler, William Peryn, Katherine Palmer, Dorothy Clement, Richard Whitford – can be seen as participating in movements of renewal that would adjust these inherited understandings. Yet in the historic process of which they were a part, though it moved strongly toward change, the past retained a shaping force. Attempts at continuity co-exist with the evolution of new forms. The Greyfriars chronicler is tolerant of some religious and social alterations, though not all. Morpheta Kingsmill retains strong ties with the members of her old community, accepting the marriage of one of them; after his house's closure Richard Whitford continues to see individual spiritual growth as foundational for social reform and hence to publish his popular spiritual tracts. The reading and writing of these English religious show them as participants in the struggle of these years, sometimes sinking, sometimes rising, in their attempts to swim through the waves of change.

CHAPTER ONE

Looking backward?
London's last anchorite, Simon Appulby (†1537)

The last anchorite of the London parish of All Hallows London Wall,[1] the priest Simon Appulby, died in June 1537. His anchorhold, which had housed a series of named occupants since at least 1402,[2] was turned over to a personal servant of London's mayor, the city swordbearer, as a piece of secular patronage. Appulby's will shows he understood that the anchorhold might not endure, although All Hallows' anchorites had for at least 150 years enjoyed the closest ties to parish and neighborhood in their northeast corner of London, located along the city wall between Moorgate and Aldgate. The passage from spiritual to secular use of this local landmark,[3] and the loss of its latest inhabitant, a man of the neighborhood, demonstrates the cultural reach of religious change.

Appulby had been the author of a popular book of meditations on Christ's life, the *Fruyte of Redempcyon*, which represented a genre overwhelmingly central for over a century. The genre's paramount example,

---

I have called Appulby London's last anchorite, since although a later anchorite's will exists, we do not know when Jane Hardy left her anchorhold. In her May 12, 1543 will she calls herself "sometime anchoress without Bishopsgate, now being of the parish of St. Bride's." There is no mention of goods; she leaves everything (unspecified) to a John Haywood "in recompense of the long charge that I have put him to." LMA: DL/C/B/004/MS09171/011, f. 97v (commissary court).

[1] The two principal writers on All Hallows and its anchorites are Charles Welch (ed.), *The Churchwardens' Accounts of the Parish of All Hallows, London Wall* (London, 1912) and Rotha Mary Clay, "Further Studies on Medieval Recluses," *Journal of the British Archaeological Association* 3rd ser. 16 (1953), 74–86. The former edited the parish accounts and the latter discovered the identity of Simon the Anker. I have quoted from their work but have checked the documents they used, expanding and infrequently correcting.

[2] All Hallows anchoritism may have begun a century earlier. City of London Letter Book E (f. 27) records the 1314 grant of "a certain tourella on London Wall, near Bishopsgate" to Sir John de Elyngham, chaplain. He intended to live there and was commanded by the mayor and aldermen to maintain it. Since he is not called an anchorite, however, the question of whether he was the cell's first inhabitant must remain open. See Welch, *All Hallows*, p. xxix.

[3] "The cell ... may have been on the site of the present vestry, which is a semi-circular chamber, built on or forming part of the old London wall"; Welch, *All Hallows*, p. xxx. Clay provided a 1905 watercolor of the structure but noted that it "did not escape part-demolition by enemy action in three attacks (1940–1)"; "Further Studies," 85.

Nicholas Love's *Myrrour of the Blessed Life of Jesus Chryst*, had been the most influential English text of lay formation since its first appearance around 1410 and *Fruyte* too was a best-seller. What *Fruyte* and its great predecessor, the *Myrrour*, offered was an approach to scripture, one that was centrally meditative but also drew on the Fathers, was accompanied by moral and doctrinal lessons, and concluded with formal prayer. Published in 1514 and 1517, then again in 1530, 1531, and 1532, *Fruyte* should be understood as a final conservative statement in the centuries-old debate about lay scriptural access, written before the disruptions of the later 1530s. Strongly endorsed by episcopal authority, like Love's *Myrrour*, Appulby's book provided for its wide audience the sort of convenient and trustworthy access to the narrative of Christ's life likely to stimulate devotion. In both his anchoritic vocation and his spiritual writing, then, Appulby serves as a marker for the familiar certainties that the 1530s would begin to dismantle.

All Hallows London Wall anchorites

This site had had a parish anchorite from at least the beginning of the fifteenth century. The reclused vocation is often thought of as flourishing in remote spots, or, when attached to an institution, as characteristically monastic in its associations. Work on continental anchoritism, however, has emphasized its late medieval presence in cities, particularly cities of the Low Countries.[4] Recently this model has been applied to England where, though rural anchoritism remained strong, "nevertheless the number of urban English anchorholds, in tandem with the wider European tradition … steadily increased until the sixteenth century, as anchoritism became an important urban phenomenon"[5] – or, as Roberta Gilchrist puts it, as anchorholds became "an integral element of the ecclesiastical topography of medieval towns."[6]

The London neighborhood where Appulby's anchorhold was located lay along the northeast section of the city wall between Moorgate on the west and Aldgate on the east, and near Bishopsgate between these

---

[4] Anneke B. Mulder-Bakker, *Lives of the Anchoresses: The Rise of the Urban Recluse in Medieval Europe* (Philadelphia, 2005), though she sees this phenomenon as gendered female.

[5] Mari Hughes-Edwards, "Anchoritism: The English Tradition," in Liz Herbert McAvoy (ed.), *Anchoritic Traditions of Medieval Europe* (Woodbridge, 2010), pp. 131–52 (pp. 140–41). She notes that agreement on the rise of urban anchoritism is registered by other contributors to this collection.

[6] Quoted in Hughes-Edwards, "Anchoritism." The figures provided by Ann K. Warren remain standard: *Anchorites and Their Patrons in Medieval England* (Berkeley, 1985), p. 20.

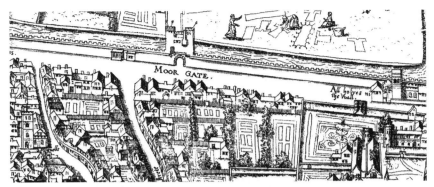

Figure 1.1 This section from London's copperplate map (after 1557) shows
Moorgate, All Hallows London Wall parish, Bishopsgate, and the Pappey, the
neighborhood of both anchorite Simon Appulby and former grey friar Albert Copeman.

two (see Figure 1.1).[7] The sponsoring parish, All Hallows London Wall,
was a poor one whose population included a large number of workers
in the leather trades. In 1427 it had been united with the nearby chapel
of St. Augustine Pappey, where in 1442 a fraternity was founded for the
aid of aged priests, housed close to the church.[8] The parish's patron was
the Augustinian Holy Trinity priory, on the city's eastern edge just inside
Aldgate, and London's only female Franciscan house, the Minoresses, lay
just outside the gate.

The men and women who lived in the cell on the north side of All
Hallows church assumed a central role in the parish's life, making a significant contribution not only spiritually but economically. The first All
Hallows anchor whom we can identify died at the opening of the fifteenth
century. Margaret Burre's 1402 will left to her daughter Amy her primer,
two linen sheets, a worn mantel, and a chest containing her best white veil.
The anchoress's servant Joan was bequeathed a white tunic, a new blanket,
and a small worn chest.[9] Another woman, Emmota Olrun, received a variety of domestic items: a metal pot for boiling, a worn brass pan, pewter
pots of two-quart and one-quart size, a towel and "all my veils black and
white, except for the white veil previously mentioned." She was also given

---

[7] M. D. Lobel, *British Atlas of Historic Towns, Vol. III: The City of London from Prehistoric Times to c.1520* (Oxford, 1989), map 4 and map titled "The Parishes."

[8] George Hennessy, *Novum Repertorium Ecclesiasticum Parochiale Londinense* (London, 1898), p. 100. Caroline M. Barron and Matthew Davies (eds.), *The Religious Houses of London and Middlesex* (London, 2007), pp. 188–89.

[9] LMA: DL/AL/C/002/MS09051/001, f. 97v, dated September 21, 1402, proved November 4, 1402 (archdeaconry court).

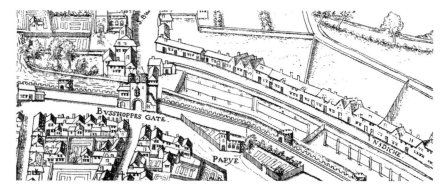

a chair and an alabaster image of the Virgin (see Figure 1.2). The quantity of the bequests, including all the anchorite's veils, suggests that Emmota Olrun might have been Margaret Burre's successor.

The anchorite's will leaves three kinds of personal possession: clothing, domestic necessities such as cooking pans or bedding, and objects of religious devotion. Margaret Burre owned three alabaster carvings, the products of a flourishing English industry.[10] Besides her image of the Virgin bequeathed to her friend, she gave two others to the church of All Hallows: a crucifixion (see Figure 1.3) and, for the high altar, an image of St. Anne.[11] This devotion, combined with mention of her daughter, suggests that like St. Anne, Margaret Burre was a widow. The anchoress's choice of All Hallows' parish priest and its two churchwardens for her executors underlines her parish ties. Her warden executors were John Surman, a carpenter, and Nicholas Bedewell, a whitetawyer (leatherworker), whose own will survives, dating from a dozen years later (1414).[12]

---

[10] The anchoress's gift was bequeathed during what Francis Cheetham calls the middle years of English alabaster production. He divides the period as follows: early (c.1340–c.1380); middle (c.1380–c.1420); later middle (c.1420–c.1450); late (c.1450–1540). *English Medieval Alabasters* (Oxford, 1984), introduction.

[11] A late-fifteenth-century account of a miraculous alabaster image of St. Anne illustrates one way in which such an image could be displayed and describes its wooden housing. The miracle, in which the case suddenly opened, occurred in the church of Daventry, Nottinghamshire, on Palm Sunday 1471. "In a pillar of the church, directly afore the place where King [Edward IV] kneeled … was a little image of Saint Anne, made of alabaster, standing fixed to the pillar, closed and clasped together with four boards, small, painted and going round about the image, in manner of a compass"; *Records of the Borough of Nottingham*, III: 18, quoted in Cheetham, *Alabasters*, p. 29. Seventy-six years after Margaret Burre's legacy, in 1478, the parish accounts show they again acquired "ij images of alabaster to the high altar"; Welch, *All Hallows*, p. 22.

[12] Nicholas Bedewell's will is LMA: DL/AL/C/002/MS09051/001, f. 314v. made April 11, 1414, proved ides of May, 1414 (archdeaconry court). Only a grant of administration survives for John Surman.

Figure 1.2 This alabaster panel of the annunciation, dated 1380–90, may be similar to the alabaster image of the Virgin that anchorite Margaret Burre left to Emmota Olrun in 1402.

Figure 1.3 This alabaster crucifixion dated *c.*1400 was acquired in London and is contemporary with the crucifixion given to the high altar of All Hallows London Wall parish in 1402 by its anchorite Margaret Burre.

were anchorites men or women
in this case?
20   Looking backward?

whitetawyers – national archives
ref C147/271 in French

In it Bedewell requested burial in All Hallows churchyard and left a legacy of 3s. 4d. to the parish fraternity of blessed Mary, a group identified with the whitetawyers.[13] In the early years of the fifteenth century, then, these first evidences of a tradition of parish anchoritism that would sustain itself for another century and a half, together with the presence of a parish fraternity, indicate the existence of an active parish life.

A gap of about fifty years intervenes between Margaret Burre's death and the next mention of the All Hallows anchorite, but in 1461 another member of the Bedewell family left a bequest to the anchor. Margaret Bedewell gave a towel "of werk" and a silver spoon to the anchor, now a priest, to say a trental for her soul (see Appendix 1).[14] Nine mentions of the anchorite in the third quarter of the fifteenth century indicate that the cell was occupied fairly continuously. Though we do not know the names of any of these anchors, two gifts were made to a woman.[15] In 1474 John Emlyn, an upholder (upholsterer) left 12d. to the anchor at London Wall and 6d. to the anchoress,[16] indicating that more than one cell existed at this site. A will of 1500 made by Jane, Viscountess Lisle, likewise shows that two solitaries were in residence at this time, since it gave 13s. 4d. to the anchor of London Wall and the same sum to the anchoress.[17] These cells may have been occupied simultaneously at some times, while at other times perhaps only one was filled. Throughout this twenty-year period (1458–78) the faithful's support of the anchorite continues, as does the anchorite's support of the church. Gifts made by this anonymous solitary of 6s. 8d. and of 4d. in 1459/60 and of 3s. 4d. in 1469/70[18] show his or her involvement in maintenance of the church fabric, while they also demonstrate that the anchorite played an economic role at least from the mid fifteenth century.

In the last quarter of the century, sometime before 1477/78, the priest William Lucas became the All Hallows anchorite and left a substantial record of his presence in the anchorhold. In that year an entry in the *Calendar of Papal Letters* noted that he had been enclosed "for several years," so he may have been the man who received John Emlyn's gift in 1474. He was granted papal permission to be absent from his cell for fifteen months in order to make a pilgrimage to Rome and other holy

---

[13] Caroline Barron, "The Parish Fraternities of Medieval London," in C. M. Barron and C. Harper-Bill (eds.), *The Church in Pre-Reformation Society* (Woodbridge, 1985), p. 16.

[14] LMA: DL/C/B/004/MS09171/005, f. 333, will of Margaret Bedewell.

[15] See Appendix 1, 1457/8 and 1474.   [16] *CPMR*, VI: 135.

[17] C. Eveleigh Woodruff (ed.), *Sede Vacante Wills: A Calendar of Wills Proved before the Commissary of the Prior and Chapter of Christ Church, Canterbury* (Canterbury, 1914), III: 130.

[18] Welch, *All Hallows*, pp. 7, 9.

places.[19] In the same year, 1478, Lucas gave the parish the substantial sum of 20s. Charles Welch notes that this represents nearly one-fourth of the parish's total receipts for that year, and perhaps this large gift was intended to replace the support All Hallows would miss while Lucas was away.[20]

The most intriguing information about Lucas, however, comes from a chancery suit that he brought against Richard West, citizen and tailor, in 1479/80, probably just after his return from Rome.[21] According to the anchor, West had approached him for a loan of £20; he answered that he had no money of his own except for the funds that had been "put into his hands and keeping ... of the goods of the said church." The anchor lent West the parish money, however, cautioning him that he must "have it again to make delivery therof unto the said parish at such time as they would call therefore." The practice of using the anchorite or his cell as a repository for valuables is found as early as the twelfth century,[22] and Rotha Mary Clay notes that the *Ancrene Riwle* warns: "Neither receive under your care the church vestments, nor the chalice ... for oftentimes much harm has come of such caretaking."[23]

The story of the loan is entwined with the narrative of Walter Andrewe, a boy whom Lucas had raised and "drew forth in virtue and caused to be learned to read, write, and to lay accounts sufficiently." The anchorite had apprenticed the boy to West, but West subsequently charged that Andrewe, together with other apprentices, had been involved in the theft from him of a great deal of cloth – wool, silk, and linen – worth over £200. West believed that Andrewe had given some of the stolen cloth to whores, to make kirtles. West had earlier repaid £10 of the anchorite's loan and he asserted at this point that he and the anchorite had mutually agreed that the remaining £10 of parish money that he owed would be forgiven him. In exchange, West would agree not to prosecute the boy and to discharge him from his apprenticeship. The anchorite contended that there was no such agreement and that he had, perhaps foolishly, returned to West the pledges he had held for the £10, simply because he feared West's retaliation against Walter Andrewe, the boy he had "brought up with him self."

Richard West was a prominent member of the Merchant Taylors' Company and had been master in (probably) 1478/79. He was presented

---

[19] Clay, "Further Studies," 80, quoting *CPL*, xiii.625.

[20] Welch, *All Hallows*, p. xxx.

[21] TNA Early Chancery Proceedings C1/66/66–69, summarized in Clay, "Further Studies," 80–81. I have provided additional detail from the document.

[22] Henry Mayr-Harting, "The Functions of a Twelfth-Century Recluse," *History* 60 (1975), 337–52.

[23] Rotha Mary Clay, *The Hermits and Anchorites of England* (London, 1914), p. 137.

as an apprentice in 1441/42 and the last mention of him occurs in July 1493.[24] His various transactions in the chamber of the Guildhall span several decades.[25] Whether he or the anchorite was in the right is uncertain, but other evidence attests to West's quarrelsome disposition. The court minutes of the Merchant Taylors' Company record a continuing dispute between West and another merchant over a period of three years, from 1487 to 1490, during which West is alleged to have commanded the other man, "Go out of my house Bench whistler" – that is, trifler or good-for-nothing.[26]

As so often, the outcome of the suit between West and Lucas is not provided by the documents. The judgment may have gone against the anchorite, however, since in the year of Lucas's death, 1486, the parish paid 15s. 11d. "in suit of plea against the executors of Sir William Lucas sometime here anchor." This large sum represents about one-fifth of the parish's annual revenue and its payment for legal fees indicates that a still larger sum was at issue: the parish money that the churchwardens were probably attempting to recover. That they thought it worthwhile to bring suit shows that they viewed the anchor's estate as capable of supporting their claim, probably for the remaining £10 of the loan. Robert Tittler points out that even as late as the seventeenth century the practice of moneylending "was still more of a social than a purely economic phenomenon. Credit was extended because of the needs of kin, neighbours, and even community."[27] Viewing Lucas's loan as part of a network of mutual obligation goes some way toward explaining the continuity of this anchoritic practice from the twelfth through the end of the fifteenth century.

Another contemporary reference allows us to see Lucas in a different context. At almost the same time as the West lawsuit, in 1480, Anne, Duchess of Buckingham, died and left 6s. 8d. to the anchorite for twenty masses and diriges. Her will refers only to the anchorite of London Wall, but in that year the holder of the cell was certainly Lucas.[28] Welch points

---

[24] Matthew Davies (ed.), *The Merchant Taylors' Company of London: Court Minutes 1486–1493* (Stamford, 2000), pp. 259, 301, 303.

[25] Reginald R. Sharpe (ed.), *Calendar of Letter Book … L: temp Edward IV–Henry VI* (London, 1912), pp. 3, 62, 88, 105, 175–76. For additional details of West's life including his 1481 election as a collector of the subsidy, see *CPMR*, VI: 147. I am indebted for these references to Dr. Matthew Davies, University of London.

[26] Davies, *Court Minutes*, p. 91. West's will, made November 3, 1496, is TNA PCC 5 Horne (Prob 11/11, ff. 48v–49). In it he leaves a psalter boke limned with gold to his son-in-law.

[27] Robert Tittler, "Money-Lending in the West Midlands: The Activities of Jane Jeffries 1638–49," *Bulletin of the Institute for Historical Research* 67 (1944), 249–63.

[28] Duchess of Buckingham's will: TNA PCC 2 Logge (Prob 11/7, ff. 14v–15v); proved October 31, 1480. Some of her accounts survive: London, BL Additional MS 34213 and two rolls: BL Additional

out that we can read in the parish accounts the actual delivery of that sum by "a man of my lady of Buckingham." The duchess's will combines great wealth and great piety. She asked that her body be conveyed to the collegiate church of Plessy, Essex, "setting all pomp and pride of the world apart," and she left 20d. to every priest of Syon, Sheen, and the Charterhouse to say five masses and diriges for her. Placing the anchor in the company of that notable trinity of devout religious houses suggests that even before the last anchorite of All Hallows' possible connection with Syon (see below), the anchor of London Wall was regarded as sharing the kind of elevated spirituality that characterized these institutions. Or perhaps the connection between the duchess and the anchorite was simply a neighborhood one. Her will makes it clear that she had been living in the "great chamber" at the Minoresses, the London Franciscan house that was near Aldgate and near Holy Trinity Priory, the parish's sponsoring institution.

The last mention of Lucas comes in the year of his death:[29] on June 15, 1486 a papal indult was issued permitting "William de Lucasa, anchorite" to choose a confessor. Both Lucas and his unknown successor died in that year.[30] The churchwardens' accounts show that 6s. 8d. was paid for the "[b]urying of the new anchor that is to say for the great bell for his knell." Lucas's replacement was probably a man named Robert Lynton, since on May 10, 1488 the Archbishop of Canterbury ordered two men to administer the goods of Lynton, the anchorite of All Hallows London Wall who had died intestate.[31] The parish received the substantial gift of 53s. 4d. from his executors,[32] about two-thirds of the annual parish income. Its substantial amount is the more surprising since Lynton had been in place only briefly, at most for two years.

The next anchor of London Wall was a man named Giles, mentioned in a will of October 27, 1491 whose testator, Richard Bodley, left the anchorite

---

29608 and Egerton 2822. She commissioned part two of New York Public Library MS Spencer 3 (Wingfield Psalter); see Kathleen L. Scott, *Later Gothic Manuscripts 1390–1490*, 2 vols. (London, 1996), II, no. 106.

[29] *CPL*, xv.417.

[30] Clay, "Further Studies," 81, notes that Lucas's name is entered in the obituary roll of the London Fraternity of Clerks under 1487 (LMA: CLC/L/PB/C/001/MS04889).

[31] Christopher Harper-Bill (ed.), *The Register of John Morton, Archbishop of Canterbury 1486–1500*, 2 vols., Canterbury and York Society 75, 78 (Leeds, 1987), I, no. 297.

[32] Welch, *All Hallows*, p. 34. The accounts in 1488 record a payment "for burying of Sir John the anchorites priest." The syntax allows Sir John to be either the anchorite or his priest. Since the reference comes just two years after Lucas's papal permission, however, it seems likely that the unknown Sir John was the man William Lucas chose as his confessor, who then would have outlived his employer by two years.

his two best gold rings.[33] Bodley was a former warden of the Grocers'
Company; since he was not a member of All Hallows parish, but wor-
shiped at St. Botolph Billingsgate, his gifts suggest that the anchorhold
at London Wall had by this time become known as a London institution rather than simply a parish one. Bodley owned a copy of the most
popular contemporary devotional book. His will leaves the *Myrrour of the
Blessed Life of Jesus Chryst* to his son William and the book survives, with
William's inscription: "Thys Booke ys Wylliam Bodleys & Elizabethe hys
wyffe" (Cambridge, Corpus Christi College MS 142).[34] The Bodley family's ownership of this book reflects mainstream lay reading taste, which
continued unchanged at least from the early fifteenth century until the
dissolution. This anchor Giles, or his successor, maintained the tradition
of financial support that plays such a large part in the relation between
All Hallows and its recluse. In 1501 the parish received "a great pax with
three images of silver by the gift of the Anchor."[35] As William Lucas had
done, this man continued to keep the parish funds: "Item Rest in Master
Anchor hands in ready money for the church xxv s" (1509–11).[36]

Simon Appulby

The last anchorite of All Hallows London Wall is the best known; some
possible traces of Simon Appulby's life before his anchoritic profession
can even be found. He may perhaps have been the priest to whom, in
1483, the Abbot of St. Albans, William Wallingford, promised the next
vacancy of the parish anchorhold at St. Michael's church, St. Albans. The
anchorhold was then occupied by a woman, Dame Margaret Smyth.[37]
Whether this man is to be identified with the London anchor is not clear,

[33] Jennifer Mary Collis, "The Anchorites of London in the Later Middle Ages," MA thesis (University of London, 1992), p. 35. The rector of All Hallows, beginning in 1486, was John Row; Hennessy, *Novum Repertorium*, gives no date at which he vacated. The next incumbent, Thomas Wilson, resigned in 1506/07 (p. 82), so it is possible that John Row was rector in 1495–97 and that the anchor's gift was made for the burying of the rector's parent ("Sr jon mother").

[34] Anne F. Sutton, "Lady Joan Bradbury (d. 1530)," in C. M. Barron and A. F. Sutton (eds.), *Medieval London Widows 1300–1500* (London, 1994), pp. 210–12. CCCC MS 142 also contains the prose lives of saints Nicholas, Katherine, and Margaret from the *Gilte Legend* of 1438, an English form of general confession, a treatise of ghostly battle, and the articles of major excommunication in English.

[35] Welch, *All Hallows*, p. 68. It was perhaps Giles who received Jane Lisle's bequest of 13s. 4d. in 1500 (see note 17 above).

[36] Clay, "Further Studies," 82.

[37] H. T. Riley (ed.), *Chronica monasterii St. Albani*, Rolls Series 28, pt. 6, vol. II (London, 1873), pp. 257–58. It is not likely that this man ever became the St. Albans anchorite, since in 1503 Elizabeth of York's privy purse expenses show a gift to the anchoress of St. Michael's (Warren, *Anchorites*, p. 184).

though the dates can accommodate a single life. If in 1483 Simon Appulby were twenty-six, the lowest age for ordination, he would have been eighty in 1537, the year in which he died.

Appulby's presence in his London neighborhood is more certain, however. In the early sixteenth century, St. Augustine Pappey was the neighborhood church closest to All Hallows. Its brotherhood for aged or poor priests annually elected a master and wardens whose duties were to visit the brethren and supervise their needs and behavior, and to audit the accounts of the collectors quarterly, receive the money, and divide it appropriately.[38] In 1505, 1506, and 1507 Simon Appulby was elected as one of two wardens of the Pappey. Two years later in November 1509 a Sir Simon Appulby, identified as parish priest of St. Foster (St. Leonard Foster Lane, a center city-parish), was one of the witnesses to the will of Roger North,[39] the father of Edward (later Baron) North. The family was prominent and bookish: Edward North's career moved from a position as counsel for the City of London to chancellor of the Court of Augmentations. Edward had two sons: Roger, second Baron North, owned the Ellesmere manuscript of Chaucer's *Canterbury Tales*, while his brother Sir Thomas was the translator of Plutarch's *Lives*.

The connection between Appulby and London bishop Richard Fitzjames is first visible in 1513. The advowson of All Hallows parish belonged to the priory of Holy Trinity Aldgate, as did the gift of the anchorhold,[40] and in 1513 Appulby made his anchoritic profession before Fitzjames in the priory of Holy Trinity, at the northeast corner of the city wall.[41] Because bishops were frequently responsible for supervision of anchorites, episcopal support was particularly vital and this traditional relationship between bishop and recluse may suggest a later commission from Fitzjames to Appulby. In the year after his anchoritic profession, 1514, Appulby published the first

---

[38] Thomas Hugo, "The Hospital of Le Papey in the City of London," *Transactions of the London and Middlesex Archaeological Society* 5 (1881), 183–221 (201), lists masters and wardens from London; BL MS Cotton Vitellius F.xvi., ff. 119v–123. In 1505 Appulby's co-warden was Nicholas Caverton; in the following two years, William Maysttherother.

[39] TNA PCC 23 Bennett (Prob 11/16/175). Appulby is not recorded as rector of this parish, hence was apparently a curate. Hennessy, *Novum Repertorium*, p. 127.

[40] *VCH London*, pp. 587 and 465, quoting John Stow, who says the founder was Maud, queen of Henry I, in 1107 or 1108. According to the cartulary of Holy Trinity, however, All Hallows London Wall was granted to the house between 1128 and 1134 by a priest named Ranulf who gave it to the convent when he entered religion at Reading Abbey. Gerald A. J. Hodgett (ed.), *The Cartulary of Holy Trinity, Aldgate*, London Record Society 7 (London, 1971), p. xvii. For the priory's situation during Appulby's life, see Manuel C. Rosenfeld, "Holy Trinity, Aldgate, on the Eve of the Dissolution," *Guildhall Miscellany* 3 (1970), 159–73.

[41] Fitzjames's register, LMA: DL/A/A/005/MS09531/009.

edition of *Fruyte of Redempcyon*, accompanied by a printed endorsement from Bishop Fitzjames.

Appulby's book: sources and context

The work was not entirely original, but is a translation from an anonymous Latin text, *Meditationes de vita et beneficiis Jesu Christi, siue gratiarum actiones*.[42] Its first edition was published by Ulrich Zell at Cologne about 1488; six more editions followed before 1500. Sometimes attributed to Thomas à Kempis, it consists of a series of meditations on Christ's life, each one ending with a prayer; the last two-thirds of these focus on the Passion. Soon after its first publication the *Meditationes* appeared again in radically shortened form, on July 9, 1489 at Strasburg. Here it became part of a handbook of prayers, the *Antidotarius Animae*, compiled by the Cistercian abbot of Baumgarten in Alsace, Nicholas Weydenbosch or Salicetus. He had received his medical degree at Paris before entering religion and in 1482 was assigned by the Abbot of Citeaux to produce the first printed liturgical books for the use of the order. By 1487 the general chapter had approved his versions of the breviary, psalter, and missal. This experience with publishing may have influenced his subsequent production of the very successful book of prayers. Abbot Weydenbosch's medical background is visible in his preface, which explains that the *Antidotarius Animae* was conceived as a manual of spiritual medicine; its *pars digestiva*, for instance, contains prayers of sorrow while its *pars purgativa* provides prayers to accompany the sacrament of confession.[43] It was a useful compilation, offering prayers for a variety of occasions.[44] ISTC records seventeen more printings before 1500 at Antwerp, Paris, Nuremberg, Venice, and elsewhere.[45]

In its original form the *Meditationes* comprised sixty chapters,[46] while in its appearance in the book of prayers these have been cut to forty. Its

---

[42] I am grateful to Dr. J. T. Rhodes, University of Durham, for permission to publish her discovery of the source for *Fruyte of Redempcyon*.

[43] ISTC lists twenty-three more editions after the first, before 1500/01; see http://istc.bl.uk, under *Antidotarius Animae*.

[44] A2v–3. For Weydenbosch's life, I follow the *Dictionnaire de spiritualité* (Paris, 1982), XI, cols. 299–301.

[45] Flora Lewis has suggested that the *Antidotarius Animae*'s indulgenced prayers may be a source for the added indulgenced prayers in English books of hours of 1510, 1511, and subsequently. "'Garnished with Gloryous Tytles': Indulgences in Printed Books of Hours in England," *Transactions of the Cambridge Bibliographical Society* 10 (1995), 577–90.

[46] Including two prayers at the beginning and one at the end. The first two editions are without *tabulae*, but a table of contents appears in the third edition, Augsburg, not after 1489; BL IA 6085.

length, in its first version, was between thirty and thirty-five thousand words; in the *Antidotarius* its length is less than ten thousand words. Whole chapters have been omitted and, while the chapter headings in the two versions are frequently identical, often Weydenbosch has retained only the first portion of a chapter.

This shortened version in the *Antidotarius* became Simon Appulby's source. He used this text as a framework, reproducing its Latin chapter titles as his own English ones, and frequently translating each chapter verbatim (for instance, his chapters 1, 8, and 9). Appulby makes the *Antidotarius's* forty chapters into thirty-one through rearrangement of material and some not very substantial omission. The Latin text of the *Antidotarius* begins each chapter with either of the phrases "Gratias tibi ago" or "laudo et glorifico te" and Simon imitates this: "Thankings be to thee lord Iesu Christ" [B 4v], "I laud and glorify thee lord" (C 1). The *Fruyte* is in the main a faithful English translation of the short version of the *Meditationes* found in the *Antidotarius*, with the addition of some new material taken from the revelations of Birgitta of Sweden. These additions are signaled in Appulby's book by marginal side notes.

Brigittine additions represent something less than one-fourth of the work's total length, while another one-fourth seems to be original to Appulby. The Brigittine material is heavily Marian: it is found in chapter 4, on Mary's life, and in chapters 16, 19–20, 22, 24, 26, and 28, which describe the Passion, often emphasizing Mary's role in it. William Bonde, Syon monk and author, recommended Appulby's book in the first edition of his own *Pylgrimage of Perfection* (1526). In a chapter on meditation at matins, Bonde suggests the use of a treatise "lately printed of the life and passion of our lord called the fruit of redemption | where ye may … find such points right well set out for this purpose."[47]

Bonde here describes how *Fruyte* can serve as a basis for what he calls meditative practice:

> I exhort all them that would practice this way: first, [to begin] every day before the service, or else when they may have time and leisure convenient to recount in their hearts with thanks the passion of our lord Jesu, with the circumstances of the same … When such contemplative persons have gathered those articles and points and hath them so perfectly in their minds that they can rehearse them and revolve them in their minds at their pleasure, then … let them begin to practice and apply their meditation in the service of God.

[47] *STC* 3277, f. CCli.

At about the same time Bonde was registering his approval of the *Fruyte of Redempcyon*, that is in the mid-1520s, another contemporary reader was incorporating Appulby's work into a personal collection of fifteen small quarto tracts. The compiler of this volume was probably the woman whose name appears twice in it, Dame Margaret Necollson, a nun either of Elstow, a Benedictine house in Bedfordshire, or of Watton, Yorkshire.[48]

Syon's resources and its instructive mission might have contributed to the appearance of Appulby's book, but that the work was part of an episcopal initiative is suggested by the unusual official recommendation it received from Bishop Fitzjames, a man whose orientation was deeply conservative.[49] *Fruyte*'s endorsement reads:

> Here endeth the treatise called the fruit of redemption, which devout treatise I Richard unworthy bishop of London have studiously read and overseen and the same approve as much as in me is. To be read of the true servants of sweet Jesus, to their great consolation and ghostly comfort, and to the merits of the devout father compounder of the same.[50]

This advertisement of the book's doctrinal orthodoxy strongly recalls the circumstances surrounding Archbishop of Canterbury Thomas Arundel's similar endorsement of Nicholas Love's *Myrrour*, around 1410. Found in seventeen manuscripts of Love's text, that memorandum, in Latin, states that Love presented his translation "for inspection and due examination" and that Arundel commended and approved it personally, ordering it to be "published universally for the edification of the faithful and the confutation of heretics or lollards."[51] The episcopal review of an English translation, the subsequent approval for dissemination either via copying or printing, and, above all, the institutional sponsorship of the work as a response to the threat of heresy are unchanged in the interval between 1410 and 1514.

---

[48] T. A. Birrell, "The Printed Books of Dame Margaret Nicollson: A Pre-Reformation Collection," in J. Bakker, J. A. Verleun, and J. v. d. Vriesenaerde (eds.), *Essays on English and American Literature and a Sheaf of Poems, Presented to David Wilkinson* (Amsterdam, 1987), pp. 27–33, for Bedfordshire; Carol M. Meale, "The Miracles of Our Lady: Context and Interpretation," in Derek Pearsall (ed.), *Studies in the Vernon Manuscript* (Woodbridge, 1990), pp. 115–36 (p. 132 n.), for Yorkshire. For more on the former house, Eileen Power, *Medieval English Nunneries c. 1275 to 1535* (Cambridge, 1922), p. 48.

[49] Emden calls him "unsympathetic to the new learning" and quotes Erasmus's dismissive comments on Fitzjames's reverence for Duns Scotus, "whose name seemed to him semidivine"; *BRUO*, II: 691–92.

[50] *STC* 22557.

[51] Michael G. Sargent (ed.), *Nicholas Love's Mirror of the Blessed Life of Jesus Christ: A Critical Edition Based on Cambridge University Library Additional MSS 6578 and 6686* (New York, 1992), p. xlv.

Heresy was an imminent threat in sixteenth-century London as well, a hundred years after Love's translation. Between 1510 and 1518 Bishop Fitzjames examined about forty Lollards in the city,[52] and in 1514, the year of Appulby's first edition, he personally interrogated the well-known Londoner Richard Hunne for heresy. Hunne was condemned posthumously after his suspicious death in December 1514 for possession of the scriptures in English, among other charges.[53] Although Appulby's book does not contain the explicitly anti-Lollard passages that characterize Love's *Myrrour* (on the eucharist, on the hierarchy, on obedience), it shares with Love's book a political posture. Both offer an approved version of the gospel narrative in place of the narrative itself. The two books represent a conservative and traditional answer to the question of scripture in English. By the early sixteenth century the substitution of scriptural summaries for vernacular scripture had become an accepted institutional response to challenge, one that printing could further facilitate.

Appulby's book: revival

Sixteen years after its first publication, *Fruyte of Redempcyon* appeared again at a moment when the question of scripture in English was being everywhere discussed in the capital. The edition is dated May 21, 1530, while a second edition appeared in 1531 and a third in 1532.[54] Because these books reprinted Fitzjames's 1514 episcopal permission to publish, it seems likely that the new bishop of London, John Stokesley, elevated in 1530, would have been responsible for the reprint. Stokesley was certainly aware of the power of the press in supporting a conservative theological position. In the following year, 1531, John Bale says that at Stokesley's request printer Henry Pepwell published an edition of John Eck's *Enchiridion locorum communium adversus Lutheranus*, a handbook of short Latin essays designed for the use of clergy in composing their homilies. At about the same time, Stokesley also ordered that another anti-Lutheran text, William Barlow's *Dyaloge Descrybyng the Orygynall Ground of These Lutheran Faccyons*, "be preached of the curates throughout all his diocese."[55]

---

[52] Susan Brigden, *London and the Reformation* (Oxford, 1989), pp. 85, 87.
[53] R. Wunderli, "Pre-Reformation London Summoners and the Murder of Richard Hunne," *JEH* 33 (1982), 209–24.
[54] *STC* 22557–22559, 22559.5, 22560. Fitzjames's note appears in all.
[55] John Bale, *Yet a Course at the Romish Fox* (Zurich, 1543), f. G7, quoted in Irwin Buckwalter Horst, *The Radical Brethren, Anabaptism and the English Reformation to 1558* (Nieuwkoop, 1972), p. 45. Susan Wabuda, "Bishops and the Provision of Homilies 1520 to 1547," *Sixteenth-Century Journal* 25.3 (1994), 556.

But although Stokesley had been created Bishop of London on March 28, 1530, he was in Italy in spring of that year and was enthroned by proxy on July 19; he did not return until October and was not personally consecrated until November 27.[56] Though his absence from London does not entirely rule out his commissioning of a reprint of *Fruyte* for May 1530 publication, there were other relevant activities in the capital that spring. Two proclamations were issued, attempting to control both importation of religiously heterodox books and translation of scripture into English.[57] The first of these proclamations preceded the publication of *Fruyte*; Richard Pynson's warrant for "printing papers against heresies" was dated March 6, 1530 and he was paid in May, sometime before the 11th.[58] This proclamation was headed "Certain heretical and blasphemous books sent into the realm by Lutherans" and it is barely possible that the May 21 re-publication of *Fruyte* was a response to it, since the final paragraph does deal with imported books and since the document concludes with a list of forbidden books. The larger thrust of the proclamation, however, as G. R. Elton noted, was the revival of laws against heresy, an initiative Elton attributed to Thomas More who had been chancellor since the previous October, in 1529.[59]

More relevant to *Fruyte*'s appearance is the May 1530 commission summoned by the king, a group of a dozen scholars of divinity from Cambridge and another dozen from Oxford, plus various important clerics, who met in London from May 11 to May 24 to discuss the issue of scripture in English.[60] During that time, in fact, on May 14 Bishop Nix of Norwich wrote in a letter that "some say that wherever they go they hear that the King's pleasure is that the New Testament in English should go forth."[61] The commission produced a document titled a "publick instrument," which they promulgated on May 24; it gave a fascinating

---

[56] Andrew A. Chibi, *Henry VIII's Conservative Scholar: Bishop John Stokesley and the Divorce, Royal Supremacy and Doctrinal Reform* (Bern, 1997), p. 15, based on Stokesley's register, LMA: DL/A/A/005/MS09531/012/001, ff. 1, 2, 5.

[57] *TRP*, nos. 122 and 129.

[58] G. R. Elton, *Policy and Police: The Enforcement of the Reformation in the Age of Thomas Cromwell* (Cambridge, 1972), p. 218, n. 5.

[59] Elton calls the proclamation "Lord Chancellor More's attempt to save the realm from heresy, the sum total of his contribution to government policy during his tenure of office"; *Policy and Police*, p. 218. See also R. W. Heinze, *Proclamations of the Tudor Kings* (Cambridge, 1976), p. 132: "In an effort to stem the tide of Protestant influence in England, the medieval heresy laws were revived and applied."

[60] For a detailed account of the meeting, Allen G. Chester, *Hugh Latimer, Apostle to the English* (Philadelphia, 1954), pp. 57–60.

[61] *LP*, IV, no. 6385.

summary of their two weeks' discussion, noting that it had been reported to the king that it was his duty to cause the scriptures to be translated into English and that he and the bishops did wrong "in denying or letting of the same."[62] Despite this explicit challenge, the discussion concluded that the king and prelates were justified in censoring English scripture and that if people would "follow such lessons as the preacher teacheth them [they] may as well edify spiritually in their souls as if they had the same scripture in English." Those present added that because of the "pestilential books" now circulating, the king and prelates did well to be cautious, but the king promised he would have the scripture translated if his subjects' behavior improved.

Much of the "publick instrument" found its way into the second proclamation on June 22, 1530.[63] This document was far more specific than the earlier proclamation in attempting to control printing and, specifically, printing of English scripture. It commanded that such books be examined by the diocesan ordinary whose name, along with that of the printer, must appear in the book. It relayed the commission's judgment that "it is thought ... not necessary the said Scripture to be in the English tongue and in the hands of the common people, but that the distribution of the said Scripture, and the permitting or denying thereof, dependeth only on the discretion of the superiors" since scripture in English might be "the occasion of continuance or increase of errors."

Though the dating, and hence the sequence of events, is unclear, spring 1530 was clearly a high point in London's struggle over scriptural access, and *Fruyte* should be seen at this time, in its second set of appearances, as a substitute for William Tyndale's New Testament whose revised edition had been printed in Antwerp on January 17, 1530. For this struggle, Bishop Stokesley was especially fitted. He particularly opposed wide availability of scripture in English. Commissioned, with others, by Thomas Cranmer as Archbishop of Canterbury to prepare an English translation of the New Testament, he responded, "I have bestowed never an hour upon my portion, nor never will ... for I will never be guilty of bringing the simple people into error."[64] Edmund Bonner, Stokesley's successor as Bishop of London, wrote to Richard Grafton: "the greatest fault

---

[62] David Wilkins, *Concilia Magnae Britannicae et Hiberniae ab Anno MDXLVI ad Annum MDCCXVII*, 4 vols. (London, 1731), III: 736–37. Edward Hall reports a similar meeting that he dates the next day, May 25; it is not certain whether there were one or two meetings; see J. J. Scarisbrick, *Henry VIII* (Berkeley, 1968), pp. 253–54, for further discussion.

[63] *TRP*, no. 129.

[64] John Strype, *Memorials of ... Thomas Cranmer*, 3 vols. (Oxford, 1812), I: 48.

that I ever found in Stokesley was for vexing and troubling poor men …
for having the Scripture in English."[65] His failure, together with More,
in eliminating the Antwerp New Testaments by buying and destroying
them is well known; in 1531 he "caused all the New Testaments of Tindal,
and many other books which he had bought up, to be brought to Paul's
church-yard and there openly burnt."[66] His predecessor Cuthbert Tunstall
had done the same; yet the progress of vernacular scripture seemed irreversible and at the end of 1535 Miles Coverdale's complete translation of
the bible appeared in English, dedicated to the king. In 1537, the year of
Appulby's death, Bishop Stokesley emphasized again during Convocation's
discussion of Coverdale's translation his own more inclusive idea of the
nature of revelation: "Yet are ye far deceived if ye think that there is none
other word of God but that which every souter [shoemaker] and cobbler
doth read in his mother tongue."[67] Appulby's meditative presentation of
Christ's life, sanctioned by an episcopal predecessor, would have appealed
to Stokesley as a suitable vehicle for familiarizing the laity with scripture
and for stimulating devotion – but that modified form of scriptural access
was now being repeatedly challenged. In July 1537, about a month after
Appulby's death, a second English translation, Matthew's Bible, reached
England and was widely welcomed.

The anchoritic vocation: closure

Appulby's relation with the parish and his manner of living continued the
traditional anchoritic patterns visible in William Lucas's life. Like Lucas, he
made frequent gifts to the parish during his life there. For at least the final
half-century of the anchorite's presence at All Hallows, the churchwardens'
accounts make clear how helpful financially his presence was. All Hallows
seems always to have struggled economically. The foundation of the parish
fraternity in 1343 stressed All Hallows' physical needs. "Its [the guild's] primary purpose was the restoration of the church. The steeple was in danger
of falling and other repairs were urgently needed."[68] Much later, in 1486, All
Hallows received a papal grant of an indulgence for those who confessed,
visited the church and gave alms, or who merely contributed, if unable to
visit. The motive was financial support: the pope wished "that the church

---

[65] A. F. Pollard, *Records of the English Bible* (London, 1911), p. 225.
[66] Strype, *Cranmer*, I: 416–17.
[67] Benson Bobrick, *Wide as the Waters: The Story of the English Bible and the Revolution It Inspired* (New York, 2001), p. 147.
[68] H. F. Westlake, *The Parish Gilds of Mediaeval England* (London, 1919), p. 27.

may be maintained in structure and furnished with everything necessary for divine worship."[69] It is possible that Lucas negotiated this benefit on his 1478 trip to Rome. Fifty years later in 1528/29 the parish was attempting a different mode of support: the churchwardens' accounts show that All Hallows sponsored a fundraising play: "Received at the play clear as it appears by the gathering book £5 8s. 9 1/2d."[70] Parish drama was almost always linked with parish financial need. In a poor parish like All Hallows, the anchorite, with his or her extra-parochial supporters from a wider London base, could provide a valuable supplement to parish income.

The religious shifts that were to affect anchoritic life were under way before Appulby's death, though their long-term effects were not yet entirely visible. The priory of Holy Trinity, the neighborhood institution where Appulby had been made an anchorite, was the first monastery in England to be surrendered, on February 24, 1532. Appulby's London neighborhood might thus be thought to have felt the coming of change early on, four years before the dissolution of the smaller monasteries began in 1536. E. Jeffries Davis proposed that the suppression of Holy Trinity was a royal trial balloon floated in the direction of further monastic dissolution and that it succeeded since there were apparently no protests.[71]

Clay discovered an application for the anchorhold's patronage on the very date of the priory's surrender, when alderman John Champneys requested from the mayor and aldermen permission to name the next anchor after Simon Appulby's death.[72] Champneys, a skinner, was elected alderman from three different wards successively and soon after his request for the anchorhold patronage he became mayor of London.[73] An important figure, he may have wished to protect the anchorhold, particularly since Appulby's executor in his own will left Champneys a gold cramp ring, suggesting that the anchorite, his executor, and the alderman were connected by ties of friendship.[74]

---

[69] *CPL*, xv.63.

[70] LMA: P69/AH5/B/003/MS05090/001, f. 41.

[71] E. Jeffries Davis, "The Beginning of the Dissolution: Christchurch Aldgate, 1532," *Transactions of the Royal Historical Society* 4th ser. 8 (1925), 127–50.

[72] Clay, "Further Studies," 84. She calls the alderman Roger Champneys, but there is no London alderman by this name. The document is COL/CA/01/01/008, f. 214v (Repertory 8).

[73] Champneys was alderman of Castle Baynard Ward 1527–33; of Broad St. Ward 1533–34; of Cordwainer Ward 1534–56, the year of his death. He was mayor in 1534/35 and was knighted on October 28, 1534. Between 1527 and 1539 he was six times master of the Skinners' Company. Alfred B. Beaven, *The Aldermen of the City of London temp. Henry III–1908*, 2 vols. (London, 1911–12), II: 26.

[74] Will of John Davell, TNA PCC 5 Alenger (Prob 11/28, f. 40), made March 26, 1540, proved May 10.

Appulby did not die, however, for five more years, and indeed 1532, the year in which Holy Trinity was dissolved, saw the publication of the last edition of his work. But for the neighborhood the political and religious situation must have been an ominous one. Since its surrender the priory had been vacant and would remain so for two years, from February 1532 to March 1534, when an Act of Parliament confirmed the king's dissolution of the house. In that month Lord Chancellor Sir Thomas Audeley was granted the site of Holy Trinity priory and all its contents. The priory's subsequent fate was a particularly brutal, perhaps emblematic one, as John Stow tells the story. Audeley offered the priory great church to the parishioners of the nearby St. Katherine Cree parish but they refused, "having doubts in their heads of after-claps."

> Then was the priory church and steeple proffered to whomsoever would take it down, and carry it from the ground, but no man would undertake the offer; whereupon Sir Thomas Audley was fain to be at more charges than could be made of the stones, timber, lead, iron, etc. For the workmen, with great labour, beginning at the top, loosed stone from stone, and threw them down, whereby the most part of them were broken, and few remained whole; and those were sold very cheap.[75]

To local residents like Appulby these events meant, at the very least, that the future was uncertain. His 1537 will, entered in the London Vicar-General's book,[76] gathers old and young within the familiar enclosure of the parish. His service as warden of the Pappey thirty years earlier is recalled; when in his will he requested the fraternity members' presence at his funeral, he was no doubt summoning a number of old friends.

Besides requesting the attendance of these aged men, the will provided for the presence of children at the funeral, who would carry the two dozen tapers that had now been bought. The tomb too had been carefully planned within the anchorhold and two parish feasts of buns, cheese, and ale were scheduled. Despite the modesty of its plan (only £1 8d. were to be spent on the food and drink), the will reaches out to encompass the neighborhood community. One bequest is particularly interesting: the will asks that his executors dispose the residue of Appulby's goods in deeds of piety and charity except for "the goods which I by my writing late gave unto John Drynkmylke."

---

[75] Kingsford, *Stow*, p. 142.
[76] Will of Simon Appulby, LMA: DL/C/330, ff. 252v–253, printed in Colin A. McLaren, "An Edition of Foxford, A Vicars'-General Book of the Diocese of London 1521–1539, ff. 161–268," M.Phil. thesis (University of London, 1973), no. 649.

Nothing had been known of this man until his name surfaced recently in another will, twelve years after Appulby's. On September 30, 1549, Drynkmylke served as a witness for William Wattes of St. Stephen Colman Street, another northeast London parish.[77] In the will Wattes left Drynkmylke 20s. "for his pains taking with me in my sickness." Wattes may in fact be one of the grey friars who signed that London house's deed of surrender ten years earlier, and whose subsequent lives are traced in the next chapter. Although his will does not include any friars' names, neither does it mention either company membership or wife. The suggestion that Wattes might be the former Franciscan of that name is strengthened by the presence of John Drynkmylke both in his will and in Simon Appulby's. The confidante of anchorite Appulby, the nurse of friar Wattes, Drynkmylke seems a representative of practical charity during religiously turbulent times.

Appulby attempted to anticipate the changes that might end both his form of life and its physical shelter. He says,

> my very mind and will is that all such books and vestments as now be within the chapel of the said anchorage shall there perpetually remain to the use of the anchor which after my decease shall supply the same room so that the same room of an anchor there be supplied within one year and a day next after my decease; otherwise and without that so be, I will that all the same books and vestments shall be put to such use as shall seem good to mine executor.

In fact, events followed the anchorite's projected timetable quite closely. Appulby's will had been made in June 1537. In July 1538 the city granted the empty anchor house to the swordbearer of London – since February, a man named Robert Smart.[78] The swordbearer had been the most important member of the mayor's household since the fourteenth century and was regularly granted housing as one of his perquisites.[79]

The All Hallows anchorite's existence was rooted in activity rather than withdrawal, much like the anchorites of continental cities of the Low Countries. Writing about such women in the twelfth and thirteenth centuries, Anneke Mulder-Bakker describes their public and pastoral functions: "The anchoritic existence actually approached that of a parish priest ... [both followed] a recognizable way of life ... serving their fellow

---

[77] LMA: DL/C/B/004/MS09171/012, f. 32v.

[78] COL/CA/01/01/010, f. 20v (Repertory 10). For other grants to him, see Repertory 10, f. 160v, 178v, 271v and Repertory 11, ff. 220, 257, 281v, 481. On November 24, 1538 he also received "all the wainscot that doth lack within the frater" of the Charterhouse (*LP*, XIII (ii), no. 903).

[79] Caroline M. Barron, *London in the Later Middle Ages: Government and People 1200–1500* (Oxford, 2004), pp. 156–58.

human beings."[80] Henry Mayr-Harting called this the "hinge function" of the twelfth-century anchorite, referring to the counsel, medicine, and practical charity an anchorite often gave to his or her community.[81] In such instances, an identification of the anchorite as neighbor, rather than as recluse, seems warranted.

The lives of Simon Appulby and William Lucas, his late-fifteenth-century predecessor, demonstrate this aspect of the vocation – identified in the twelfth century and actively pursued in the fifteenth and sixteenth. Both appear deeply committed to the daily life of parish and neighborhood. The importance of the anchorite's presence to the parish's financial wellbeing may be particularly surprising. Lucas's custody of parish funds, Appulby's service to the nearby fraternity for aged priests, both men's role as economic guarantors for a poor parish and as spiritual directors for clients throughout the city and neighborhood – these services point to the centrality of the anchoritic presence and suggest the disruption implicit in the erasure of these centuries-old functions. The passage into private ownership first of Holy Trinity priory in 1534 and then of Appulby's anchorhold in 1538 removed traditional social supports that had sustained a communal way of life, though in mixed and partial ways.

The vocation of the solitary, poised between religious and lay life, thus seems to have ended unequivocally. In the later attempts to maintain communal religious life abroad, outside England, there could be no place for the cultural and economic complexity that defined anchoritism. Neither could reformed religious life at home, after the dissolution, admit the elaborate system of intercessory prayer at the heart of the vocation. With Appulby's death this particular form of spirituality, urban anchoritism, disappeared from London.

The audience for Appulby's writing, too, seems to have vanished. After 1532, the *Fruyte of Redempcyon* was not published again, and its approach, part of a centuries-old institutional effort to provide a limited, firmly guided access to scripture, was finally marginalized in favor of a more open scriptural reading practice. Yet the meditative approach to Christ's life and hence to the New Testament that was central to *Fruyte* would be at the heart of Ignatius Loyola's *Spiritual Exercises* less than a decade after Appulby's death, in the 1540s. As one commentator says of the *Exercises*: "the role assigned to the imagination ... the invitation to make oneself present to the event ... the emphasis laid on the imitation of Jesus in

---

[80] Mulder-Bakker, *Lives of the Anchoresses*, pp. 13–14 and see Chapter 6.
[81] Mayr-Harting, "Functions," 344.

his sufferings, all that belongs to the tradition of the last centuries of the Middle Ages."[82] Imaginative meditation on the Passion as in *Fruyte of Redempcyon* would continue, both in recusant spirituality and elsewhere, to be a foundational spiritual practice, though it would no longer replace scriptural reading. Appulby's volume thus suggests the difficulty in labeling as final even the period's most profound religious changes.

[82] Alexander Brou, *Ignatian Methods of Prayer* (Milwaukee, 1949), p. 135.

CHAPTER TWO

The Greyfriars Chronicle *and the fate of London's Franciscan community*

The fate of London's Franciscan friars at the dissolution poses an intriguing problem, since one of them who remained in the capital until the middle of Mary's reign composed an eyewitness account of these turbulent times. The notes – almost jottings – that we call the *Greyfriars Chronicle* are written in a manuscript with other Franciscan material (London, BL MS Cotton Vitellius F.xii). In it the so-called "Register" that just precedes the chronicle lists the many eminent persons buried in the friars' huge church, gives an account of the London foundation, and offers some general Franciscan history. This "Register" portion of the manuscript was edited by C. L. Kingsford, who believed it was put together by a friar of the house about 1520.[1]

To the manuscript, in a different hand, was added the *Greyfriars Chronicle* that begins as a London list of mayors and sheriffs, with brief commentary. It ends with an account of events in the capital over eighteen years between the 1538 dissolution of its Franciscan house and 1556. It was almost certainly written by a friar who took the manuscript away with him at the house's closure and continued to write in its blank pages.[2] Though its interest in religious matters is clear, despite its writer's mendicant origins the *Greyfriars Chronicle* provides what may seem a remarkably neutral account of the changes in mid-century London. We would, of course, wish to know its author's identity. Equally obscure is the question of what happened to other members of the community after the house's deed of surrender was signed on November 12, 1538.[3] Though many of their stories

---

[1] C. L. Kingsford, *The Grey Friars of London* (Aberdeen, 1915).
[2] This chronicle has been twice edited: J. G. Nichols (ed.), *Grey Friars of London Chronicle*, Camden Society 53 (London, 1852); R. Howlett (ed.), *Monumenta Franciscana*, Rolls Ser. (1882), II: 143–260. Quotations have been taken from the latter edition; references to this edition are given after quotations in the text.
[3] Joseph Hunter, "Appendix II: A Catalogue of the Deeds of Surrender...," in *Eighth Report of the Deputy Keeper of the Public Records* (London, 1847), p. 28, from TNA E 322/135.

are lost, some of these men have left traces in London records of their subsequent careers, both conservative and reforming,[4] and the detailed wills
of two of them allow us to speculate about the chronicle's authorship.

The manuscript

Because Cotton Vitellius F.xii was damaged by fire in 1731 and its folios
re-mounted on guard leaves, it is not possible to be certain of its original
collation, nor to tell at which point it was joined with the material that
now precedes it. Kingsford followed the manuscript's title ("Registrum …
que sepeliunter in ecclesia … fratrum minorum London") in calling the
first three sections (of five) the "Register," but suggested that the manuscript might most correctly be described as a collection of materials for the
history of the London grey friars.[5] Its first section, ff. 274–316, is headed
"Hic est titulus monumentum …"[6] The second section Kingsford calls
"the Register proper, giving a brief account of the foundation of the convent and of its buildings with a summary of deeds relating to the site." It is
headed "Prima fundacio fratrum minorum Londoniense" and runs from
f. 317 to f. 329. The third section comprises lists of Franciscan martyrs,
saints, bishops, and other notables, is headed "Nomina illorum … mar-
tyrizati …," and is found on ff. 330–37. The fourth section, the *Greyfriars
Chronicle*, opens with "Names of baillives, custodies, mayors, and sheriffs"
and begins with 1 Richard I (1189). It is found on ff. 338–65v, where it
concludes in the middle of a verso. The fifth section, a genealogical table
or diagram from Adam and Eve to Edward VI, opens, "Considering the
length …" and runs from f. 366 to f. 393v. The manuscript's 119 paper
folios are thus divided into five parts, the last two of equal length (27 ff).

Kingsford noted that in the first section, "an attempt seems to have
been made to keep up this part of the record by the regular entry of further burials down to 1530."[7] Thus, for instance, burials dated "1526" appear
on ff. 301 and 304v, "1528" on f. 298, "1530" on ff. 276v and 290v, and

---

[4] The main sources investigated, using the names of the 1538 signatories, were the Diocese of
London index to bishops' registers 1306–1829 (LMA: DL/A/A/016/MS18318); Register Bonner,
1539–49; 1553–59; Register Ridley, 1550–53 (LMA: DL/A/A/006/MS09531/012/001 and 002); George
Hennessy, *Novum Repertorium Ecclesiasticum Parochiale Londinense* (London, 1889); will indexes to
PCC, consistory, and commissary court wills; *L&MCC*; and biographical registers of Oxford and
Cambridge.

[5] Kingsford, *Grey Friars*, p. 1.

[6] The older foliation used in the Cottonian catalog is crossed out in the MS; the most recent foliation,
used here, is one number higher.

[7] Kingsford, *Grey Friars*, p. 1.

"1531" on f. 283. These entries are not in the hand that wrote the *Greyfriars Chronicle*, but in a considerably more skillful one. The chronicle hand, in fact, is awkward, its character worsened by the scribe's regular use of a pen nib too broad for the constricted spaces in which he was writing. A different hand, a graceful secretary, has provided content summaries of the chronicle events at the top of each folio from the reign of Henry VI (f. 344v) to the end of the first year of Edward VI's reign (f. 356).

The second section, however, as Kingsford observed, ends with "English versions of two fourteenth-century leases" (ff. 327–29v) and a memorandum of a further lease, dated Mcccccxxviij, during the mayoralty of John Rudstone (1528–29). These entries are in the hand of the Greyfriars chronicler. Writing in the manuscript at the same time as another friar in the late 1520s, ten years before the dissolution, the chronicler's interest in history was already well established, as his provision of these older documents shows. In addition, his own chronicle, part four of the manuscript, was probably begun before the dispersal of his house. Mary-Rose McLaren notes the variety of its sources and suggests it was written in "a place with access to a variety of manuscripts" like the Greyfriars library.[8] The language of its opening closely resembles that of *Arnold's Chronicle* (*STC* 782, 1503?), although some substantial differences in the form of names suggest that the chronicler might have been using multiple sources.[9] His retention and continuation of the manuscript after the closing of his house is not surprising. Having probably already begun to compose his chronicle in the manuscript and having written in it over several years, at the dissolution he may have considered it his own.

Evidence from the manuscript's fifth and final section strengthens the view of this author as consciously a historian. It has not previously been noticed that this item, written in three columns and at a right angle to the reader, is a version of a well-known genealogical roll-chronicle. Appearing both in Latin (long and short versions) and English (long and short versions), it was influenced by Peter of Poitiers's (†1205) *Compendium Historiae in Genealogia Christi*. Like that work, it begins, "Considering the length and hardness of holy scripture … I have put the names and the works

8 Mary-Rose McLaren, *The London Chronicles of the Fifteenth Century: A Revolution in English Writing* (Cambridge, 2002), p. 117.
9 For instance, in regnal year 1 Ric.5, Arnold has Walter Brown, the friar has Walter Ermeny. In 1 John 9, Arnold has as sheriffs Serle, mercer, and Hugh de Saint Albons, while the friar has Roger Wynchester and Edmond Hardelle. The account of King Richard's death is substantially different. Nonetheless, McLaren, *London Chronicles*, sees the relation between Arnold and Vitellius from the reign of Edward IV on as "very close."

of the holy old fathers by order and by row … to bring it into this little work to take away length." It provides a diagrammatic line of descent for English kings from Adam and Eve. Many versions survive: Albinia de la Mare, who classified them, listed five examples of the long English version,[10] and our manuscript apparently belongs to this group since the incipit of MS Cotton Vespasian F.xii is identical with that found in these manuscripts, all of which end with Edward IV except for BL Kings MS 395. Both the Kings manuscript and Cotton Vespasian F.xii have been continued to the reign of Edward VI. Kingsford, who first described this group of genealogical rolls, says the text's "purpose was educational and it has no [historical] value,"[11] yet he cites in Lansdowne Roll 6 "some brief notes of interest as expressing Tudor opinion." Such notes are found in Vitellius F.xii as well.

This section is written in the same hand as the chronicle that precedes it and consists of a traditional diagrammatic genealogical table with its colored roundels enclosing rulers' names, connected by colored lines. At the end, the roundel for Edward VI has been drawn and his name entered, but no summary of that reign has been written and the final paragraph belongs to Henry VIII. "This was a great wise man and he did many victorious acts … and in his time he put down the bishop of Rome's power in England and also put down all religious persons within this his realm of England" (f. 393v). The matter-of-fact perspective that obtains throughout the *Greyfriars Chronicle*'s accounts of religious change here becomes an endorsement, surprising on the lips of one of the suppressed "religious persons."

The chronicler's views

The writer's position is not entirely easy to evaluate. Religious events that we would expect him to find reprehensible, like the execution of the Carthusians, of Thomas More and John Fisher, and of his fellow Franciscan John Forest, and even the closure of his own house, are registered with careful neutrality. Indeed the Greyfriars' closing does not even receive a separate entry. Instead, we read: "Also this year [1538] was all

[10] Albinia de la Mare (ed.), *Catalogue of the Collection of Medieval Manuscripts Bequeathed to the Bodleian Library, Oxford, by James P. R. Lyell* (Oxford, 1971), pp. 80–85. Kathleen L. Scott lists nineteen illustrated MSS, many unknown to de la Mare, for instance no. 116 in *Later Gothic Manuscripts 1390–1490*, 2 vols. (London, 1996), II: 315–17.

[11] C. L. Kingsford, *English Historical Literature in the Fifteenth Century* (New York, reprint edn., 1972), p. 164.

the places of religion within the city of London suppressed in November"
(p. 202). From then on the writer refers to his former home as "the church
sometime the Grey friars" (pp. 208, 213, 215, 216) and, later, "the house in
London for the poor, the which was sometime the Grey Friars" (pp. 237,
238). Expressions of emotion involving religious matters are few, although
he notes "much speaking against the sacrament … that some called it jack
of the box, with divers other shameful names" (p. 215), and he is sarcastic at the prison treatment of Bishop of London Edmund Bonner: "the
great gentleness that was showed … [in] taking away his bed" when he
refused a bribe (p. 226). The chronicler appears shocked, as some of his
contemporaries were, by the intemperate preaching of former friar John
Cardmaker; on Cardmaker's sacramental views he comments, "what an
erroneous opinion is this unto the lay people" (p. 224).

On the other hand, in 1534 he observes that "this year was the bishop of
Rome's power put down" (p. 197). That descriptive phrase itself might be
thought a declaration of position. Elsewhere, consistently, it is "the pope"
(pp. 192, 254), though the chronicler may merely be repeating the language of the Act of Supremacy, particularly current in the year of its passage. This reductive epithet, however, is used again in the summing-up of
Henry VIII's reign at the end of the manuscript.

More troubling to the Greyfriars author are matters involving cultural
change. He finds variance in observance confusing, noting that some kept
particular holy days and some did not, and once he adds, "Almighty God
help it when his will is" (p. 228). Erasure from the calendar of many traditional saints' days had been mandated in July–August 1536 and the effects
had subsequently been extremely divisive. Not only was parish life affected
in its celebration of the liturgy, since that life depended upon the regular
rotation of feasts and festivals, but the abrogation "raised the issue of the
legitimacy of the royal supremacy in stark terms" – that is, whether the
king was empowered to effect those disruptive changes.[12]

When strong anger *is* expressed it is in a political context, not a religious one, and treason regularly draws condemnation. The northern rebels
"there suffered as they were worthy" (p. 201) and Protector Somerset too
deserved his fate: "Almighty God would not suffer it for his great mis-
chief" (p. 225). The ruler is consistently given his subject's blessing, and
despite their very different religious positions both Edward and Mary
receive fervent wishes for success ("God of his mercy send him good luck

---

[12] Ethan H. Shagan, *Popular Politics and the English Reformation* (Cambridge, 2003), pp. 55–59, gives
a variety of instances showing the intense feeling on both sides of this change.

and long life, with prosperity," p. 214; "God save her grace and long to continue and prosper her in goodness," p. 244). Certainly here what has been called "the sacred duty of obedience to the monarch rather than the pope" is strongly felt.[13]

The author's positions may seem difficult to reconcile with one another: traditional sacramental beliefs, distaste for the pope, anxiety at the pace of religious change if not its content – all combined with intense, consistent loyalty to a series of rapidly changing rulers. Yet such fluidity was not uncommon in the two decades just after the dissolution and perhaps even, as here, among professed religious. More mysterious than its variations are the account's silences, perhaps attributable not only to a contemporary need for caution but, it may be, to a notion of authorial neutrality peculiar to the chronicle genre.

The Greyfriars house in 1538: religious positions

At the dissolution the community was described by its head, warden Thomas Chapman, as eager for change. We might thus expect that a substantial portion of these London conventual Franciscans, unlike the Observants,[14] would have welcomed the new order. In September and December, 1538, almost the entire house – twenty-six men – received capacities, that is, release from vows and entitlement to a benefice such as a secular priest might hold.[15] Seven of this number, however, did not sign the deed of surrender two months later, on November 12. It seems likely that these seven left before the end; they might represent the more radical (or the more politically adroit) quarter of the house.[16] The remaining

---

[13] Lucy E. C. Wooding, *Rethinking Catholicism in Reformation England* (Oxford, 2000), p. 6; and see Shagan, *Popular Politics*, p. 45, mentioning a letter by John Fewterer, Confessor-General of Syon, invoking scriptural support for royal authority "and for the bishop of Rome nothing at all."

[14] Keith Brown, "The Friars Observants in England 1482–1559," PhD dissertation (Oxford, 1987), provides a full account of the London Observants. Greyfriars warden Chapman is anxious to distinguish his friars from them in his letter to Cromwell (see below): "Whatsoever the king's grace and you shall command me to do I shall do it with all readiness and so will all my brethren. I dare depose for them that we are not observant."

[15] The earliest overview, a bleak one, of the financial situation of ex-religious was provided by Gerald A. J. Hodgett, "The Unpensioned Ex-Religious in Tudor England," *JEH* 13 (1962), 195–202. His conclusions have been discussed by D. S. Chambers, *Faculty Office Registers 1534–1549* (Oxford, 1966), pp. xlviii–xlix. For London Greyfriars members listed there, see pp. 148–49, 165 (William Caterick), 167 (Adrien Cornelius).

[16] Robert Best, William Clerke, Thomas Collyns, Robert Frost, Lewis Hollywell, Gavin Jonys, Hugh Norrys. Clerke was serving at St. John Walbrook when he made his conservative will on June 14, 1544; see Ida Darlington (ed.), *London Consistory Court Wills 1492–1547*, London Record Society 3 (London, 1967), no. 203.

nineteen capacitied friars, plus seven signatories whose names appear for the first time since they either did not apply for or did not receive dispensations, make up the November total of twenty-six who put their names to the closing document. Counting the seven who received capacities in September but were not present at the closure, the house would originally have contained thirty-three men.

Some information is available about a dozen of the twenty-six signatories, just under half those who signed. When they have left wills, as five of them have done, their careers and beliefs are visible in more detail. Seven can be glimpsed only fleetingly (George Hovy, John Mathew, Lewis Pestell, John Richardson, John Thornall, Edmund Tomson, John Tomson), while three died too early to be considered as candidates for authorship of the chronicle (William Caterick, Thomas Chapman, William Wattes). The wills of two others, John Baker and Albert Copeman, show some of the adaptations that allowed these ex-friars to continue to live and work in the capital. They are full enough to admit some speculation and will be discussed below.

Ten of the twelve signers stayed in London and most of them managed to achieve an ecclesiastical position of some sort. In fact, the appointment of former Franciscans to London parishes, even to rectorships, seems to have been more common than we might expect. (Susan Wabuda comments that the movement of mendicants into parish ministries "was among the most ambivalent solutions that the English Reformation offered.")[17] Their origins were various: the best known was John Cardmaker, former warden of the Exeter Franciscan house, who was vicar of St. Bride's from 1543 and was eventually martyred in 1555.[18] Edward Ryley, former warden of the Aylesbury house, was in 1556 rector of St. Mary Ax and, in 1560, of St. James Garlickhithe.[19] John Joseph, a Canterbury friar and a zealous reformer, was one of Cranmer's chaplains and, in 1546, rector of St. Mary-le-Bow.[20] Thomas Cappes, on the list of Oxford Franciscans requesting a capacity, was in 1540 a chaplain at St. Mary Magdalen Old Fish St. and, two years later, at St. Michael Wood St.[21] In 1548 Thomas Kirkham DD, former warden of the Doncaster Grey Friars, was appointed

[17] Susan Wabuda, *Preaching during the English Reformation* (Cambridge, 2002), p. 129.
[18] Thomas S. Freeman, "Cardmaker, John (c. 1496–1555)," *ODNB* (2004), online: www.oxforddnb. com/view/article/4613 (accessed June 29, 2009).
[19] A. G. Little, *The Grey Friars in Oxford* (Oxford, 1892), p. 287.
[20] Little, *Grey Friars*, pp. 288–89.
[21] Little, *Grey Friars*, p. 293; John Strype, *Ecclesiastical Memorials Relating Chiefly to Religion, and the Reformation of It, and the Emergencies of the Church of England, under King Henry VIII, King Edward VI and Queen Mary I*, 6 vols. (Oxford, 1822), I, pt. 1: 566.

to St. Martin Outwich and Guy Elton was instituted vicar of St. Leonard Shoreditch in 1576.[22] Except for Ryley, all were reformers and Cardmaker, Joseph, and Kirkham preached at St. Paul's. Finally, one friar of the London house who left before the closure and hence did not sign in 1538 became the vicar of St. Martin in the Fields: Robert Best.[23]

An effort was mounted about 1553 to restore the London Franciscan friary, particularly since the buildings were intact. Those responsible were the Observant friar William Peto and the Dominican friar William Peryn, whom Mary appointed that year as the head of the restored Dominican house at St. Bartholomew's. (Peryn and his book, the *Spirituall Exercyses*, are the subject of Chapter 5, below.) Asked whether the restoration was supported by other friars, the narrator of this account, John Howes, replied: "There were five or six other poor friars which had been friars in the house before, but they only depended upon Peryn and Peto."[24] Perhaps the house's chronicler, whose account ends in 1556, was one of those who agitated for return in 1553. Certainly we know that in this year Baker, Copeman, Richardson, Edmund Tomson, and Best were alive and in London.

The warden

Warden Thomas Chapman's religious and political position is represented by three letters he wrote in 1538,[25] two to Thomas Cromwell and a third to Richard Neville – actually, as the letter makes clear, for the eyes of Archbishop Thomas Cranmer, since Neville was one of Cranmer's "most trusted servants" and steward of his household.[26] Like so many letters of the late 1530s they are filled with an intense anxiety about the future and, specifically, about the dispensations that Cromwell had evidently prom- ised to the house. In each of his letters Chapman touches on the subject of the religious habit, which symbolizes the old order that must be repu- diated.[27] The house's willingness to change is repeatedly stressed. So, for instance, to Cromwell: "I put no confidence in my coat ... and that shall appear when so ever [you] shall command us to change ... and we will

---

[22] Little, *Grey Friars*, p. 290.   [23] Little, *Grey Friars*, p. 286.

[24] William Lempriere (ed.), *John Howes' MS., 1582* (London, 1904), pp. 69–70.

[25] Printed in Kingsford, *Grey Friars*, letters IX–XI.

[26] Diarmaid MacCulloch, *Thomas Cranmer: A Life* (New Haven, 1996), p. 202, identifying Neville as from Northamptonshire, not Kent.

[27] "Once the dignified flag of orthodoxy, the cowl shifted under the weight of Protestant polemic to become the vivid symbol of menace." Wabuda, *Preaching*, p. 125.

obey gladly."[28] Again, to Neville: "[St. Paul] prohibiteth the thing that is good enough when it is or may be occasion of evil and ... the coat that we wear and the fashion that some of us use is the occasion of evil ... We think long every one of us till we have changed our coat."[29] Finally, to Cromwell again: "you commanded me to send the names of my brethren, whereupon you might send a dispensation of our papistical slanderous apparel ... I think long till your dispensation come for my brethren and so think they also."[30] A fourth document, dated the day of the surrender and signed by Chapman and twenty-five friars,[31] does not reveal anything of the head's or the house's personal sentiments, since although it repudiates "papistical ceremonies, wherein we have been ... practiced and misled in times past," the identical language is found in letters from the Franciscan houses of Aylesbury, Bedford, Coventry, and Stanford.[32]

Whether Chapman's letters should be considered sincerely felt forecasts of a new order or simply the efforts of a harried superior on behalf of his house, their tone is unmistakably urgent, even frantic. In February 1538 all English friaries had been placed under the supervision of Richard Ingworth, once prior provincial of the Dominicans, and as David Knowles observes, "they had lost their independence as separate orders ... They had little property and no treasure, and their dissolution ... brought very little revenue to the Court of Augmentations."[33] The bureaucratic delays in receiving dispensations were so severe that the visitors themselves pleaded with Cromwell on behalf of the displaced. D. S. Chambers notes, "[t]he friars suffered most from the shortcomings of the administration. They experienced difficulty in obtaining capacities quite apart from exclusion from the pension lists and the struggle to obtain preferment. The Commissioners themselves expressed pity," and he asks, "in some cases did [the dispensations] never arrive?"[34]

---

[28] Kingsford, letter IX. *LP*, XIII (i), no. 880, SP 1/131/f.256. It was written before the burning of friar John Forest on May 22, 1538, so perhaps in April.

[29] Kingsford, letter x, British Library MS Cotton Cleopatra E.iv, f. 38.

[30] Kingsford, letter XI, British Library MS Cotton Cleopatra E.iv, f. 115. It is printed in Ellis, III: 236–38.

[31] *LP*, XIII (ii), no. 808. The document is printed from William Trollope's *A History of the Royal Foundation of Christ's Hospital* (London, 1834), pp. 21–22, in Kingsford, *Grey Friars*, pp. 217–18.

[32] Thomas Rymer, *Foedera, conventiones, literae et cujuscunque generis acta publica inter reges Angliae*, 3rd edn. (1741), VI, pt. 3: 23–24. The letter from the Carmelites of Stanford is identical, only changing "grey coat" to "white coat." The dates are October 1–8, 1538.

[33] David Knowles, *The Religious Orders in England, Vol. III: The Tudor Age* (Cambridge, 1961), p. 360.

[34] For instance, the Oxford friars' capacities were entered in the register on July 31, 1538, but they had not been received by the end of August. Chambers, *Faculty Office Registers*, pp. lii–lv.

To some extent Chapman was no doubt doing what he thought best for his community in emphasizing, perhaps overstressing, its reforming consensus. The letter to Neville, however, despite its assurances, sounds a less confident note and suggests a more realistic assessment of opinion within the house. "I am warden, and have labored to amend it [the occasion of evil, mentioned earlier and represented presumably by the old way] and it passes my ability; whereupon I perceive that it is … time to call for more help than we have among us." Having suggested division, he hastens to stress uniformity again: "There is not one in our house but he would gladly change his coat" – if they had livings. The warden says that he has a plan to provide such livings, one he wishes to outline for Archbishop Cranmer, although the latter has recently commanded "that we should not come in to speak with him,"[35] hence the letter is addressed to Neville. Chapman's message appears even more consciously crafted if we understand him to have been aware of the archbishop's strong dislike of friars.[36]

Twenty friars were given one-time payments,[37] but only Chapman received a pension, in the amount of £13 6s. 8d.; unusually, he did not stay in London. A. B. Emden discovered his 1545 appointments to two benefices in Sussex, at Winchelsea and Rye. His pension ceased to be drawn by July 1547.[38] He may be the man whose inscription is found in a copy of Syon author William Bonde's 1531 *Pylgrimage of Perfection*: "Liber Thome Chapman scriptoris" on the title page and again on the verso of the last leaf.[39] *Pylgrimage* would have been a suitable book for Chapman to own: this 600-page, comprehensive work was intended, as its author says, for superiors "that hath other in cure," though its summary of traditional teaching and devotion cannot have represented Chapman's own views at the end of the 1530s.[40]

The rest of the house

Reforming beliefs like Chapman's were held too by former friar William Caterick. His dispensation is dated some time later than the rest of the

---

[35] Kingsford, *Grey Friars*, letter x.

[36] MacCulloch, *Cranmer*, p. 144: "his particular *bête noir* … Friars in general were regarded by the evangelicals as a chief source of poison against their cause."

[37] Caroline M. Barron and Matthew Davies (eds.), *The Religious Houses of London and Middlesex*, Centre for Metropolitan History (London, 2007), p. 126, quoting *VCH London*, p. 506, which gives the number of twenty, citing *LP*, XIV (ii), no. 236, p. 73, but no names are provided in *LP*.

[38] *BRUO 1501–1540*, p. x.

[39] CUL Sel.3.49; *STC* 3278.

[40] J. T. Rhodes, "Syon Abbey and Its Religious Publications in the Sixteenth Century," *JEH* 44 (1993), 11–25 (21–22).

community's, on December 4, 1538, the month after the surrender of the London house. It was awarded at Cambridge, probably because he had been studying at that well-known center of reform. He was admitted to the bachelor's degree at about this time, in 1537/38. Emden notes that in 1546 he was vicar of Burwell St. Mary's, Cambridgeshire, when he was dispensed to hold a second benefice and was admitted as rector of St. Alban Wood Street, London, on January 26 of the same year.[41] He had been the curate of St. Alban earlier, however, at least from April 27, 1543, when he witnessed and signed a parishioner's will there.[42] His achievement of a London rectorship is surprising, since Caterick had been called before London's Vicar-General in March 1544 and Susan Brigden speculates that he had been evangelizing.[43] The living, with its generous salary of £16 8s. 4d., was in the gift of the provost and fellows of Eton and provost Robert Aldrich, whom his biographer calls "a true Henrician Catholic in his belief," was a conservative in religion who accepted reunion with Rome under Mary.[44] It may have been sympathy for an ex-friar which allowed Aldrich to overlook the specifics of Caterick's position.

Caterick made his will on September 21, 1548 "in perfect health," but the will was proved less than three weeks later, on October 9, 1548.[45] Of its twenty-five lines, nineteen provide a strong statement of faith, "trusting only that God the father will extend his mercy upon my wretched soul for his dear son's sake Jesus Christ, desiring all his faithful members both now with him in rest and also here in his militant church to pray to him with me for his great mercy." Such repeated requests for mercy characterize reforming wills, but perhaps the invocation of what would formerly have been called the communion of saints is more traditional, though Caterick is careful to specify that the dead are at rest and not in purgatory. After burial "in the earth," and "like a Christian man," half his goods were to be given to the poor of his parish and half to his poor kinsfolk. The only persons mentioned in Caterick's will are his executor Henry Edwards and his overseer "my trusty friend Thomas Ionston," both untraced.

---

[41] *BRUO 1501–1540*, p. 107; John R. H. Moorman, *The Grey Friars in Cambridge, 1225–1538* (Cambridge, 1952), p. 162.

[42] Will of Ann Rian; see Darlington, *London Consistory Court Wills*, no. 194.

[43] Susan Brigden, *London and the Reformation* (Oxford, 1989), p. 403.

[44] Angelo J. Louisa, "Robert Aldrich (1488/9–1556)," *ODNB* (2004; online edn. May 2010), online: www.oxforddnb.com/view/article/315 (accessed July 3, 2010). Tim Card, *Eton Established: A History from 1440 to 1860* (London, 2001), pp. 40–41. Sir Thomas Smith, the Eton provost appointed in December 1547 by Protector Somerset, would probably have been more sympathetic to Caterick's views. For the salary, *L&MCC*, no. 57.

[45] LMA: DL/A/A/006/MS09531/012/001, f. 214.

We do not know how many other friars might have shared these views. Chapman's and Caterick's positions were the most clearly reforming and they were among the more successful of these ex-friars, since as graduates they received parish rectorships. (Chapman signed the surrender as "doctorem.") The views of a third man, John Richardson, were apparently quite different. Though he does not seem to have attended either university, Richardson was likewise awarded a London parish – a stroke of luck for which Mary's brief reign was responsible. In 1557 he became rector of St. George Botolph Lane through the patronage of Philip and Mary and thanks to the entry into religion of the former rector Richard Edwards.[46] Before his St. George appointment, in 1548, he was a chantry priest at St. Paul's and/or at Guildhall College,[47] and at St. Paul's he served as chaplain to Gabriel Dunne, one of the major canons and formerly the last abbot of Buckfast, Devon.[48] Dunne's sympathies were with the old faith: his will leaves money for an alabaster altar of the annunciation to be his monument in St. Paul's and he made bequests to Sebastian Westcote and John Heywood, perhaps the most traditional members of the St. Paul's community.[49] Despite what seem his conservative sympathies, John Richardson's brief 1560 will is cautiously formulated, only invoking the Trinity, Father, Son and Holy Ghost, three persons in one God.[50] Its bequest of 20s. to Jesus Commons, a college of priests on Dowgate Hill whose library John Stow praised,[51] must be almost the last gift to that institution. Of its end about this time nothing is known, though Richardson's bequest might suggest a refuge for traditionalists.[52] He also left an unspecified sum at the discretion of his executors to a Master Richard Pytt, who had served Bishop of London Richard Fitzjames's chantry at St. Paul's and

---

[46] LMA: DL/A/A/006/MS09631/012/002, f. 472.

[47] *L&MCC*, nos. 108 and 92.

[48] Marie-Hélène Rousseau, *Saving the Souls of Medieval London: Perpetual Chantries at St. Paul's Cathedral c.1200–1548* (Farnham, 2011), p. 166.

[49] John Stephan, "The Last Will and Testament of Gabriel Dunne, Abbot of Buckfast," *Buckfast Abbey Chronicle* 27 (1951), 173–82.

[50] LMA: DL/A/A/006/MS09531/012/001, f. 151v; also Consistory Court Register Bullock, f. 25v.

[51] Barron and Davies, *Religious Houses*, p. 190. Catherine Jamison, "Notes on Jesus Commons," *Notes and Queries* 173 (1937), 92–93, says the site "had no frontage on Dowgate," although the map in M. D. Lobel, *British Atlas of Historic Towns, Vol. III: The City of London from Prehistoric Times to c.1520* (Oxford, 1989), places it there.

[52] Henry A. Harben, *Dictionary of London* (London, 1918), p. 321, says it was "discontinued about 30 years before Stow wrote his *Survey*," i.e. about 1565. Kingsford, *Stow*, I: 231. Lobel, *City of London*, p. 78, says "dissolved temp. Eliz. I." Since Jesus Commons was not near St. George Botolph Lane, Richardson's bequest probably represents a conservative charitable intention and we might wonder whether in 1560 Jesus Commons provided some support for ex-religious.

was probably one of the six fellows of Whittington College at its closure in 1548.[53] Richardson's identity as an ex-friar is strengthened by the presence in the will of Sir William Smith, his overseer, probably the friar of that name who was at the Oxford convent in 1528.[54] One more London Franciscan received a parish, this time outside the capital. John Thornall, doctorem, who signed the surrender in 1538, is registered in Emden as identical with a Berkshire rector who does not appear after 1556.[55]

It is often assumed that appointments as chantry priests sustained many ex-religious, and indeed at the closure of the chantries in 1548 the names of several men are identical with those of former grey friars. At St. Bride Fleet Street, John Mathew was one of two chantry priests serving the brotherhood of Our Lady, sharing a salary of £13 6s. 8d.[56] At St. Alphage parish, Lewis Pestell was the stipendiary priest for John Graunt's chantry; his salary was about the same, £6 13s. 4d.[57] The chantry of John Dowman at St. Paul's Cathedral provided a salary of £8 to chaplain John Tomson.[58] Margaret Bowker says, "[i]n the 1540s, when the full force of inflation was beginning to be felt, it was impossible to live on a salary of £5 or less without any additional benefit in kind."[59] The level of financial support in London for these common positions, £6-plus, would have been somewhat above this minimum.

Thanks to a 1544 Court of Augmentations lawsuit about post-dissolution rentals in the former Greyfriars precincts, we catch a glimpse of two more ex-friars.[60] Both testified in the suit, asserting that they knew the parts of the building in question, since they were "friars of the said late Grey friars." George Hovy (he signs thus, though the clerk writes "hoby") asserted that he was a chaplain of the parish of St. Botolph Aldersgate,

[53] Rousseau, *Saving the Souls*, p. 115. *L&MCC*, no. 96. Cambridge, Emmanuel College MS 237, a copy of ps-Chrysostom *Opus Imperfectum* carries a gift inscription to Richard Pytt from John Thornton, a chaplain of Whittington College. M. R. James (ed.), *Catalogue of the Manuscripts of Emmanuel College Cambridge* (Cambridge, 1904), pp. 136–37. The name of Richard Pytt "Bathonienses" is found in five early printed books whose dates range from 1506 to 1532, but this man seems an unlikely candidate for Richardson's legatee, due to his location. It may be he who received the MA from Oxford in 1511; see *BRUO 1501–1540*, p. 470.

[54] *BRUO 1501–1540*, p. 527.

[55] *BRUO 1501–1540*, p. 564. John Thornall, Franciscan, Oxford convent 1510–25, B.Th. 1523, DD 1525, rector of Stanford Dingley, Berkshire, 1546, and rector of Bradfield, Berkshire, vac. 1556. Little, *Grey Friars*, pp. 279–80, gives more details of his Oxford career.

[56] *L&MCC*, no. 107.

[57] *L&MCC*, no. 83. The parish accounts mention him in 1547/48: "Paid to Sir Lewys for his half year's wages, £3 5s. 8d." LMA: P69/ALP/B/006/MS01432/001, f. 100.

[58] *L&MCC*, no. 109.

[59] Margaret Bowker, *The Henrician Reformation: The Diocese of Lincoln under John Longland 1521–1547* (Cambridge, 1981), p. 102.

[60] TNA E 321/37/18.

aged thirty-six. The position placed Hovy very near his old home, since St. Botolph was just north of the Greyfriars. George Hennessy says that three years later in 1547 Hovy was appointed perpetual curate there,[61] that is, pastor, since the incumbents from *c.*1399 all bear that title. The church-wardens' accounts show that before that he was paid £7, a sum roughly comparable to those received by Mathew, Pestell, and John Tomson. The salary of the other friar who testified in the lawsuit with Hovy, Edmund Tomson, is unknown.[62] Tomson called himself a chaplain of St. Clement Danes, aged forty-three. Earlier, in a 1540 will, he had been left the large sum of 20s. by a Robert Turner, whose parish is not specified. Turner asked Tomson to pray for "my soul and all Christian souls" and it may be that the friar was Turner's ghostly father.[63] Tomson appeared a second time in another property dispute, a Star Chamber suit of 1552 where he says he was a Franciscan for twenty-four years; thus he would have entered the order in 1514. C. J. Sisson found Tomson's name in a third suit, where he testified, in 1578, that he was eighty-three years old.[64] These calculations of Tomson's age conflict slightly,[65] but in 1578, exactly forty years after the house's dissolution, he must have been almost the last London grey friar.

The Franciscans considered so far all managed to obtain positions that supported them either adequately or comfortably. The livelihood of another member of the community is less clear. William Wattes studied theology for eight years at Oxford and Cambridge (he must have known Thomas Chapman, the London warden, for about two decades, since both were at the Oxford convent in 1517).[66] He has been identified as the "doctor Wattes" whose activities are described in a January 1540 travelers' conversation.[67] Nine months after the Greyfriars' dissolution Wattes had

---

[61] Hennessy, *Novum Repertorium*, p. 105 for Hovy, giving no date of death or vacancy.

[62] Tomson is mentioned in Thomas Chapman's letter IX, which says Tomson had been given the sum of 12s. probably intended for John Forest (*LP*, XIII, no. 880). Little, *Grey Friars*, p. 288. Edmund and John Tomson's surnames are spelled identically on the Greyfriars deed of surrender.

[63] Darlington, *London Consistory Court Wills*, no. 141.

[64] C. J. Sisson, "Grafton and the London Grey Friars," *The Library* 4th ser. 11 (1930), 121–49. The earlier two mentions of Tomson were first published by Kingsford, *Grey Friars*. 1544 Court of Augmentations suit: E 315/235, f. 69; E 321/37/18; E 321/12/35. 1552 Star Chamber suit: STAC 3.1/83, 4/49 and 4/50 and 5.V9/22. 1578 suit: C 24/361/75 and 121.

[65] Tomson's stated age of forty-three in 1544 yields a birth date of 1501. His stated age of eighty-three in 1578 yields a birth date of 1495. The latter date is more probable, based on his statement that he had been a Franciscan for twenty-four years, since this would mean he entered the order in 1514 (1538 minus twenty-four), at which time an age of nineteen rather than thirteen seems more likely. (Age 43 may be a transcription error for 48, which would give a birthdate of 1496.)

[66] *BRUO 1501–1540*, pp. 107, 611.

[67] MacCulloch, *Cranmer*, pp. 260–61; also Richard Rex, "The Friars in the English Reformation," in Peter Marshall and Alec Ryrie (eds.), *The Beginnings of English Protestantism* (Cambridge, 2002),

preached and "read to great audiences in London all last summer [1539] and had converted many from the new opinions." The following month, February 1540, he was in the stocks at Canterbury bridewell "after having been accustomed to mouth it [preach] elsewhere in opposition to the gospel."[68] At his London hearing, it was reported that "an alderman of Gracious Street"[69] and another person (a second account says it was the Master of the Rolls, i.e. Sir Christopher Hales) offered "to be surety for his forthcoming" or "to be bound for him in 1000 l."[70] They claimed to be representing 10,000 Londoners assembled "to have fetched him from the bishop of Canterbury with strength."[71]

It seems possible that the William Wattes who died ten years later in 1549 was this popular conservative preacher. He was then living in the parish of St. Stephen Coleman Street, where he asked to be buried in the churchyard.[72] None of the names mentioned in the will are Franciscans, but the will suggests a celibate since it reveals no marriage or children, or, indeed, trade membership. Its largest bequest is faithful to the spirit of Franciscan poverty: 30s. were to be given in 2d. increments to the poor of St. Stephen's. Wattes left small bequests of a shilling each to six men, and similar sums to two kinswomen. A postscript gave 20s. to John Drynkmylke "for his pains taking with me in my sickness." This must be the man mentioned in the will of another notable former religious, Simon Appulby, the subject of Chapter 1, who just before the dissolution in 1537 referred to goods "which I by my writing late gave unto John Drynkmylke."[73] Appulby was the anchorite of the parish of All Hallows London Wall; like St. Stephen Coleman Street it lay in the north-central area of the city.

Two wills: John Baker (†1570) and Albert Copeman (†1572)

In the last Franciscan wills we have, dated 1570 and 1572, it is possible to see traces of circles still connected to the old beliefs, though sometimes

pp. 38–59 (p. 55). Rex points out that Wattes also preached in Lent 1537 at Salisbury, before the closing of the London house.

[68] *LP*, xv, nos. 31 and 259, printed in Hastings Robinson (ed.), *Original Letters Relative to the English Reformation*, 2 vols., Parker Society (London, *1847*), II: 627.

[69] The northern part of Gracechurch Street lay in Bishopsgate ward (pp. 33–44), whose alderman from 1532 was Robert Pagett, merchant tailor. The southern part was in Bread Street ward (pp. 45–54), where Henry Huberthorn, merchant tailor, was chosen in 1537. Alfred P. Beaven, *The Aldermen of the City of London temp. Henry VIII–1908* (London, 1911–12).

[70] *LP*, XV, no. 31 and XIV (ii), no. 750.

[71] *LP*, XIV (ii), no. 750.

[72] LMA: DL/C/B/004/MS09171/012/f. 32v.

[73] LMA: DL/C/330, ff. 252v–53. See Mary C. Erler, "A London Anchorite: Simon Appulby, His *Fruyte of Redempcyon* and Its Milieu," *Viator* 29 (1998), 227–39.

accommodating change as well. The opening statement in the 1570 will of John Baker is explicitly reforming: he gives his soul to God, "my only maker and redeemer ... trusting to be saved by the only death and passion of my lord and savior Jesus Christ and to be in the number of them that shall be saved."[74] Despite this evangelical formula, Baker's will reveals enduring ties with his previous life. He was living nearer than any other friar except Hovy to his old home, the Greyfriars, and still in the area of Smithfield. St. Bartholomew the Less, the parish to which Baker now belonged, had been constituted from the monastic church of St. Bartholomew's Hospital and had been made parochial on January 13, 1547. When Henry VIII granted the hospital to the city, "the church within the site of the hospital [was] called the church of St. Bartholomew the Less in West Smithfield."[75] It lay north of the parish of St. Botolph Aldersgate, between Aldersgate Street on the east and Duck Lane on the west.[76] Like Baker, other ex-religious remained in the neighborhood. In 1547 the first vicar of Baker's new parish St. Bartholomew the Less, Thomas Hikkelyn, was one of the canons of the hospital who had been present at the chapter acknowledging the royal supremacy in 1534.[77]

Not only was Baker dwelling near the former Greyfriars, he also requested burial in the cloister of his old home, "over against the school-house door there" – that is, the door of Christ's Hospital, the school established in the early 1550s in the former Greyfriars precincts. Baker was adroit enough to foresee the arrangements necessary for his unusual request. He left 20s. to the children of Christ's Hospital school, on condition that the treasurer or master obtain "license that my body may be buried and laid in the place before recited."[78]

[74] LMA: DL/C/0358/001, ff. 124v–25v (Consistory Court Register Bullock). The will is signed "John Baker," though at the head of the will the scribe has written in error "John Bartillmewe of the parish of little St. Bartellmewe." Christ Church Newgate's register shows the burial, on August 14, 1572, of "John Baker, old preest who died in St. Bartholomew's," but this is probably an error for 1570. The original register survives, written in 1586 by the churchwardens of that year, who must have made the mistake, copying at some distance in time. Willoughby A. Littledale (ed.), *The Registers of Christ Church, Newgate, 1538 to 1754*, Harleian Society Registers 21 (London, 1895), p. 270. And see C. L. Kingsford, "Additional Material for the History of the Grey Friars, London," *Collectanea Franciscana II*, British Society for Franciscan Studies 10 (Aberdeen, 1922), p. 76. Kingsford thought Baker "so far the last of the Grey Friars of London of whom we have knowledge," but Copeman's will is dated 1572 and Edmund Tomson was living in 1578.

[75] E. A. Webb, *The Records of St. Bartholomew's Priory and of the Church and Parish of St. Bartholomew the Great, West Smithfield*, 2 vols. (Oxford, 1921), I: 276.

[76] Webb, *St. Bartholomew's*, II, map facing p. 131.

[77] Norman Moore, *The History of St. Bartholomew's Hospital*, 2 vols. (London, 1918), II: 160–61.

[78] A president (not a master) was the nominal head of Christ's Hospital, supervising a body of sixteen governors elected for two-year terms, who ran the institution. One of them was elected treasurer; a John Jackson, company unknown, held the post from 1561 to 1574 during the period of Baker's will. Carol Kazmierczak Manzione, *Christ's Hospital of London, 1552–1598* (Selinsgrove, PA, 1995), pp. 46, 179.

Greyfriars had both a great and a little cloister. Richard Whittington's library stood above the ground floor on the north side of the great cloister. A document from 1546, eight years after the dissolution of the house, testifies that at that point the library still had twenty-eight desks and twenty-eight double settles (wooden benches with arms and high backs). "And also there be certain old books upon the said desks."[79] In requesting burial in the cloister Baker seems to have been arranging to lie not far from the historic library.

Other traditionalists were living in the precincts at this time. In Mary's reign the governor of Christ's Hospital William Vikers, son of the famous physician Thomas Vikers or Vicary, gave leases of desirable housing in the Greyfriars precinct to two Catholic controversialists, perhaps as a political move to prevent re-establishment of the convent. John Storey, who had been Bonner's commissary general, and William Chedsey, one of Bonner's chaplains, were installed there and John Christopherson, the Marian bishop of Chichester, received a similar lease. Storey and Chedsey were still alive when Baker died and presumably still living in the precinct where he requested burial. Indeed, John Howes says that Storey used his dwelling there to conduct interrogations of suspected evangelicals, so that religiously the character of this formerly Franciscan space was decidedly mixed.[80]

Baker calls himself bachelor in divinity.[81] Though he did not have a clerical appointment after the dissolution, the level of the will is prosperous. The number of garments recorded in the will, their quality, and the specificity of their details are all somewhat unusual. Three cassocks were described,[82] one of frieze furred with white lamb and edged with black lamb, one of grosgrain lined with cotton, and a third simply of cloth (plus one everyday gown). More surprising is the damask coat furred with white lamb, while another friend received the choice of "one of my damask coats with my pair of satin sleeves to take off and on."

Several of those remembered in the will, perhaps like Baker himself, had accommodated to the new dispensation while retaining Catholic leanings. The printer John Cawood, to whom Baker left a gold ring with his name

[79] Moore, *St. Bartholomew's Hospital*, II: 250.
[80] Lempriere, *John Howes' MS.*, pp. 67–68.
[81] A John Baker received the B.Can.L. in 1512/13 from Cambridge, though perhaps this is the man recorded as entrant in theology in that year (Moorman, *Grey Friars in Cambridge*, p. 150). Moorman says this man "came to Cambridge from Canterbury and went afterwards to London"; p. 132. Another John Baker received the BA in 1516/17 (*AC*, I (i), pp. 70–71).
[82] At this time cassocks could be worn by either men or women.

in it, had been appointed royal printer by Mary to replace the reforming Richard Grafton, and under the queen Cawood was one of the wardens of the re-founded fraternity of the Holy Name of Jesus in St. Paul's, a well-off and conservative group. Brigden calls him a "promoter," one of the informers who were responsible for arrests of the godly.[83] He continued as royal printer under Elizabeth (with Richard Jugge), and as Alec Ryrie notes, he cannot have been regarded as entirely a traditionalist, since his premises were searched for suspect books in 1557. Like Baker, too, he prospered: by 1556 he was the wealthiest member of the Stationers' Company and a significant benefactor, serving for years as master and in various company offices.[84]

The John Eden who was one of Baker's two executors might be the man accused of Catholic sympathies after Baker's death. One of the city attorneys, he had been deprived of his post around 1580 because he was "known to have brought up his children beyond the seas in the Roman Catholic religion." The subsequent sarcastic letter from members of the Privy Council to the mayor makes amusing reading ("thanking them for the zeal shown, not only in his removal, but also in refusing to re-admit him, although they had been requested to do so")[85]. In 1577 the diocesan returns of recusants show the wife of John Eden, no valuation given, living in the parish of St. Olave Silver Street.[86] A John Eden who was left £6 13s. 4d. by Stephen Gardiner, Bishop of Winchester, in 1555 may or may not be the same man. Gardiner's father's will had left his children in the care of a Thomas and a Richard Eden, and Gardiner himself had been taken to Paris as a young teenager in the household of an Englishman named Eden. The editor of the bishop's letters suggests that Gardiner's will bequests, to a John and a Thomas Eden, were made to members of this family.[87]

---

[83] Brigden, *London and the Reformation*, p. 626.

[84] Alec Ryrie, "Cawood, John (1513/14–1572)," *ODNB*, online: www.oxforddnb.com/view/article/4958 (accessed September 14, 2011).

[85] Margaret R. Kollock, *The Lord Mayor and Aldermen of London during the Tudor Period* (Philadelphia, 1906), p. 95. In 1586 Eden petitioned for the city office of alnager (inspector of woolen cloth). Kollock cites for 1586 *Calendar of State Papers Domestic 1581–90*, vol. CLXXXVII (London, 1865), p. 311, and for 1581, W. H. Overall and H. C. Overall (eds.), *Analytical Index to the Series of Records Known as the Remembrancia … City of London AD 1579–1664 in the Library of the Guildhall* (London, 1878), pp. 124–26.

[86] Patrick Ryan, SJ, "Diocesan Returns of Recusants for England and Wales, 1577," *Miscellanea XII*, Catholic Record Society 22 (London, 1921), 46.

[87] For Gardiner's will, J. G. Nichols and John Bruce (eds.), *Wills from Doctors' Commons*, Camden Society 83 (Westminster, 1863), pp. 42–47; J. A. Muller, *Stephen Gardiner and the Tudor Reaction* (New York, 1926), p. 4, n. 9.

Baker's 1570 legacy of what seems to be the collected works of St. Bernard, made to a Master John Norden, raises the question of whether this might be the eminent surveyor (*c*.1549–1625), caught at an early moment in his life. Since Norden entered Hart Hall, Oxford, in 1564 and graduated BA in 1568 and MA in 1573, it is possible that he received from Baker the work of the twelfth-century doctor while still a graduate student, though Baker's will was made in August 1570, before Norden's master's degree was awarded. If John Norden the surveyor and John Norden the devotional writer are the same man, however (as the author of Norden's *ODNB* entry believes), that man held reforming religious views. The preface to his extremely popular book of prayers, *A Pensiue Mans Practise* (first edition 1584, *STC* 18616), thanks God for Elizabeth, "so pure a guide of true religion," while his *Mirror for the Multitude* (1586, *STC* 18613) uses the extreme language of controversy ("mad minsters of the Romish Confederacy"). A contemporary of the same name caused confusion, as the surveyor himself noted in a 1599 letter to Robert Cecil: "I was by some unfortunately mistaken for another of my name … The Norden pretender was a Kentishman, I, born in Somersetshire."[88] It seems that St. Bernard's great subjects – the ascent of the soul to God and the depiction of mystical experience – were more likely to have been appreciated by the unknown Kentishman.

Two men who played important roles in Baker's will were members of London's medical community and because of their centrality in Baker's life, we might wonder whether Baker himself belonged to this community. He does not appear, however, in Pelling and White's list of London physicians and irregular medical practitioners. What that list does reveal is that Baker was living in an extremely medical neighborhood. Nine sixteenth-century practitioners were based in the parish of St. Bartholomew the Less, as Baker was.[89] This location, inside the precincts of St. Bartholomew's Hospital since 1547, would be immensely desirable for medical personnel. Of course, membership in this parish would have been inspired by various motives: perhaps for Baker, remembrance, while for others, convenience.

---

[88] Hatfield House, Cecil MS 103/27.2, quoted in *ODNB*; and see for Norden, Stan A. E. Mendyk, "*Speculum Britanniae*": *Regional Study, Antiquarianism and Science in Britain to 1770* (Toronto, 1989), ch. 3. Hasted mentions a John Norden (†1580) buried in the parish church of Rainham in southeast Kent. Edward Hasted, *The History and Topographical Survey of the County of Kent*, 12 vols. (London, 1998), VI: 5.

[89] Margaret Pelling and Frances White, *Physicians and Irregular Medieval Practitioners in London 1550–1640* (2004), online: www.british-history.ac.uk, under "St. Bartholomew the Less."

Baker's other executor, with Eden, was William Conway, an apothecary. His 1586 will identifies him as a grocer,[90] and indeed apothecaries were a subgroup within that company. As Caroline Barron points out, they were subordinated both to the masters of the grocers and of the physicians, the latter of whom, as she says "were anxious to control the free-ranging activities of the apothecaries."[91] That Conway was a fairly successful practitioner is shown by his lay subsidy assessment in 1582 of £12,[92] and by his will which leaves his son William "the use and benefit of the two shops [the location was unspecified, but Bucklersbury, off Cheapside, was the apothecaries' district] and the still house and all the wares in the same with all my books and implements belonging to my art." A harmonious relation with the College of Physicians is either commemorated or perhaps anticipated by a large gift to them of £5 "to be disposed at the discretion of the president and censors."

Conway lived in the large extramural parish of St. Sepulchre, outside the city walls to the northwest and hence in the same quarter of the city as Baker.[93] St. Sepulchre was unusual in having retained a parish house after the 1548 dissolution of the chantries, and Conway's bequest in 1586 suggests the continuity of traditional parish celebrations and recalls Stow's description of such parties earlier in the sixteenth century. He left £4 "for a recreation for my honest and good neighbors of the church quarters and others," and 40s. to buy linens for the use of the church house.[94] His namesake son William was admitted pensioner to Gonville and Caius College, Cambridge, on February 6, 1577 at age fifteen, when he was registered as the son of William "citizen and druggist of London."[95]

Henry Wotton, Baker's overseer, was the eminent son of a famous father, Edward (1492–1555), physician and naturalist and the first reader

[90] TNA PCC 46 Windsor (Prob 11/69/362). And see R. G. Lang, *Two Tudor Subsidy Assessment Rolls for the City of London: 1541 and 1582*, London Record Society 29 (London, 1993). Henry Wotten might have continued in his father Edward's house in the parish of St. Alban Wood Street (in 1541, no. 86).

[91] Caroline M. Barron, *London in the Later Middle Ages: Government and People 1200–1500* (Oxford, 2004), pp. 286–87. Margaret Pelling and Charles Webster, "Medical Practitioners," in Charles Webster (ed.), *Health, Medicine and Morality in the Sixteenth Century* (Cambridge, 1979), pp. 165–235 (pp. 178–79).

[92] Lang, *Tudor Subsidy*, no. 337.

[93] Brigden says that in Edward's reign St. Sepulchre's was a hotbed of papistry; *London and the Reformation*, p. 627.

[94] Although the 1548 Chantry Certificate does not list a parish house for St. Sepulchre, the parish's Edwardian inventories show that in 1549–51 the wealthy merchant adventurer Emmanuel Lucar bought the church house for £26 13s. 4d. H. B. Walters, *London Churches at the Reformation* (London, 1939), p. 212.

[95] AC, I (i), p. 382, which says his school was Grey Friars, presumably Christ's Hospital.

in Greek at Corpus Christi College, Oxford. Henry (*c.*1527–*c.*1597) graduated MB from Christ Church in 1562, received his MD in 1567, and like
his father was Greek reader at Corpus Christi. He was admitted a candidate of the College of Physicians in 1564, became a fellow in 1572, and was
censor in 1581 and 1582. Interestingly, he was recommended by the College
of Physicians for the post of physician to St. Bartholomew's Hospital in
1585, but was rejected.[96] His parish is unknown; he does not appear in the
1582 lay subsidy.[97] Other beneficiaries in Baker's will may have provided
a further sense of his activities, but I have been unable to trace Marcus
Leighley and his wife; William Turke, gentleman; John Fisher, salter, and
his son Philip; Thomas Aides, fishmonger; William Kenham, brewer; and
John Pole of St. Faith's parish.

The last Franciscan to be considered, Albert Copeman, signed the dissolution document in 1538, but he is not listed as applying for or receiving
a capacity. Nevertheless he must have gotten one because the 1548 Chantry
Certificate lists him as a chaplain of William Trystor's chantry at St. Vedast
Foster Lane, where he received annually £6 13s. 4d., though "of poor quality and learning and having no other income."[98] He was thirty-nine in
that year; we next meet him a quarter of a century later as the parish clerk
of St. Botolph Bishopsgate, where he made his will on February 25, 1572
and was buried the next day.[99] His age would have been sixty-three. The
original will survives in a pretty hand, not Copeman's given his next-day
burial.[100] Like Baker, Copeman commends his soul to God, but in language much more neutral than Baker's: "I give and bequeath my soul into
the hands of almighty god and my body to be buried in the churchyard of
St. Botolph's."

It is not possible to say at what date after 1548 Copeman received this
parish post, but it might have been during the St. Botolph rectorship of
Hugh Weston, appointed by Bishop Bonner, between May 10, 1544 and
December 8, 1558.[101] Weston was an extreme conservative, one of Mary's
chaplains, and chosen by her as dean of the restored Westminster Abbey,

---

[96] William Munk, *The Roll of the Royal College of Physicians of London*, 2nd edn., 5 vols. (London, 1878), I: 70–71.

[97] Lang, *Tudor Subsidy*, p. 30. The man of that name in 1541 at St. Magnus, worth £200, is probably too early.

[98] *L&MCC*, no. 5.

[99] St. Botolph Bishopsgate register, LMA: P69/BOT4/A/001/MS04515/001, unfoliated [f. 25], "Sir Albart Copeman preist."

[100] LMA: DL/C/419/81, also in Consistory Court Register Bullock, ff. 171v–72.

[101] Hennessy, *Novum Repertorium*, p. 111.

hence it might be thought that he would be conscious of the fortunes of ex-religious. The parish registers begin only in 1558, while the surviving churchwardens' accounts begin in 1567 and record an annual salary to the parish clerk, not named, of £4. In addition the clerk received an annual stipend of 4s. for arranging a Sunday bread distribution, made to thirteen poor people ("his fee for to call in the bread into the church and to see it set down upon some decent place in the church for the poor").[102] Service as a parish clerk thus yielded considerably less than the £6 13s. 4d. paid earlier to Copeman when he was employed as a chantry priest at St. Vedast's. He must have supplemented his St. Botolph's salary, however, since his will refers to "my cupboard in my shop and all that is in it." Since as clerk Copeman would have been responsible for entry of births, deaths, and weddings in the register, we might hope to see evidence of his handwriting, but the register from 1558 on was re-copied, as its title page notes: "new written according to her Majestys injunctions … Anno Domini 1599,"[103] and the old register does not survive.

The largest of Copeman's debts (33s. 2d.) was owned to Annes Heaton. Later bequests make it clear she was his housekeeper or caretaker and she received most of his furniture and two gowns. More curious is the 20s. Copeman owed to the alderman, who in this neighborhood was, as he says, the alderman of the steelyard.[104] Remaining monies, ranging from 12s. down to 2s. 2d., were owed to Leonard Hopkyns, John Wygens, Garet the tailor, and William Lomley (amount left blank), all parishioners, except Lomley.[105]

Baker and Copeman are the only London grey friars whose wills mention books. Copeman's English bible went to Barnet (or Barnard) Noster, a younger friend and parishioner whose two daughters were born in 1574 and 1579 and who died in 1597, twenty-five years after Copeman.[106]

---

[102] St. Botolph Bishopsgate churchwardens' accounts, LMA: P69/BOT4/B/008/MS04524/001, f. 4. This parish charity was founded in 1567 by mayor and parishioner William Alleyn and by the Corpus Christi guild of the Skinners' Company and in that year Alleyn gave St. Botolph's a book to record both the bread charity and the parish accounts. LMA: P69/BOT4/B/008/MS04524/001, f. 3.

[103] St. Botolph Bishopsgate register, LMA: P69/BOT4/A/001/MS04515/001.

[104] "The Hanse merchants … elected their own alderman who … was allowed to hold a court for the Hanse merchants and to act on their behalf." Barron, *London*, p. 87.

[105] Of these names, John Wygens (Wiggens) was buried January 20, 1577 from St. Botolph's while Leonard Hopkyns is probably the Leonard Hopkinson who was married October 17, 1559, buried June 9, 1582. A. W. Cornelius Hallen (ed.), *The Registers of St. Botolph, Bishopsgate London*, 3 vols. (London, 1889, 1893), I: 280; III: 288. The parish had over thirty members named Garet (and variations). William Lomley does not appear in the parish register.

[106] Hallen, *Registers*, I: 92, 96, 320.

He left the unspecified residue of his books to one John Dugdall, named as servant to Lord Giles Paulet, together with "my folding table and the joined form to it and also my trundle bed." Dugdall does not appear in the parish records but the mention of the Paulet family establishes that the legatee was the father of historian William Dugdale, since connections between the Paulet and Dugdale families were extensive.[107] John Dugdall would have been twenty at this time and it may be that the former friar had taught him. That he served as one of the witnesses to Copeman's will on the day before the latter's death means that Dugdall was nearby.

Ten years later he accompanied William Paulet, grandson of the marquis of Winchester and son of Lord Giles Paulet, to St. John's College, Oxford as his tutor (guardian).[108] In that year, 1582, John Dugdall himself matriculated at the age of thirty. He studied civil law but took no degree, continuing to live in Oxford and to work as a clerk of accounts and steward of their courts for St. John's until 1598.[109] We do not know whether during these Oxford years, the 1580s and 1590s, Dugdall still owned Albert Copeman's library.

Copeman left to the Honorable Giles Paulet the remainder of the lease of his house "wherein I now dwell" in exchange for the discharge of certain listed debts. This connection is perhaps the most significant element in Copeman's will. Lord Giles was a younger son of William Paulet, the Elizabethan minister and first marquis of Winchester (1474/75–1572) whose religious positions during his career were notably various. In a 1574 list headed "Catholicks in Inglonde," however, three of Winchester's sons were listed:[110] John Paulet, second marquis of Winchester (*c.*1510–76), Lord Giles Paulet (after 1521–80), and Lord Chidiock Paulet (in or before 1524–74).[111] Chidiock's recusancy is re-affirmed by a second list of "names and

---

[107] Jan Broadway, "Unreliable Witness: Sir William Dugdale and the Perils of Autobiography," in Christopher Dyer and Catherine Richardson (eds.), *William Dugdale, Historian, 1605–1686: His Life, His Writings, and His County* (Woodbridge, 2009), pp. 34–50.

[108] St. John's had been founded in 1554 under Philip and Mary by the Catholic Sir Thomas White and "its statutes laid down precise regulations for divine worship in accordance with the Sarum use," although twelve fellows were deprived between 1567 and 1574 for Catholicism, Edmund Campion being the most celebrated. W. C. Castin, *The History of St. John's College Oxford 1598–1860* (Oxford, 1958), p. 5; James McConica, *The History of the University of Oxford, Vol. III: The Collegiate University* (Oxford, 1986), p. 411.

[109] William Hamper, *The Life, Diary, and Correspondence of Sir William Dugdale* (London, 1828), pp. 5–6, quoting Anthony Wood's Bodleian MS 8560. I am grateful to Dr. Jan Broadway, Queen Mary College, University of London, for information about the Dugdale family.

[110] John Bannerman Wainewright, "Two Lists of Influential Persons Apparently Prepared in the Interests of Mary, Queen of Scots, 1574 and 1582," *Miscellanea VIII*, Catholic Record Society 13 (London, 1913), 89.

[111] These dates are taken from *ODNB*; only the heir, John, is listed in *CP*, XII (ii), pp. 762–64.

addresses of papists" from 1578. It mentions "Lord Chidiock Paulet, the Spittle, without Bishopsgate" and notes that "Robert Hare and Saunders of the Inner Temple ... repair to Lord Paulet."[112] His older brother John lived in the neighborhood as well. Describing the street leading out from Bishopsgate, Stow notes first the Dolphin Inn just outside the gate, "then is there a faire house of late builded by *Iohn Powlet*."[113] The house stood opposite St. Botolph Bishopsgate church,[114] at which Giles Paulet was a parishioner.

This neighborhood outside Bishopsgate was contiguous with Simon Appulby's northeast neighborhood around All Hallows London Wall. Its features – the Spital, its open-air pulpit, the fields behind it – can be seen in sharp detail on the portion of the copperplate map depicting the Moorgate–Bishopsgate area, shown earlier as Figure 1.1.[115] Nancy Pollard Brown's identification of the Spital precinct as an area of Catholic householders concentrates on the period from Jesuit Robert Southwell's 1586 return to England through the early seventeenth century,[116] but Copeman's will, made in 1572, indicates that the precinct and the nearby parish of St. Botolph Bishopsgate may have had this character earlier in the 1570s, as the 1578 list of papists cited above also suggests. Several precinct buildings, for instance, were leased in 1580 to the recusant and antiquarian Robert Hare.[117] The lease refers to the great cost and charge that he "heretofore hath bestowed" on the properties, evidence that Hare's occupancy pre-dated 1580.[118] Hare certainly knew his neighbors the Paulet

---

[112] Wainewright, "Two Lists," 89. The editor cites *Calendar of State Papers Domestic 1566–79, Addenda* (London, 1871), pp. 510–11, for the 1578 list and adds that "Mass was being said" at the Spitle. In 1564 Bishop Horne of Winchester reported on Chidiock's Catholicism, and he refused to sign the Act of Uniformity. See Bindoff, "Chidiock Paulet (by 1521–74), of Wade, Hampshire," in *House of Commons*, III: 70–71, giving a different birth date than *ODNB*.

[113] Kingsford, *Stow*, I: 165. Stow was writing this section in 1594–98.

[114] Lobel, *City of London*, map 2.

[115] This section of the copperplate map is reproduced in Peter Whitfield, *London: A Life in Maps* (London, 2006), pp. 32–33, who says "the most striking feature of this plan ... is the obvious spread of dwellings outside Bishopsgate, where ... large houses with sizeable gardens extend northwards, enjoying the space and air outside the confines of the City, almost foreshadowing the later growth of suburbia."

[116] Nancy Pollard Brown, "Paperchase: The Dissemination of Catholic Texts in Elizabethan England," *English Manuscript Studies 1100–1700* 1 (1989), 120–43. Brown says that at the dissolution, houses in the Spital precinct passed to the marquis of Winchester and that in 1542 he transferred them to Stephen Vaughn, "one of his household officers" (p. 123). Winchester did not own Spital property, however, and Vaughn was not in his service – though Robert Hare was (see below).

[117] Elisabeth Leedham-Green, "Hare, Robert (c. 1539–1611)," *ODNB* (2004; online edn. June 2008), online: www.oxforddnb.com/view/article/12366 (accessed January 23, 2011); see also G. M. Coles on Robert Hare in P. M. Hasler, *The House of Commons (1558–1603)*, 3 vols. (London, 1981), II: 254.

[118] London County Council, *Survey of London, Vol. XXVII: Spitalfields* (London, 1957), p. 47.

brothers: his father Sir Nicholas Hare, Master of the Rolls under Mary, had been a client of their father, the marquis of Winchester,[119] and one writer attributes Nicholas Hare's parliamentary election to Winchester's influence.[120] Robert Hare himself was in the service of the marquis from as early as 1558.

Giles Paulet appears frequently in the parish records of St. Botolph Bishopsgate. The births of his four children, Elizabeth, Mary, Anne, and William (and the death of Mary at age two) are recorded in the parish register in quick succession between 1561 and 1564, several of them only eleven months apart. In 1568/69 the parish paid "for mending the window where my lord Gyles sitteth," and in 1570/71 for mending Lord Giles's pew. His wife died in July 1572; her forename is not given.[121]

If the Paulet brothers were adherents of the old faith, their London dwellings standing near each other in this conservative neighborhood, Lord Giles's patronage of an elderly former friar, now a parish employee, would seem thoroughly consistent. Indeed the payment of debts that Copeman requested from Lord Giles does speak of patronage given and received. It was Giles Paulet, in fact, who probated Copeman's will – promptly, about ten days after his death, on March 5, 1572.[122]

Authorship of the *Greyfriars Chronicle*

The extent to which these twelve former friars remained close to their former home is considerable.[123] Three hardly moved from the neighborhood: Baker at St. Bartholomew the Less; Copeman in his first post at St. Vedast; Hovy at St. Botolph Aldersgate. Five remained in the western half of London: Caterick at St. Alban Wood Street; Mathew at St. Bride; Pestell at St. Alphage; Edmund Tomson at St. Clement Danes; John Tomson at St. Paul's. Three moved to the eastern half of the city: Copeman in his second post at St. Botolph Bishopsgate; Richardson at St. George Botolph Lane; and Wattes at St. Stephen Colman Street. Two found employment

---

[119] The copperplate map shows that the Bishopsgate neighborhood would have been close to their father's mansion, the former Austin friary just south of All Hallows London Wall, which the Marquis of Winchester was granted between 1540 and 1550. See Kingsford, *Stow*, I: 176–77; II: 300.

[120] Roger Virgoe, "Hare, Nicholas (by 1495–1557) of Bruisyard, Suff. and London," in Bindoff, *House of Commons*, II: 296–97.

[121] LMA: P69/BOT4/B/008/MS04524/001, ff. 5, 10v, 12, 13v. Hallen, *Registers*, I: 79 (2), 81, 82, 271.

[122] The will had named one John Cooper as its executor, but this sentence was crossed out.

[123] Claire Cross notes that several Yorkshire friars likewise "attempted to stay in the vicinity"; "The End of Medieval Monasticism in the North Riding of Yorkshire," *Yorkshire Archaeological Journal* 76 (2006), 155.

outside London: Chapman in Sussex and Thornall in Berkshire. Where the rest of the community went and how they lived is unknown.

Baker's will and Copeman's are extensive enough to offer some purchase for speculation about the identity of the Greyfriars chronicler, the man who recorded London's political and religious events between 1538 and 1556. Baker's final statement of reliance on Christ's mercy uses the familiar godly language of reform. His continuing residence near the former Greyfriars, however, and his request for burial in its cloister signal an attachment to his former life, congruent, it might seem, with the wish to record the continuing development of the events in which he had played a part. His medical connections, the unknown source of his prosperity, his interest in dress, and his library make him an intriguing figure, one whom it is hard to sum up satisfactorily.

Copeman's patronage by a recusant younger son and his location in a neighborhood with several Catholic households suggests his sympathies were traditional, although his position as a parish employee must have necessitated some acceptance of the current religious status quo. His ownership of a collection of books and particularly his gift of them in 1572 to John Dugdall, the historian's father, might suggest a shared interest in history, although John Dugdall's life is too hidden for us to do more than wonder about his reading. Copeman's composition of the *Greyfriars Chronicle* cannot be more than a possibility. Yet the movement of the manuscript over the last quarter of the sixteenth and the first quarter of the seventeenth century, as far as we can trace it, is entirely within the circles we might expect would find its contents deeply valuable. Its first editor, J. G. Nichols, noted that it had been owned by historian John Stow who copied considerable portions, those recording the friary's earlier history and the burials, into his own manuscript BL Harley 544.[124] Stow also corrected a few passages from 1538 to 1556 in the *Greyfriars Chronicle*, indicating that he read and knew this history.[125] A connection between John Dugdall and John Stow sometime in the 1570s can only be conjectural, but a possible link might be the recusant antiquarian Robert Hare, who lived in the Spital area from at least 1580 and probably earlier, and who knew Stow from the early 1570s.[126]

---

[124] Kingsford, *Stow*, I: xci; II: 345.

[125] Nichols, *Grey Friars*; Kingsford, *Stow*; and more recently Alexandra Gillespie, "Stow's 'Owlde' Manuscripts of London Chronicles," in Ian Gadd and Alexandra Gillespie (eds.), *John Stow (1525–1605) and the Making of the English Past: Studies in Early Modern Culture and the History of the Book* (London, 2004), p. 59.

[126] Kingsford, *Stow*, I: lxviii, lxxii.

From Stow the manuscript passed into the possession of historian William Camden before coming to rest in the great collection of Camden's friend, traveling companion, and former pupil Robert Cotton, where it now resides.[127] We know that Camden owned the manuscript before Cotton did thanks to a letter around 1623 from Augustine Vincent to Cotton, which says, "I pray you lend me your book of burials in the Minories that was Mr. Camdens."[128] Camden's interest in the Franciscan manuscript is likely to have been this register of tombs and burials in the large Franciscan church, since in 1600 he published his own overview of the monuments of Westminster Abbey, *Reges, reginae, nobilis et alii in ecclesia collegiate B. Petri Westmonasterii sepulti*. If so, he probably owned the Greyfriars manuscript before 1600. Points of contact between Camden and Stow were many: Kingsford printed an undated letter in which Camden asks Stow for the loan of his book on "the foundations of the abbeys in Lincolnshire, Warwickshire, Derbyshire, and Nottinghamshire," and Harley MS 530 which contains this letter also includes some corrections by Camden for Stow's *Survey of London* that Kingsford says are incorporated in the printed text.[129] Oliver Harris notes that Camden and Stow knew each other at least by 1574, three years after Camden had left Oxford, on the evidence of a letter in that year from John Dee to Camden.[130]

Consequently the progression of the manuscript from Stow to Camden to Cotton seems certain. A final, odd instance of the manuscript's readership may be mentioned: after the manuscript entered Cotton's collection, William Dugdale knew and used it. During the Civil War, Dugdale and John Selden sorted and bound Cotton's papers.[131] Either at this time or earlier Dugdale wrote his name on the first folio and, like Stow, copied excerpts from it into a manuscript of his own, Bodley Dugdale 15.[132] Can the two Dugdales, father and son, each have known the manuscript – Dugdale

---

[127] Wyman H. Herendeen, "Camden, William (1551–1623)," *ODNB* (2004; online edn. January 2008), online: www.oxforddnb.com/view/article/4431 (accessed June 10, 2009). He points out that their friendship was supported by proximity since Cotton's house abutted the walls of Westminster School where Camden was headmaster.

[128] Colin G. C. Tite, *The Early Records of Sir Robert Cotton's Library: Formation, Cataloguing, Use* (London, 2003).

[129] Kingsford, *Stow*, I: lxxiii, lxxxix. He quotes herald Ralph Brooke's testimony that Stow had an annuity of £8 from Camden in return for Stow's transcripts of Leland's papers (I: xxv).

[130] Oliver Harris, "Stow and the Contemporary Antiquarian Network," in Gadd and Gillespie (eds.), *John Stow*, pp. 27–35 (p. 33). Ian Archer points out that at least from 1586 both were members of the Society of Antiquaries and "rubbed shoulders" at their discussions. "John Stow, Citizen and Historian," in Gadd and Gillespie (eds.), *John Stow*, p. 14.

[131] Kevin Sharpe, *Sir Robert Cotton 1586–1630: History and Politics in Early Modern England* (Oxford, 1979), p. 82.

[132] Tite, *Early Records*, p. 171.

père as the recipient of the book from Albert Copeman, Dugdale *fils* as its reader several decades later?

In the end we cannot be sure of the chronicle's author or the manuscript's first owner. Nonetheless, if a transmission something like that outlined above took place, we might speculate that despite his 1548 assessment as "of poor quality and learning," it was the Franciscan Albert Copeman who composed this unparalleled account of London life in the years just after the dissolution. The manuscript gives us a welcome means of access to the lives of these London Franciscans and to the ways in which they encountered both religious change and the economic and cultural shifts that resulted. The elements of stability that they negotiated for themselves included continuing residence in London, institutional positions, and occasionally a degree of contact with former associates. At the center of such efforts at continuity is the Greyfriars manuscript, its *Chronicle* an expression of its author's conviction that the contemporary account he had added to its earlier record constituted a worthy record of his period's uncertainties.

CHAPTER THREE

Cromwell's nuns:
Katherine Bulkeley, Morpheta Kingsmill, and Joan Fane

That there were religious at the dissolution whose sympathies lay more with the new order than with the old seems undeniable. The warden of the London Greyfriars, author of revealing letters to Thomas Cromwell, was one such, and indeed Cromwell's correspondence provides information about others. Various heads of religious houses, both male and female, were part of the minister's remarkable network of contacts. Cromwell's comprehensive development of clients and supporters throughout England has been well studied in its secular manifestations. Mary Robertson says, "[h]e selected from among existing families of local influence those individuals who could best serve as the liaison between court and country. These were appointed to local office (or confirmed in offices already held), consulted, watched, encouraged, rewarded, and personally admonished if necessary."[1] The pattern of oversight for religious institutions was similar. Cromwell's practices here have been considered part of an effort to centralize ecclesiastical authority under the crown, and it has recently been suggested that in fact the attention given to religious houses by Cardinal Wolsey and Cromwell from the mid-1520s may have been partly responsible for the ease with which English religious institutions were dissolved.[2] An anonymous Elizabethan writer puts it even more plainly: "He placed abbots and friars in divers great houses ... which men were ready to make surrender of their houses at the king's commandment."[3]

During the final years of the 1530s, Cromwell appointed at least three women as heads of larger houses, each of the houses valued at well over £300 annually. Family connections were a crucial element in these

---

[1] Mary L. Robertson, "'The Art of the Possible': Thomas Cromwell's Management of West Country Government," *Historical Journal* 32 (1989), 793–816 (813).

[2] Martin Heale, "'Not a Thing for a Stranger to Enter Upon': The Selection of Monastic Superiors in Late Medieval and Tudor England," in Janet Burton and Karen Stover (eds.), *Monasteries and Society in the British Isles in the Later Middle Ages* (Woodbridge, 2008), pp. 51–68 (p. 61).

[3] Wright, *Suppression*, p. 114.

preferments, since all three women had brothers who were closely allied with Cromwell. In each case religious sympathy seems to have been a factor as well. Abbess of Godstow, Oxfordshire, Katherine Bulkeley's six lively and charming letters to Cromwell suggest a relation close to friendship and they state her evangelical position explicitly, in language not unlike that of Greyfriars warden Thomas Chapman. From Morpheta Kingsmill, last prioress of Wherwell, Hampshire, only one letter to Cromwell survives, and though the letter shows her to advantage as the defender of her house's rights of patronage, it is Kingsmill's will that opens the question of her beliefs, suggesting either an accommodation with her family's involvement in reform or, perhaps, a careful neutrality. Finally, it is neither letters nor will, but private reading that reveals the sympathies of the last prioress of the Dominican nuns of Dartford, Kent. When Joan Fane owned and gave away a copy of radical printer-poet Robert Crowley's 1550 edition of *Piers Plowman*, her interest in social change and her sympathy for the poor, so central to the medieval poem, had family roots. All three women were relatively young, born probably between 1495 and 1505, hence somewhere in their thirties when elevated.[4] Fane died around 1556; Bulkeley and Kingsmill lived until 1570. Though their positions were varied, all reflected to some degree the religious sympathies of their families and, most visibly, of their brothers – like themselves, dependants of a great patron, Thomas Cromwell.

Katherine Bulkeley

Abbess Katherine Bulkeley belonged to an important Welsh family who dominated their region; her brother Sir Richard Bulkeley was a notable courtier and client first of Wolsey, then of Cromwell, whom his enemies accused of such ambition that he would "suffer no man to live in the country but himself."[5] In 1537 when he was acting chamberlain of north Wales, he wrote Cromwell asking for an appointment for his relative Arthur (later Bishop of Bangor), and in 1538 he requested a dissolved friary for himself.[6] Cromwell's accounts for 1537 show that in that year he had lent Bulkeley £200.[7] A letter from Bulkeley to Cromwell in 1536 recounts

[4] Bulkeley was Godstow's second most junior nun at a 1520 visitation, hence perhaps aged about twenty. Kingsmill had been Prioress of Wherwell in 1529 at a previous election. Fane was said to have been over thirty when elected in 1537.

[5] Glanmore Williams, *Wales and the Reformation* (Cardiff, 1997), pp. 43, 55, 65.

[6] *LP*, XII (ii) no. 998; XIII (ii), no. 892.

[7] *LP*, XIV (ii), no. 782.

a reproof from the latter, who had told Bulkeley that "all is words that I do and no deeds." Bulkeley's reply abases himself: "I know right well it lieth in your hands to undo me for ever with a word of your mouth."[8]

It may be that Cromwell had a hand in the resignation of the old Godstow abbess Margaret Tewkesbury, who had ruled since 1517. Her message to him asking for approval of her enclosed resignation letter,[9] while it does not necessarily indicate Cromwell's initiative in the matter, at least shows his careful management of the situation. She wrote on September 28, presumably 1534, since episcopal assent to Katherine Bulkeley's election was issued on March 16, 1535.[10] Bulkeley had been a nun of Godstow since before 1520. In that year she was second from last in the seniority list,[11] hence among the youngest members of the house and perhaps aged only about thirty-five when she became abbess. Six months later on September 27, 1535, John Tregonwell wrote his master Cromwell that on his visit to Godstow he "found all things well and in good order."[12] We know nothing about the details of the Godstow election, but Cromwell's influence was later acknowledged by the abbess herself: "it hath pleased your lordship to be the very mean to the King's majesty for my preferment." Elsewhere, like her brother she used the language of clientage easily, telling Cromwell "you have of nothing brought me to all that I have by your mere [utter] goodness, never deserved of me in any part."[13]

An early message of hers sends Cromwell a present of "a dish of old apples, whereof some be a twelvemonth old, and some two year old," along with his fees.[14] In another letter, her thanks for his preventing the mayor and citizens of Oxford "from entering the commons which I and my tenants have held 400 years" is jaunty, and this communication is accompanied by a gift of Banbury cheeses, an Oxford specialty.[15] She offered Cromwell the stewardship of Godstow in flattering terms, deprecating its fee, only 40s., but pointing out that "you shall have at your

---

[8] Williams, *Wales*, p. 59, quoting TNA SP 1/112/20 (*LP*, XI, no. 1329).

[9] *LP*, VII, no. 1197, printed in Ellis, III: 116.

[10] Smith, *Heads*, III: 648, citing Lincoln Episcopal Register XXVI, f. 257. At the surrender Abbess Tewkesbury was still living, though aged over eighty. She requested an additional 20 marks to add to her current pension of 20 marks; *LP*, XIV (ii), no. 539.

[11] A. Hamilton Thompson (ed.), *Visitations in the Diocese of Lincoln 1517–1531*, 3 vols., Lincoln Record Society 33, 35, 37 (Hereford, 1940–47), III: 153.

[12] *LP*, IX, no. 457 (TNA SP1/97, pp. 37–38).

[13] *LP*, XIII (ii), no. 758; *LP*, XIII (i), no. 441, printed in Green, *Letters*, III: xxxii, pp. 69–70.

[14] *LP*, XI, no. 570, printed in Green, *Letters*, III: xxxiii, pp. 71–72.

[15] *LP*, XIII (i), no. 1262.

commandment twenty or thirty men to do the king service thereby"[16] and revealing that Godstow had recently sent men to the north in the rebellions of 1536/37.

It is clear that the arrival of Cromwell visitor Dr. John London in early November 1538 came as a great surprise to Bulkeley. The conflict between the abbess and the visitor was both religious and personal. The abbess wrote Cromwell that "as your lordship doth well know, [London] was against my promotion and hath ever since borne me great malice and grudge."[17] Though he was Oxford-based, like Bulkeley, London has been thought an odd choice to be one of Cromwell's visitors, as his own convictions were conservative.[18] In the 1520s he was the Bishop of Lincoln's commissary to the University of Oxford, where he was warden of New College, and Margaret Bowker calls him "very vigilant" in seeking out heresy.[19] Cromwell himself described London as "a great papist and hinderer of good learning"; hence, perhaps, the minister's prevention of London's attempts to close Godstow.[20]

Bulkeley's two last letters, both written in November 1538, offer both a compelling self-defense and a powerful statement of belief. On November 5, in the midst of London's visit and in response to his charges of self-aggrandizement, she wrote, "I have not alienated one halfpenny of the goods of this monastery, moveable or unmovable, but have rather increased the same ... I have not offended and am and will be most obedient to [the king]." Cromwell's intervention at this point, in 1538, gave Godstow only one further year. Bulkeley's final letter of November 26, 1538, which thanks Cromwell for the stay, also notes that in accordance with Cromwell's wishes she has transferred ownership of the house's

---

[16] Eileen Power explains that "abbeys holding from the king in chief had to perform many services appertaining to tenants in chief" including the duty to send men for the king's service, and she mentions Shaftesbury, Nunnaminster, Wilton, and Barking as performing this service. *Medieval English Nunneries c. 1275 to 1535* (Cambridge, 1922), p. 185. *LP*, XIII (i), no. 441, Green, *Letters*, II: xxxii.

[17] BL Cotton Cleopatra E.IV, f. 228; *LP*, XIII (ii), no. 758; Wright, *Suppression*, pp. 229–31; Cook, *Letters*, CXXXVI, pp. 212–14.

[18] G. R. Elton, *Policy and Police: The Enforcement of the Reformation in the Age of Thomas Cromwell* (Cambridge, 1972), pp. 352–53.

[19] Margaret Bowker, *The Henrician Reformation: The Diocese of Lincoln under John Longland 1521–1547* (Cambridge, 1981), p. 182. Ethan H. Shagan is more explicit, calling London "a persecutor of Oxford evangelicals in the 1520s"; *Popular Politics and the English Reformation* (Cambridge, 2003), p. 200.

[20] For London, *BRUO 1501–1540*, pp. 359–60. Diarmaid MacCulloch, *Thomas Cranmer: A Life* (New Haven, 1996), p. 300, calls London "a flamboyant figure"; see also David Knowles, *The Religious Orders in England, Vol. III: The Tudor Age* (Cambridge, 1961), pp. 354–55. He died in the Fleet in 1543, having been charged with perjury in the prebendaries plot, an attempt to prove Cranmer an evangelical.

demesnes and stock to royal physician George Owen, though "no man living, under the King, could have had it of us with our good wills, saving your lordship."

The abbess must still have hoped to preserve Godstow, however, since it is in this final letter that she appeals to Cromwell on the basis of what looks very much like a shared system of belief ("as my very trust and comfort is in you, I beseech you to continue my good lord, as I trust you shall never have cause to the contrary"). Her reforming principles are immediately invoked: like warden Chapman, she disparages the religious habit: "not doubting but this garment and fashion of life doth nothing prevail toward our justifying before God. By whom, for his sweet son Jesus' sake, we only trust to be justified and saved." Religious practice at Godstow has been reformed: "there is neither pope nor purgatory, image nor pilgrimage, nor praying to dead saints, used or regarded amongst us: but all superstitious ceremonies set apart, the very [true] honour of God and the truth of his holy words ... is most tenderly followed and regarded with us." The two letters constitute an able and convincing refutation of the central charges made against religious houses: personal corruption and papistry.

Godstow surrendered a year later on November 17, 1539, and in March 1540 Dr. Owen bought the abbey for £558. It became his home, but by the early eighteenth century, the buildings were in ruins (see Figure 3.1). Katherine Bulkeley had ruled for only a little under five years (1535–39). At the collapse of her house she retired to a life with her family at Cheadle, Cheshire, where her 1559 will commends her soul to Almighty God, to Jesus Christ his only son, and to the Holy Ghost, but does not invoke the Virgin or saints.[21] The will is full of nieces and nephews and suggests a happy domestic life with plenty of creature comforts, sustained by her generous pension of £50.[22] We know from an inscription in a window, now destroyed, that in 1556 she built the church's chancel and glazed the windows,[23] and she probably lived in the parsonage there, where she had a 1552

[21] G. J. Piccope (ed.), *Lancashire and Cheshire Wills and Inventories from the Ecclesiastical Court, Chester*, Chetham Society 33 (Manchester, 1851), pp. 54–56. For more detail on the abbess's life, see Mary C. Erler, "Religious Women after the Dissolution: Continuing Community," in Matthew Davies and Andrew Prescott (eds.), *London and the Kingdom: Essays in Honour of Caroline M. Barron* (Donington, 2008), pp. 142–43.

[22] *LP*, XIV (ii), no. 539, November 17, 1539. The house was assessed at £319 18s. 8d. Dugdale, *Monasticon*, IV: 360.

[23] J. P. Earwacker, *East Cheshire: Past and Present*, 2 vols. (London, 1877), I: 204. "Orate pro anima Dominae Katherinae Bulkele quondam Abbatissae de Godstow quae hoc sacellum construxit Anno Dni MCCCCClvi et omnes fenestras vitriari fecit."

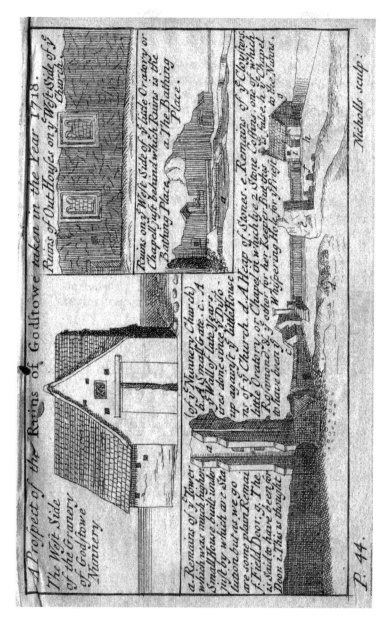

Figure 3.1 "A Prospect of the Ruins of Godstowe taken in the Year 1718," from *Memoirs of the Antiquities of Great Britain*, 1723.

lease.[24] She was left all his Oxfordshire lands by Thomas Powell, a former fellow of All Saints College, Oxford, a married cleric who had become rector of St. Thomas, Godstow in 1535, the same year Bulkeley became abbess, and who from 1545 was rector of Cheadle, where she retired. Their lives were certainly connected: he requested burial at Cheadle in the chancel when he died in 1551.[25]

Yet religious positions in her family were not uniform and she was close to more conservative persons as well. One of the three executors of her will was her nephew Thomas Bulkeley, who served Bishop of Peterborough David Pole, an important figure in the restoration of Catholicism under Mary. Pole's will left Thomas Bulkeley a book and £5.[26] Her nephew Dr. Arthur Bulkeley, for whom her brother had sought promotion, was likewise conservative. When he held the living of St. Peter's in the Bail, Oxford, before he became Bishop of Bangor, he was accused of praemunire for upholding the authority of the Bishop of Rome;[27] however, Williams calls him "a cautious and conservative Henrician ecclesiastical lawyer" and "the personification of the ecclesiastical trimmer."[28]

Morpheta Kingsmill

The religious position of Morpheta Kingsmill, last abbess of Wherwell, is more enigmatic. Like Bulkeley, she ruled only for the last years of her house's life, from 1535 to 1539. For her also the connection of a brother with Cromwell was probably at least partly responsible for her elevation.[29] Only one of her letters survives, written in defense of her house's rights to Thomas Wriothesley and, through him, to Cromwell. She complains of the behavior of John Cooke, long-serving registrar of the Bishop of Winchester, a notoriously difficult and corrupt figure.[30] Her style is

---

[24] Earwacker, *East Cheshire*, I: 206.

[25] *BRUO 1501–1540*, p. 460.

[26] Thomas F. Mayer, "Pole, David (d. 1568)," *ODNB* (2004; online edn. May 2010), online: www.oxforddnb.com/view/article/22445 (accessed November 15, 2011).

[27] Bowker, *Henrician Reformation*, p. 140.

[28] Williams, *Wales*, p. 143. In 1542, however, he ordered his clergy to teach parishioners the paternoster in Welsh as well as English, four years before the publication of the first book in Welsh – a substantial pastoral initiative; p. 145.

[29] We might notice, however, that in 1529 at the election of her predecessor, Abbess Anne Colte, Morpheta Kingsmill was prioress. *LP*, IV (iii), no. 5838.

[30] *LP*, XIII (i), no. 8. For Cooke, see Ralph Houlbrooke, *Church Courts and the People during the English Reformation 1520–1570* (Oxford, 1979), p. 26: "At Winchester, John Cooke, principal registrar from 1524 until at least 1564, caused trouble for most of the bishops under whom he served." See also J. A. Muller, *Stephen Gardiner and the Tudor Reaction* (New York, 1926), pp. xxiii, xxxi.

spirited and hard-hitting: she asks that her appointee "may enjoy our gift
… and not such as may buy it of Mr. Cooke."

Kingsmill's 1570 will has been much noticed, since most of her bequests
went to seven nuns of her community, and her executor, Elizabeth Foster,
was likewise a former member of Wherwell.[31] Besides the nuns, the
only other legatees were the abbess's sister-in-law and three women who
were apparently servants: goodwife Skeyle, Alice Skeyle "my maid," and
Morveth Skeyle, clearly a namesake, plus one Joan Penke. On the basis
of the will, it has been suggested that the women lived together or near
each other.[32] Yet the will has several curious elements. Its religious statement is extremely brief, and it is hard to know whether to call it guarded
or non-committal. It says merely, "I bequeath my soul to Almighty God
my only maker and redeemer." Absent is any reforming mention of the
Son's redeeming power or, on the other hand, any conservative allusion
to the intercession of the Virgin and saints. Strikingly, the will includes
no religious mementoes of any kind, the legacies being mainly bedding.
Though the eldest of the former nuns (based on the order of the pension list)[33] is called Mistress Pekeryng, the others' names are given without
any title: Jane Woodloke, Morveth Vyne, Joan Mate, Elizabeth Hacker,
Joan Dolinge, and Elizabeth Foster. The original twenty-four have been
reduced to seven; all except Pekeryng come from the bottom half of the
seniority list. Since many nuns had died in the thirty-one years since 1539,
it is likely that this living group, if that is what it was, was originally larger.
In the will Elizabeth Hacker is further described as "now Edmund Bathe's
wife" and Bathe is both one of the will's witnesses and one of the three
men who made the accompanying inventory.[34] His presence suggests the
abbess's acceptance of the marriage and of a move beyond celibacy.

Unlike Bulkeley's will, Morpheta Kingsmill's makes hardly any mention of family. The abbess's brother John had died in 1556 and though
she leaves a "counter [counting] table" to John's widow, she makes no
other gifts to relatives. Since John Kingsmill and his wife had seventeen
children this absence seems remarkable, and perhaps suggests a degree
of estrangement. In the year before her will, 1569, the abbess had signed

[31] Hampshire Record Office (HRO) 1570B/099/1.
[32] Francis Aiden Gasquet, *Henry VIII and English Monasticism* (London, 1935), p. 477, quoted by
David Knowles and R. Neville Hadcock, *Medieval Religious Houses: England and Wales* (London,
1971), p. 267, and others, including Diana Coldicott, *Hampshire Nunneries* (Chichester, 1989),
pp. 143–44.
[33] *LP*, XIV (ii), no. 564.
[34] Coldicott, *Hampshire Nunneries*, p. 144.

a document requested by her brother's executors, releasing his estate of any claims by her.[35] Since he had died thirteen years earlier, such caution seems unusual, though it points to earlier financial arrangements between the brother and sister. What is noteworthy is the sense of obligation to her earlier abbatial responsibilities. To four named parishes she left 2s. each: Wherwell, Goodworth Longparish, Bolingdon, and Totington were four of the manors that had belonged to Wherwell at the dissolution.[36]

The inventory reveals that the abbess had been living in a dwelling that could not have housed a community: it consisted of a hall, parlor, chamber, and kitchen. Diana Coldicott says it is "impossible to know whether she continued to live in her former abbess's lodging," yet that does seem indicated. Coldicott points out that in 1539 the abbess's lodging was among the monastic buildings "assigned to remain."[37] Also remaining were the houses within the quadrant and it is likely that the nuns lived in these, though chapter house, frater, dormitory, convent kitchen, and "all the old lodgings between the granary and the hall door" were judged "superfluous." We do not know whether or not they were demolished.

Elizabeth Shelley

Hampshire was a county radically divided along religious lines, with a strong conservative presence. Though Wherwell's intentions are not clear, an unequivocal example of nuns attempting to continue a religiously based community life comes from Hampshire, where the Anglo-Saxon foundation of St. Mary's Winchester or Nunnaminster, led initially by its last abbess Elizabeth Shelley, managed to sustain a living group for almost two decades after the dissolution. The surviving wills of several nuns, each of which mentions others in the community, illustrate the gradual attrition of the group by death.[38] Abbess Shelley's will comes first, in March 1547; the last to be proved is Jayne Wayte's in 1565.[39] The formulaic preface in

[35] HRO 19M61/550–3, 1301.   [36] Dugdale, *Monasticon*, II: 642.

[37] Coldicott, *Hampshire Nunneries*, p. 144. The commissioners' report is printed in Dugdale, *Monasticon*, II: 639–40.

[38] Gasquet, *English Monasticism*, pp. 452–53; John Paul, "Dame Elizabeth Shelley, Last Abbess of St. Mary's Abbey, Winchester," *Papers and Proceedings of the Hampshire Field Club and Archaeological Society* 23.2 (1965), 60–71; Coldicott, *Hampshire Nunneries*, pp. 144–45; Joan Greatrex, "On Ministering to 'Certayne Devoute and Religiouse Women': Bishop Fox and the Benedictine Nuns of Winchester Diocese on the Eve of the Dissolution," in W. J. Sheils and Diane Wood (eds.), *Women in the Church*, Studies in Church History 27 (Oxford, 1990), pp. 223–35.

[39] Elizabeth Shelley, HRO 1547B/078; Edborough Stratford (two copies) 1553U/110 and 1552U/60; Agnes Badgecroft 1556B/04; Jayne Wayte 1565B/82 (year of death is the first element in the shelf mark).

Elizabeth Shelley's will, so different from the neutral language of Morpheta Kingsmill's prefacing statement, aligns her unequivocally with traditional belief, as she commends her soul to Almighty God, creator and redeemer thereof, and to his blessed mother Mary Virgin, and to all the holy company in heaven.[40] Better supported than Kingsmill, perhaps, by the city community surrounding the cathedral, she not only leaves bequests to six nuns, each referred to as "my sister," but to the almswomen in the nearby "systrenhouse" (Coldicott suggests she continued to visit them[41]) and to her chaplain and her ghostly father, as well as – like Kingsmill – to female servants and godchildren. Though the will does not mention religious objects, we know from other sources that she left a little chalice to Winchester College, specifying that Nunnaminster "shall have it again in case it be restored and come up again."[42] All this is quite different from Kingsmill's will.

One matter in Abbess Shelley's will has not been explored. Like Morpheta Kingsmill, she seems to have kept in contact with a married nun from her former community. She mentions a "bill obligatory" for £20, dated April 24, 1546 and negotiated with "my syster Johane Everard, of Sydesworth … wedowe." The title "my sister," which she has used for each previously mentioned nun, in combination with "widow" suggests a loan of this large sum to a former nun, about a year before her will was written in March 1547. The commissioners' list of nuns in 1539 includes three Joans: Frye, Gaynesford, Eyers.[43] The first woman was identified by Coldicott as having a shop in Romsey,[44] the second is mentioned by that name in one of the nuns' wills. Joan Eyers might be a candidate for Joan Everard, under her married name, as might the two unprofessed novices Jane Morton and Joan Ridford.

Where did Abbess Shelley and her remaining nuns live? Coldicott has explored the possibilities thoroughly, pointing out that an inventory shows the abbess's lodging as "a sizeable house" that included hall, kitchen, buttery, and seven separate chambers including the great chamber in the gallery, as well as places called the long house, wood house, and fish house.[45] Like Wherwell's, Nunnaminster's buildings in 1539 were divided into two groups: those destined to remain, including the abbess's lodging, were let in 1540

[40] HRO 1547B/078.
[41] Coldicott, *Hampshire Nunneries*, p. 141.
[42] Paul, "Last Abbess," 70, citing Winchester College Muniments 21875.
[43] Dugdale, *Monasticon*, IX: 456. The list of those receiving pensions, on p. 457, printed from an Augmentation Office record, differs slightly.
[44] Coldicott, *Hampshire Nunneries*, p. 145.
[45] Coldicott, *Hampshire Nunneries*, pp. 143–44.

to Thomas Tichborne who had been the abbey's clerk, with a notation that they were then still occupied by the abbess. Coldicott says, "[s]he probably continued to reside in the abbey lodging with a few of the former nuns until her death in 1547. It is open to doubt whether the other ladies continued to live there after that."[46] The living group probably consisted in 1539 of eight persons, dwindling down to the last survivor twenty-six years later.

Whether the nuns continued to live in the Nunnaminster buildings after the abbess's death or lived nearby, they appeared still to their Winchester contemporaries as a group. Evidence that these nuns succeeded in registering an identifiable presence is provided by no less an observer than John Bale. The reformer had been appointed rector of Bishopstoke, Hampshire, in June 1551. In his pamphlet *An Expostulation or Complaynte Agaynste the Blasphemyes of a Franticke Papist of Hamshire*, written in late 1551 or early 1552, he refers to "the superstitious nuns of Winchester, disobeying both the bishop [at this time the reformer John Ponet] and his chancellor [the conservative Edmund Stuarde, one of the overseers of Abbess Shelley's will] concerning their apparell, and utterly condemning the preachings that are now."[47] So we know that the women of Nunnaminster's rump community continued to wear their habits in 1551, about a dozen years after the community's closure and after Abbess Shelley's death in 1547. That they continued to own some books is shown by a mention in nun Agnes Badgecroft's will of "certain old books" and by the survival of a historic psalter listing Nunnaminster's abbesses through 1418, which probably continued to be used in the house's last days since the feasts of Thomas Becket are erased in obedience to the 1538 royal edict.[48]

Bale's text complains bitterly about the clergy of Winchester Cathedral and of Winchester College who had maintained various traditional forms of worship, or in Diarmaid MacCulloch's phrase, "spectacularly prolonged older religious habits into Edward's reign."[49] Precisely these men

[46] Coldicott, *Hampshire Nunneries*, pp. 151–52. Tichbourne's lease is TNA E315/212, f. 133.

[47] *STC* 636, sig. C iii verso. For Stuard, see Houlbrooke, *Church Courts*, pp. 24–25.

[48] The psalter is one of five surviving books from Nunnaminster; see David N. Bell, *What Nuns Read: Books and Libraries in Medieval English Nunneries* (Kalamazoo, MI, 1995), pp. 214–16. It was first owned by someone from Romsey Abbey; see N. R. Ker, *Medieval Manuscripts in British Libraries*, 4 vols. (Oxford, 1969–92), IV: 218–19; H. G. Liveing, *Records of Romsey Abbey* (Winchester, 1906), pp. 285–302. Around 1517 Bishop Fox gave MS copies of the *ordo* for female religious profession to his four Hampshire nunneries, Nunnaminster, Wherwell, Wintney, and Romsey. The first two survive: Nunnaminster's copy is CUL Mm 3.13, Wherwell's is Oxford, Bodleian MS Barlow 11; see Mary C. Erler, "Bishop Richard Fox's Manuscript Gifts to His Winchester Nuns: A Second Surviving Example," *JEH* 52 (2001), 1–4.

[49] Diarmaid MacCulloch, *Tudor Church Militant: Edward VI and the Protestant Reformation* (London, 2001), p. 112.

are visible in Abbess Shelley's will as supporters and friends. The upward progress, for instance, of her friend, the co-supervisor of her will John White, illustrates the power of Winchester conservatism. In 1537 he had been appointed headmaster of his old school, Winchester College, and in 1542 its warden, at which time he became chaplain to the Bishop of Winchester Stephen Gardiner. White was named on a *c.*1551 list of people who were receiving Catholic books sent from abroad.[50] Although in that year, when Bale was writing his criticism of the city of Winchester's thoroughgoing traditionalism, White was excommunicated for preaching conservative doctrine, three years later he was appointed Bishop of Lincoln and in 1556 he succeeded his mentor Gardiner as Bishop of Winchester.[51]

White's career, although subject to the winds of change, gives some indication of the continuity of old forms in Hampshire and hence of the viability of the sheltered and supported position held by the Nunnaminster women. At the same time, Hampshire had a substantial Protestant presence, and Abbess Kingsmill's brother John was at the center of reforming activity at the time of the dissolution. Ronald Fritze says, "[d]uring the late 1530s he worked closely with Cromwell's protégé Thomas Wriothesley and both men greatly benefited from the dissolution of the monasteries."[52] A 1538 letter from Kingsmill thanks Wriothesley for preferring him to the Lord Privy Seal, "whom he finds, as Wriothesley said, most liberal to his friends." The letter contains a request for a prebend in Cromwell's patronage, either for Kingsmill himself or for a friend of his sister the abbess, "if his Lordship and Wriothesley esteem it too small for them."[53] The degree of Morpheta Kingsmill's involvement in this search for patronage is difficult to calculate from this letter, but at the very least she did not resist her brother's efforts – efforts that were also advanced by social means. John Kingsmill's letter to Wriothesley asks that he and his wife be remembered to Mistress Wriothesley, suggesting that the Kingsmills and the Wriothesleys had established some social contacts. In the next year, when Wherwell was dissolved, John Kingsmill was one of the royal commissioners who signed the list of granted pensions, not only for his sister's house but for

---

[50] Susan Brigden, *London and the Reformation* (Oxford, 1989), p. 454, citing *HMC Salisbury MSS* 1.346.

[51] T. F. Kirby, *Annals of Winchester College* (London, 1892), pp. 246–49.

[52] Ronald H. Fritze, "Kingsmill Family (per c. 1480–1698)," *ODNB* (2004; online edn. 2008), online: www.oxforddnb.com?/view/article/71875 (accessed January 12, 2010).

[53] *LP*, XIII (i), no. 1190.

the other Winchester houses of Nunnaminster and St. Swithins,[54] and as
a commissioner he was jointly responsible for making an inventory of
the church goods of Hampshire.[55] As the minister's *Remembrances* show,
Cromwell originally intended that his sister's house, Wherwell, should
go to John Kingsmill at the dissolution, though in the end he did not
receive it.[56]

While both Hampshire nunneries maintained remnants of their communities, the directions taken by Nunnaminster and Wherwell contrast
vividly, both in the shape their surviving groups took and in the motives
for such efforts. The houses had about the same number of nuns, respec-
tively 24 and 25, but while Nunnaminster was a much larger establish-
ment, having 102 persons including servants, corrodians, and children,
Wherwell was worth twice what Nunnaminster was, according to the 1536
Valor: £339 as opposed to £154.[57] Historically part of the cathedral complex, and thus linked to Winchester's cathedral and college both physically and emotionally, Nunnaminster attempted a continuity that formed
part of a conservative resistance. This effort to continue their way of life
constituted a statement of traditional belief.

Wherwell's collective intention is not so explicit. Abbess Kingsmill's
will, if it has a religious dimension at all, must be reforming and if this
is so, there can have been no question of maintaining common worship or common traditional liturgical life. Perhaps the motives of the
Wherwell ex-nuns were not religious at all, but personal or economic.
The glimpse we have of them about thirty years after the dissolution
may show a successful adjustment to massive social change. If they did
live close to one another we might speculate that a combination of available convent buildings and the abbess's substantial annual pension of
£40 made it possible to continue a form of living that both resembled
their old pattern and differed radically from it. But whether or not the
Wherwell nuns formed a living community is perhaps less important
than the will's illustration of a continuity that included a married nun
(and her husband) and thus suggests the centrality of personal or local
bonds over credal ones.

---

[54] *LP*, XIV (ii), nos. 520, 523.
[55] *VCH Hampshire*, II: 67.
[56] Cromwell's remembrances, *LP*, XIV, no. 425 (BL MS Titus B.1.469), "Mr Kingysmyll for
Wharwell."
[57] Dugdale, *Monasticon*, II: 445–46.

Joan Fane

Like Bulkeley and Kingsmill, another religious superior, Joan Fane (or Vane) of Dartford, Kent, owed her position to Cromwell, whose hand is extremely visible in her election. Her long-serving predecessor Elizabeth Cressener (1488–1537) died on a Tuesday in December, presumably December 11, 1537,[58] having attempted to ensure a smooth succession – and possibly to exclude Cromwell, with whom she had earlier litigated – by summoning both the Dominican provincial John Hodgkin and Bishop of Rochester John Hilsey to her bedside. Hilsey immediately wrote Cromwell endorsing Joan Fane: "although there are in the house many elder than she is, yet there is none better learned nor more discreeter woman, she being herself above thirty."[59] A Cromwell dependant and originally a Dominican friar at Bristol (later, from 1534, provincial of the English Dominicans), Hilsey was a reformer.[60] On April 1, 1534 he and the Augustinian provincial had been commissioned to visit all the friars' houses in England and to exact assent to the oath of succession, the Boleyn marriage, and Henry's headship of the church.[61] Dartford had received the visitors in May 1534, at which time all its members swore the oath, and it may be from this meeting that Hilsey knew Joan Fane. A second letter of his praises Fane again, but notes that the Dominican provincial does not "bear his mind towards her" and intends to ask Cromwell to retain confirmation of the Dartford election in his own hands.[62] Forestalling this, Cromwell sent Sir William Petre to Dartford, and Petre notified the Lord Privy Seal that on December 17 he had "taken the compromise for the election," that is, secured the convent's sealed assent relinquishing the choice to Cromwell.[63]

On January 20, 1538 the Prioress of Dartford sent Cromwell £100 via the Bishop of Rochester.[64] Palmer lists the disbursements authorized by Fane in her short time as prioress: "three offices, three leases, eleven annuities and one grant of church presentation."[65] The difference between

---

[58] Though this and the subsequent letters on the Dartford election are undated, the year is probably 1537, as the first lease issued by new prioress Joan Fane is dated January 2, 1538 (C. F. R. Palmer, "History of the Priory of Dartford in Kent," *Archaeological Journal* 36 (1879), 241–71 (266).

[59] *LP*, XI, no. 1324 (TNA SP 1/112, f. 212).

[60] S. Thompson, "John Hilsey (d. 1539)," *ODNB* (2004; online edn. September 2010), online: www.oxforddnb.com/view/article/13325 (accessed October 27, 2010). Thompson says, "[d]uring his short episcopate he showed himself concerned to appoint those favoured by Cromwell to religious houses."

[61] *LP*, VII, no. 587 (18).

[62] *LP*, XI, no. 1325. Palmer, "History," gives a full account on p. 266.

[63] *LP*, XI, no. 1326.

[64] *LP*, XIV (ii), no. 782.

[65] Palmer, "History," 266.

this scattering of Dartford's resources and Bulkeley's cautious and correct behavior at Godstow is notable, as Bulkeley wrote: "I have not alienated one haporth of the goods of this monastery, moveable or unmovable, but have rather increased the same, nor never made lease of any farm or piece of ground belonging to this house other than has been in times past always set under convent seal for the wealth of the house."[66] Margaret Vernon, the subject of the next chapter, wrote similarly to Cromwell on leaving her house, Little Marlow: "I have but singly provided for myself to maintain it withal, because your mastership commanded me that I should nothing embezzle or take away but leave the house as wealthy as I could, which commandment I followed: I hope all shall be for the best."[67]

Only one letter of Joan Fane's survives, a graceful plea to Cromwell that he review personally the case of Bridget Browning, an underage girl not professed, who should have left Dartford after the 1535 injunction against profession under the age of twenty-four.[68] The house was dissolved sometime between April 1, 1539 when the suffragan Bishop of Dover wrote Cromwell requesting it and October 18, the date pensions were assigned.[69] Fane was thus prioress for only about the last year and a half of her house's life.

Significantly, Prioress Fane was not among the remnant of the Dartford house that lived together in Kent after the dissolution[70] and that moved abroad at Elizabeth's accession to maintain their communal life at various sites in the Low Countries.[71] Dartford's strong efforts at continuity were unusual and are matched only by Syon's – the two female houses among the six re-established under Mary. Thus the absence of Dartford's superior from these plans suggests some division in the house. In fact, Joan Fane effectively disappears after 1539, though she is recorded as receiving her generous annual pension of £66 13s. 4d. until 1556.[72] This large sum is probably a result of Dartford's high valuation at £380 9s. 1/2d., even higher than Wherwell's £339.[73]

[66] Wright, *Suppression*, p. 231.
[67] Green, *Letters*, II: lxxiv; Cook, *Letters*, XLIII.
[68] Green, *Letters*, III: xxxix, pp. 85–87, September 9 [1538]; Cook, *Letters*, XC, p. 143.
[69] Palmer, "History," 267; *LP*, XIV (i), no. 661.
[70] Paul Lee, *Nunneries, Learning, and Spirituality in Late Medieval English Society: The Dominican Priory of Dartford* (York, 2001).
[71] Godfrey Anstruther, *A Hundred Homeless Years: English Dominicans 1558–1658* (London, 1958), pp. 6–15.
[72] Lee, *Nunneries*, p. 223.
[73] Palmer, "History," 264, quoting the *Valor Ecclesiasticus*.

The Fanes were an established Kent family living at Hadlow, near Tonbridge,[74] and the prioress's brother Sir Ralph had been in Cromwell's service from 1531 to 1538, when his patron recommended him to Henry VIII and he was appointed a gentleman pensioner, serving at court until the death of Henry.[75] Subsequently he became a client of Edward Seymour, Duke of Somerset and Lord Protector to Edward VI, with whom he shared reforming social and religious beliefs. After Somerset was executed in January 1552, Fane was accused of treason and hanged in February; probably, his biographer says, "as an example to the rest of Somerset's clientele."[76]

As Ralph Fane's relation to Cromwell was a factor in his sister's election, so in turn her position as prioress allowed him substantial benefits. Fane received from Dartford a ninety-nine-year lease of the manor of Shypbourne for £5 annually, and on January 3 a life grant of stabling and provision for six horses and two servants at the monastery. On February 20, 1545, after the monastery's closure, Fane purchased Shypbourne manor; he had earlier received an annuity of £20 in lieu of his stabling. When in 1556 Cardinal Reginald Pole renewed the house's fees, annuities, and pensions, Elizabeth, widow of Sir Ralph Fane, received the £20 annuity.[77]

Reception of the cardinal's grant must have been ironic for Elizabeth Fane, who was an ardent promoter of the reformed religion.[78] John Foxe calls her "a special nurse and a great supporter" of imprisoned controversialists, among whom were Laurence Saunders, John Bradford, Thomas Rose, and Nicholas Ridley.[79] Five prison letters to her from the eventual

---

[74] Edward Hasted, *The History and Topographical Survey of the County of Kent*, 12 vols. (reprint edn., London 1998), V: 177–93.

[75] Fane appears in Henry VIII's will as one of the senior servants of the crown who were to be rewarded with various posts. W. K. Jordan, *Edward VI, The Young King: The Protectorship of the Duke of Somerset* (Cambridge, MA, 1968), p. 64. For his fall, W. K. Jordan, *Edward VI, the Threshhold of Power: The Dominance of the Duke of Northumberland* (London, 1970), pp. 87–88, also pp. 53, 83, 91, 94, 97.

[76] J. Andreas Löwe, "Fane, Sir Ralph, b. before 1510, d. 1552," *ODNB* (2004; online edn. May 2010), online: www.oxforddnb.com/view/article/22445 (accessed July 14, 2012). Lowe dates his birth "before 1510." Based on John Hilsey's letter (see above), his sister Joan was probably born *c.*1505.

[77] Palmer, "History," 266–69.

[78] Betty Travitsky, "Fane (Brydges), Elizabeth (d. 1568)," *Bibliography of English Women Writers 1500–1640*, online: www.itergateway.org/mrts/earlywomen/index.cfm?action=showwriter&id=268; Cathy Shrank, "Fane, Elizabeth (d. 1568)," *ODNB* (2004; online edn. May 2010), online: www.oxforddnb.com/view/article/68050 (accessed February 10, 2011).

[79] John Foxe, *Acts and Monuments*, ed. George Townsend, 8 vols. (London, 1843), VII: 234ff; VIII, appendix 6. Her activity has been summarized by Thomas Freeman, "'The Good Ministrye of Godlye and Vertuouse Women': The Elizabethan Martyrologists and the Female Supporters of the Marian Martyrs," *Journal of British Studies* 39 (2000), 8–33 (25). See also John N. King, *English Reformation Literature: The Tudor Origins of the Protestant Tradition* (Princeton, NJ, 1982), pp. 97, 218, 477.

martyr John Philpot survive, and one of hers to him.[80] John Strype says
that Lady Fane sent John Bradford three questions regarding the mass and
in his reply he says he has "already written" a little book on the subject,
which he will send her.[81] This would be *The Hurt of Hearing Mass*. What
may have been the first work of Anne Cooke, later the wife of Sir Nicholas
Bacon, was dedicated to Lady Fane,[82] a translation from Italian of sermons
by the Italian reformer Bernardino Ochino. Anne Cooke was aged only
about twenty at the time (1548). Her preface to a later expanded edition
of the sermons (1551; *STC* 18767) is addressed "to the right worshipful and
worthily beloved Mother the lady F" and attributes "any good use in me"
to "your many and most godly exhortations" (including Lady F's frequent
reproofs of Cooke's "vain study in the Italian tongue," criticized "since
God thereby is no whit magnified").[83]

Lady Fane and the radical poet-printer Robert Crowley knew each
other well. In 1550 he published her work, now lost, *Certain Psalms in
Number 21 with 102 Proverbs*. In the next year Crowley dedicated to her
his own poem "Pleasure and Pain, Heaven and Hell, Remember These
Four and All Will Be Well" (*STC* 6090), a diatribe against the rich's
oppression of the poor in which Christ speaks a versified expansion
of his words at the Last Judgment (Matt. 25) to those saved and condemned: "I made you rich to feed the poor" (l. 152). Crowley's preface
calls Fane "a right worthy patroness of all such as labor in the lord's
harvest."[84]

[80] Robert Eden (ed.), *The Examinations and Writings of John Philpot*, BCL, Parker Society 34
(Cambridge, 1842), letters XIV–XVIII (Philpot to Fane). Fane's letter thanks him for the book he
sent her and says, "[b]ecause you desire to show yourself a worthy soldier, if need so require, I will
supply your request for the scarf you wrote of, that you may present my handywork before your
Captain, that I be not forgotten in the odours of incense." Philpot had written earlier, "[t]he scarf
I desire as an outward sign to show our enemies, who see not our glorious end"; Eden, *Philpot*,
p. 260.

[81] John Strype, *Memorials of … Thomas Cranmer*, 2 vols. (Oxford, 1812), I: 522–23. For the letter, *STC*
5886, Miles Coverdale, *Certain Most Godly, Fruitful, and Comfortable Letters* (1564), p. 335, accessed
on EEBO.

[82] John N. King and Mark Rankin, "Print, Patronage, and the Reception of Continental Reform:
1521–1603," *Yearbook of English Studies* 38 (2008), 49–67.

[83] "Lady F" was previously identified as Anne Fitzwilliam, Anne Cooke's mother's maiden name,
by Franklin B. Williams, Jr., *Index of Dedications and Commendatory Verses in English Books before
1641* (London, 1962), p. 64. Cooke has been called the best of Ochino's three translators, who
included Richard Argentyne and John Ponet; M. A. Overell, "Bernardino Ochino's Books and
English Religious Opinion 1547–80," in R. N. Swanson (ed.), *The Church and the Book*, Studies in
Church History 38 (Woodbridge, 2004), pp. 201–11.

[84] Robert Crowley, *The Select Works of Robert Crowley*, ed. J. M. Cowper, EETS ES 15 (London, 1872),
pp. 105–27 (p. 107).

Against this background, the discovery of an inscription in a copy of Crowley's 1550 edition of *Piers Plowman* (*STC* 19906 and 19907) suggests something of Prioress Fane's religious position. The inscription reads: "This ys William Morse booke of the gyft of my Ladye Ioane ffane sometyme priories of Darteford in Kent 1556" (Oxford, Bodleian Library, 4° Rawl. 271) (see Figure 3.2).[85] The reformers' view of *Piers* as anticipating the sixteenth-century criticisms of the institutional church would at first glance make ownership of this work by a former nun seem surprising. Yet Joan Fane's family connections and particularly her sister-in-law's patronage of Crowley suggest a different reading. It was almost certainly through Elizabeth Fane that Joan Fane obtained a copy of Crowley's *Piers* and she may have found its criticisms admissible, though in that poem religious women receive their share of obloquy.

> I am Wrath, quod he, "I was sum tyme a frere
> …
> I was the priouresses potagere [cook] and other poure ladyes
> And made hem ioutes [broths] of iangelynge
> …
> Of wykked words I, Wrath, here wortes [stews] i-made,
> Til "thow lixte" [liest] and "thow lixte" lopen [ran] oute at ones
> And eyther hitte other vnder the cheke.[86]

Despite the triviality and anger found in religious life, Langland hopes for a return to a state of innocence:

> Ac there shal come a kyng and confesse ȝow religiouses
> And bete ȝow, as the bible telleth for brekynge of ȝyore reule
> And amende monyales [nuns] monkes and chanouns
> And putten hem to her penaunce *ad pristinum statum ire*.[87]

Although Crowley's 1550 publication of *Piers* has been called "the poem's official recuperation for Protestant England," its value and interest had crossed confessional lines earlier than this. In 1532 Sir Adrian Fortescue copied the poem, with marginal notes and comments, in London BL MS Digby 145. Fortescue was executed in 1539; his death has traditionally been attributed to a refusal of the Act of Supremacy and the seventeenth century

---

[85] Lawrence Warner, "New Light on Piers Plowman's Ownership ca. 1450–1600," *Journal of the Early Book Society* 12 (2009), 183–94 (186). He points out that the copy contains the title page and preliminaries of Crowley's third edition and the text of his first (both 1550).

[86] W. W. Skeat (ed.), *The Vision of William Concerning Piers the Plowman*, 2 vols. (Oxford, 1886), I: 140, 142 (Passus V: 136, 158–59, 162–64).

[87] *Piers Plowman*, I: 308, 310 (Passus X: 317–20).

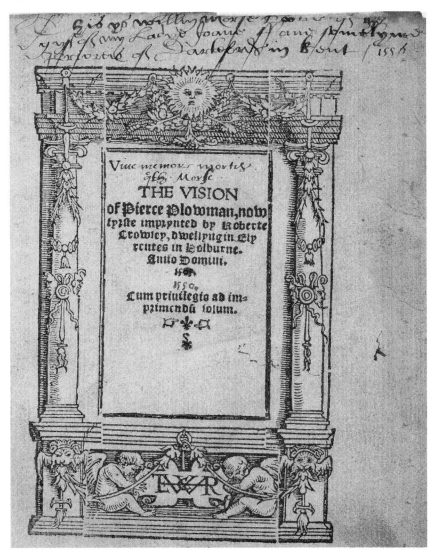

Figure 3.2 The ownership inscription on the title page of Robert Crowley's 1550 edition
of *Piers Plowman*: "This ys William Morse booke of the gyft of my Ladye Ioane ffane
sometyme priories of Darteford in Kent 1556."

regarded him as a martyr, though recent commentary finds the reasons for his death unclear.[88] His beliefs were traditional, at the very least, however, and John Bowers has suggested that his transcription of the poem "might be construed as a last-ditch reforming effort mounted against the forces of a stronger Reformation movement ... His notations seem to have revived a pre-1381 view of *Piers* as a poem of sweeping social vision whose moral insights might be applied to the current political scene to repair rather than discard existing religious institutions."[89] Fortescue's interest in the poem in the 1530s, perhaps like Joan Fane's in the 1550s, suggests that the understanding of *Piers* as a visionary call to action remained constant in the sixteenth century, an understanding congruent with both a traditional religious position and a reforming one.

Since the record of Fane's pension payment ceases after 1556, the date of the book's inscription, it probably passed at her death to William More. Lawrence Warner, who discovered the inscription, identified him as the son of Christopher More of Loseley, Surrey. Proximity suggests that it may indeed have been the owner of Loseley, the More family seat two miles southwest of Guildford, to whom the prioress gave her copy of *Piers*. Loseley was approximately twenty-five or thirty miles from the western portion of Kent – Tonbridge, Hadlow, Penshurst Place – where the Fane family had properties.[90] Ralph and Elizabeth Fane lived at Hadlow, two miles from Tonbridge, and we might speculate that after 1540, the approximate date of their marriage, Joan Fane lived with them.

In 1556 when he received the book, William More would have been aged thirty-six, at the beginning of his career as a distinguished public servant; he was later called "the most trusted agent of Elizabeth's government in Surrey."[91] He was at various times deputy lieutenant for the county, sheriff, Member of Parliament for both Surrey and Guildford, and in these positions, the queen and council's man. Eight years later in 1564 Bishop Robert Horne listed him in a group headed "The Justices of Surrey. Favorers," that is, of reform,[92] but his religious preference had already been made clear. S. T. Bindoff points out that in the first parliament of Mary's

[88] Richard Rex, "Fortescue, Sir Adrian (c. 1481–1539), landowner and alleged traitor," *ODNB* (2004; online edn. May 2010), online: www.oxforddnb.com/view/article/9936 (accessed April 23, 2012).

[89] John M. Bowers, "*Piers Plowman* and the Police: Notes Toward a History of the Wycliffite Langland," *Yearbook of Langland Studies* 61 (1992), 1–50 (38, 41).

[90] Bindoff, *House of Commons*, III: 515.

[91] *VCH Surrey*, 4 vols. (reprint edn. London, 1967), I: 379, 382, portrait facing p. 384; II: 28, 139, 623; III: 7–8 (ref.).

[92] Mary Bateson, "A Collection of Original Letters from the Bishops to the Privy Council, 1564," *Camden Miscellany* 9 (London, 1893; reprint edn. 1965), iii–84 (56).

reign (1553), he was one of those who "stood for the true religion," that is, Protestantism.[93] His own inventory of his notable book collection survives, though *Piers* is not listed.[94]

For Robert Crowley and Elizabeth Fane, perhaps the most prominent aspect of their reforming beliefs was their concern for social justice. Somerset's circle, to which Fane's husband had belonged, also championed the common people against landowners and made efforts to restrain enclosure in various ways. This, of course, is the message that reformers read in the fourteenth-century poem *Piers Plowman*: a hope for a just society benefiting the poor and a condemnation of self-interest among the clergy and the rich. It appears that this hope was shared by William More, the Elizabethan administrator, and by Joan Fane, the Dominican prioress who gave him Piers's book.

Houses of religious women seem the last place to look for adherents of Thomas Cromwell and indeed the nature of the ties between these women and the Lord Privy Seal varies a good deal. The almost flirtatious tone of Katherine Bulkeley's letters indicates that she knew him personally, as when she promises to see him when the king comes to Woodstock.[95] On the other hand, the evidence does not quite allow us to claim this sort of familiarity for Morpheta Kingsmill or Joan Fane. Partly because their houses were relatively large and valuable, all three received substantial pensions that enabled them to live in comfort. Katherine Bulkeley was granted £50 (Godstow was valued at £319); Morpheta Kingsmill received £40 (Wherwell was assessed at £339); and Joan Fane's pension was 100 marks (£66 13s. 4d.), since Dartford was valued at £380.

Two sets of obligations are visible in these narratives. At the dissolution, the bonds created by religious community were undoubtedly a central concern for superiors like these. For Bulkeley, however, the physical distance between her religious home, Godstow, and her retirement home, Cheadle, probably made the matter of her nuns' subsequent history less pressing. But certainly the question of how or whether to recognize ties established with sister religious is visible in Kingsmill's and in Fane's lives. Though it is impossible to claim anything but a partial degree of agency in the living solutions that each found, Kingsmill attempted, it appears

---

[93] Bindoff, *House of Commons*, II: 625–26.
[94] John More, "Extracts from the Private Account Book of Sir William More, of Loseley, in Surrey, in the Time of Queen Mary and of Queen Elizabeth," *Archaeologia* 36.2 (1855), 284–310. A summary is given by Elizabeth McCutcheon, who estimates the collection at around 140 books: "A Mid-Tudor Owner of More's *Utopia*, Sir William More," *Moreana* 18 (1981), 32–35.
[95] *LP*, XIII (i), no. 1262.

successfully, to sustain a local communal life, albeit perhaps not a religious one. (Elizabeth Shelley's solution, equally local, tried to maintain the traditional form of institutional religious life, but without institutional support.) Fane made a different decision, choosing not to be part of Dartford's struggles to stay together in the interests of a continuing religious commitment. Like Bulkeley's, her affiliation may instead have been with a religious position shaped by family – and perhaps modified by events, since the only record of her after the dissolution comes from 1556, almost twenty years later.

Family ties indeed surface insistently and in all three histories the political and religious positions of the dominant male family member is clear. Though the valuable administrative positions held by these women were to some degree simply counters in the ongoing relations between Cromwell and his male allies, these nuns' elevation demonstrates the often considerable extent to which women operated within such alliances, through the power of the family.

Their positions were various; it seems correct to call Katherine Bulkeley an evangelical, while Joan Fane's sympathy with institutional reform is less easily classifiable. Most challenging is Morpheta Kingsmill because of her possible participation in a form of living strongly associated with institutional religious life, yet not clearly delineated as religious. All three were aligned with change. In serving Cromwell, Sir Richard Bulkeley, John Kingsmill, and Sir Ralph Fane – and their sisters – all served the cause of religious reform.

CHAPTER FOUR

Cromwell's abbess and friend: Margaret Vernon

Although the relationships between Thomas Cromwell and the nuns Katherine Bulkeley, Morpheta Kingsmill, and Joan Fane are intriguing, the long connection between the minister and another nun, Margaret Vernon, falls into another category entirely. Intimate, chatty, and thoroughly personal, her twenty-one letters provide rare evidence of a sustained friendship between this female administrator and her famous patron, a friendship that may have been based on shared religious perspectives and that included other members of Cromwell's circle.[1]

The earliest mention of her has been thought to come from two years of accounts that give her name as prioress of the nunnery of St. Mary de Pré, near St. Albans, Hertfordshire. The accounts run from Michaelmas 1513 to Michaelmas 1515 and their summary in *Letters and Papers* is thoroughly unremarkable.[2] David M. Smith in his magisterial catalog of heads of religious houses asked whether this could be the later superior of Little Marlow, Buckinghamshire, and of Malling, Kent, but indexed her as two different persons.[3] The discovery of a previously unnoticed record, however, of a royal pardon extended to Margaret Vernon, prioress, and the convent of Sopwell, Hertfordshire, on November 20, 1509,[4] makes it likely that the Sopwell and the Pré prioresses are the same woman, given the physical closeness of the two Hertfordshire houses, either near or in St. Albans, and the dependence of both upon the great Benedictine abbey in that city. Vernon thus had an administrative career unparalleled by

---

[1] Because the previous dating of Margaret Vernon's letters has been approximate, a suggested chronology has been provided in Appendix 4.

[2] *LP*, II, no. 959 (TNA SP1/11, ff. 101–05). For instance, the accounts contain rentals from listed tenants, payments for church expenses, and felling and carriage of timber for repairs of rental properties in the town of St. Albans and elsewhere.

[3] Smith, *Heads*, index.

[4] *LP*, I, no. 438 (1 m. 23), (TNA C 67/56), not known to the *VCH* writer on Sopwell.

any English nun, as head of four houses: Sopwell, St. Mary de Pré, Little Marlow, and, finally, Malling.

In 1490, twenty years before Vernon became Prioress of Sopwell, Archbishop of Canterbury John Morton accused St. Albans abbot William Wallingford of a series of crimes involving the two nunneries of Sopwell and Pré, both of which were under the abbey's jurisdiction. The general charges included changing the prioresses of both houses at his will, "substituting for good women the evil and corrupt, and deputing brethren to rule these nunneries … who dissipate and consume the goods of the priories." The specific charges included overlooking a sexual liaison between Pré prioress Helen Germyn and one of his monks.[5] Minnie Reddan demonstrated that much material for the archbishop's accusations came from Sopwell prioress Elizabeth Webbe, who in 1480–81 had successfully sued the Abbot of St. Albans for unjust removal, and in 1500–01 was still prioress.[6] At this latter date Margaret Vernon was most likely a nun of Sopwell, since she was prioress only eight years later, in 1509. Four years after that, in 1513, she was Prioress of Pré. Earlier, in 1490, a Sopwell nun Amy Goden had succeeded the disgraced Pré prioress Helen Germyn, and such a transfer of leadership from Sopwell to Pré is likely to have occurred in Vernon's case as well. Pré was dissolved by the pope in May 1528 and annexed to the abbey of St. Albans, then held by Cardinal Wolsey. Its last prioress had died a year earlier and its three nuns had left. Pré thus became one more building-block in Wolsey's long campaign to fund his two new colleges.

It is against this background of political struggle and sexual scandal that Vernon's inquiry about promotion in her early letters to Cromwell must be read.[7] The letters make it clear that she knew Wolsey and that she and Cromwell were close. It seems likely that they met through the legal and administrative work that Cromwell was doing for Wolsey at this time. Merriman says, "[b]y far the greater portion of Cromwell's correspondence during the years 1525–1529 is connected with the suppression of the monasteries or the foundation of Wolsey's colleges"[8] – a massive job involving

---

[5] Christopher Harper-Bill (ed.), *The Register of John Morton, Archbishop of Canterbury 1486–1500*, 2 vols., Canterbury and York Society 75 (Leeds, 1987), I: p. 13, no. 50.

[6] *VCH Hertfordshire*, III: 407–32. See also David Knowles, "The Case of St. Albans Abbey in 1490," *JEH* 3 (1952), 144–58.

[7] *LP*, IV (iii), no. 5970, calendared under September 1529, so dated by Smith, *Heads*; printed in Green, *Letters*, II: xxi, pp. 520–23, summarized in *VCH Buckinghamshire*, I: 359, along with two other letters from Vernon to Cromwell (*LP*, IV, nos. 5971 and 5972; TNA SP1/55, ff. 173–76 for all three letters).

[8] R. B. Merriman (ed.), *The Life and Letters of Thomas Cromwell*, 2 vols. (Oxford, 1968), I: 51.

work with over thirty institutions.[9] It was Cromwell who kept the accounts of income from the many foundations closed in order to found Wolsey's two new institutions, and it was he who negotiated the legal work to suppress them. We can even trace a possible geographical connection when, in 1525, Wolsey commissioned three men, Cromwell among them, to survey six monasteries and their possessions.[10] Medmenham, one of the six, was about five miles from Little Marlow.

Vernon's letter asks what Cromwell's employer Wolsey wished to do about the headship of the London house of St. Helen's Bishopsgate and we later learn that she and Cromwell had discussed offering the cardinal a payment of £100 for the position. Since at this point, probably in 1528, she was head of her third house (she had been prioress of Little Marlow at least since 1521, when Smith discovered a mention of her there),[11] Vernon was entirely qualified for the larger position she requested.

Though the three nuns discussed in the preceding chapter were all appointed to headships from inside their houses, Margaret Vernon's application for St. Helen's was part of a growing trend to appoint religious superiors from outside, which Martin Heale has traced from the 1490s.[12] He points out that when such external appointments became common, "in effect a job market was created, comparable to that created for ecclesiastical benefices" – a market "reflected in correspondence between members of the lay and ecclesiastical elites" and involving payment of the sort that Vernon negotiated here. Heale provides a table of such appointments, but does not note one example particularly relevant to Vernon's case, which shows how unremarkable such transfers were becoming. In 1534 the nuns of Minster in Sheppey, Kent, resigned the choice of their new prioress to the Archbishop of Canterbury, whereupon Thomas Cranmer appointed his sister Alice, a nun of Stixwould, Lincolnshire. Geoffrey Baskerville, who discovered this appointment, thought that both Cranmer and Cromwell were deeply involved in similar practices, the former after his archiepiscopal appointment in March 1533, the latter after the fall of Wolsey in 1529.[13] Such external appointments worked to strengthen the power of a centralized administration and to reduce the power of individual houses – a

[9] David Knowles, *The Religious Orders in England, Vol. III: The Tudor Age* (Cambridge, 1961), p. 416, provides a list of monasteries suppressed by Wolsey.

[10] Merriman, *Life and Letters*, I: 48.

[11] Smith, *Heads*, III: 664.

[12] Martin Heale, "'Not a Thing for a Stranger to Enter Upon': The Selection of Monastic Superiors in Late Medieval and Tudor England," in Janet Burton and Karen Stover (eds.), *Monasteries and Society in the British Isles in the Later Middle Ages* (Woodbridge, 2008), pp. 51–68 (p. 61).

[13] G. Baskerville, "A Sister of Archbishop Cranmer," *English Historical Review* 51 (1936), 287–89.

subject particularly crucial in the 1530s as the question of monastic reform became more and more pressing.

Discussion of payment is almost always part of the correspondence surrounding these appointments. The tone is matter of fact and the offer of *douceurs* is not confined to any particular confessional position. This is the note struck by Vernon's letter to Cromwell:

> Pleaseth it you to understand that there is a goldsmith in this town, named Lewys, and he showeth me that Master More hath made sure promise to parson Larke that the sub-prioress of St. Helen's shall be prioress there afore Christmas-day. Sir, I most humbly beseech you to be so good master unto me as to know my lord's grace's [Wolsey] pleasure in this case, and that I may have a determined answer whereto I shall trust, that I may settle myself in quietness the which I am far from at this hour. And furthermore, if it might like you to make the offer to my said lord's grace of such sum of money as we were at a point for, my friends thinketh that I should shortly be at an end.[14]

Parson Larke whom Vernon mentions is John Larke, Thomas More's chaplain whom in 1530 he would nominate as vicar of his own parish church of Chelsea.[15] St. Helen's held the advowson of four city churches and two of these, St. Mary Axe and St. Ethelburga, were close enough to the nunnery to be regarded almost as part of its precinct. St. Ethelburga fronted on Bishopsgate Street, just north of St. Helen's Gate, and its rector since January 30, 1504 had been John Larke.[16] His physical closeness to St. Helen's clarifies Larke's involvement in the struggle over its headship. In addition, at some time during a later prioress's tenure he was also steward of St. Helen's, with an annual salary of £12 and use of a chamber within the priory precinct.[17] A contemporary lawsuit mentions that he seemed to be in charge of the house.[18] He was a conservative in religion who was charged with plotting against the royal supremacy and executed

---

[14] *LP*, IV (iii), no. 5970.

[15] Susan Brigden, *London and the Reformation* (Oxford, 1989), p. 354, referring to Cresacre More's *Life of More* and noting that Larke was a pluralist, cited in October 1540 by the Chelsea churchwardens for neglecting the church and holding the benefice vacant, and giving more information about his life.

[16] Robert Newcourt, *Repertorium Ecclesiasticum parochiale Londinense* (London, 1716), I: 346.

[17] *VCH London*, p. 74.

[18] An undated Star Chamber suit between Mary Rollesley, Prioress of St. Helen's, and Thomas Parker and Mary his wife (and others) states that the convent steward Sir John Larke promised them an indentured lease of their lodging in the close in order to get them to pay for expensive repairs. The money was to be later refunded, but they did not receive either the lease or the refund. STAC 2/17/217; 24/228; 25/185, summarized by Catherine Paxton, "The Nunneries of London and Its Environs in the Later Middle Ages," PhD dissertation (University of Oxford, 1992), p. 89.

on March 7, 1544.[19] The sub-prioress at the time of the letter is most likely
Mary Rollesley, who later became St. Helen's last head. Vernon's letter
thus allows us to see More and Cromwell, the two most powerful laymen
in the city, pitted against each other over the St. Helen's appointment – as
they would be over larger matters in the years following.

The period at which the headship of St. Helen's was vacant is extremely
cloudy. According to the *LP* editor, Prioress Isabel (or Elizabeth) Stampe
resigned on November 12, 1528,[20] while David Smith dates the resignation
August 22, 1528.[21] Mary Rollesley became St. Helen's head, however, at
least by December 21, 1528, on which date she issued a lease as prioress.[22]
Hence we might conclude that More's prophecy, cited in Vernon's letter,
was correct, and that Rollesley indeed became the new superior before
Christmas 1528.

Vernon's three letters suing for St. Helen's would thus fall within a
four-month period between late August and late December 1528. The first
letter to Cromwell asks what Wolsey's intention is. The second letter knows
that Wolsey intends to sponsor her and asks Cromwell if Wolsey will keep
his promise. The third does not mention Wolsey at all (his indictment
for praemunire was still in the future, on October 9, 1529), and it relies
entirely upon Cromwell: "I beg your favor in this matter, that all men
may see that I am your prioress, which is more comfort to me than to be
made abbess of Shaftesbury." The tone is both intense and intimate, quite
different from the matter-of-fact, even jocular, earlier letters. The terms in
which Vernon makes the request for preferment lead us to wonder about
the nature of the relationship: "I beseech this of you for my sake and for
the love you bear to your son Master Gregory." (Cromwell's only son was
at this time being schooled at Little Marlow, where Vernon was responsible for him.)

The impressive final letter must come after Wolsey's death on November
29, 1530, since it speaks of "my lord cardinal's days" as past and thus probably comes from early 1531. In it she notes that "certain of my friends" had

---

[19] The indictment, from *LP*, XVIII (ii), pp. 325–26, is printed by James Gairdner, *Lollardy and the Reformation in England: An Historical Survey*, 4 vols. (London, 1908), II: 412. And see Margaret Bowker, *The Henrician Reformation: The Diocese of Lincoln under John Longland 1521–1547* (Cambridge, 1981), p. 139.

[20] *LP*, V, no. 20, note 10, citing "a document on the Lord Treasurer's Memoranda Roll, 22 Henry VIII, Pasch. Rot. 2."

[21] Smith, *Heads*, III: 667–68, is probably incorrect in giving the date of both Isabel Stampe's resigna- tion and the election of her successor, last head Mary Rollesley, as August 22, 1528, citing TNA E 368/304, Easter m. 2. (the same document as that cited by the editor of *LP*, V, no. 20, note 10; see note 20 above), but this seems unlikely given Vernon's three letters requesting the post.

[22] Smith, *Heads*, gives the modern reference: TNA E 303/8/24.

"moved [Cromwell] for the house of St. Helen's, as master Marshall one."[23] This letter gives more detail about the politics of the appointment, mentioning that the king's saddler has offered 200 marks to have the position for his sister. The parallels between the St. Helen's appointment and the situations of the three nuns described in the preceding chapter are suggestive. The king's saddler was Robert Acton (later Sir Robert) whose convictions, like those of the Cromwell clients in Chapter 3, were reforming. Hugh Latimer, Bishop of Worcester, in 1537 wrote to his friend Cromwell assuring him that Acton was "faithful and hearty in all good causes, no man more ready to serve God and the king and your lordship's hearty lover to his power."[24] His sister Joyce was Prioress of Westwood, one of the smaller houses assessed at £75, with longstanding family ties, since at least six nuns named Acton were members of Westwood over the centuries. She retired in 1536 with a pension of £10 and her brother Robert gained some of the priory lands.[25] Like Abbess Bulkeley and Prioresses Kingsmill and Fane, her convictions were probably reforming, since her 1564 will left 10s. to buy a bible for a local church. Unlike these women, Joyce Acton did not succeed in receiving a major appointment but the path of the appeal, through Henry's great minister, and the similarity in religious position, were the same.

In this last letter on the subject of St. Helen's, Margaret Vernon seeks to establish her decision not to pursue the appointment for reasons both practical ("payment of this great sum") and spiritual ("burdened in conscience"). She mentions that the king has given the appointment to "master Harper," unidentified, who says he has been offered 200 marks for the position, "which proffer I will never make unto him ... for the coming in after that fashion is neither godly nor worshipful" – that is, neither religious nor respectable. The complex personal factors involved in negotiating for an elevated position like this are made further visible in the next sentence: "And besides all this I must come by my lady Orell's favor, which is a woman that I would least meddle with." Lady Orell, the widow of Sir Lewis Orell, with her second husband Thomas Parker was involved not only in the Star Chamber case mentioned above (see note 18), but also

[23] It is impossible to identify this person with certainty: candidates might include George Marshall, an Essex priest and member of the Christian brethren (see Brigden, *London and the Reformation*, pp. 25, 253, 389, 401), or William Marshall, the translator and reformer.

[24] Hugh Latimer, *Sermons and Remains of Hugh Latimer*, ed. George Elwes Corrie, Parker Society, 2 vols. (Cambridge, 1845), II: 387.

[25] Margaret Goodrich, "Westwood: A Rural English Nunnery with Its Local and French Connections," in Joan Greatrex (ed.), *The Vocation of Service to God and Neighbor* (Turnhout, 1993), pp. 43–57.

in a chancery suit with Prioress Mary Rollesley about their rent of a tene-
ment in St. Helen's close (TNA C1/553/80).

As Prioress Vernon presents them, the practical and spiritual reasons
not to pursue the position are overwhelming and the letter concludes on
a high note.

> And though I did, in my lord cardinal's days, proffer a hundred pounds
> for the said house, I beseech you consider for what purpose it was made.
> Your mastership knoweth right well that there was by my enemies so many
> high and slanderous words and your mastership had made so great instant
> labour for me, that I shamed so much the fall thereof that I forced [cared]
> little what proffer was made, but now I thank our Lord that blast is ceased,
> and I have no such singular love unto it; for now I have two eyes to see in
> this matter clearly – the one is the eye of my soul, that I may come without
> burden of conscience and by the right door and laying away all pomp and
> vanity of the world, looking merely upon the maintaining and supporta-
> tion of the house which I should take in charge.[26]

Three of the undated letters give progress reports on Cromwell's son
Gregory, who was at this time staying with Prioress Vernon at Little
Marlow. It was his earliest schooling, since in one letter Vernon says
Gregory can construe his paternoster, ave, and creed, often the first
task for students after learning the alphabet. In another letter Vernon
reminded Cromwell that he promised "that I should have the governance
of the child till he was twelve years old." The third letter says that Gregory
and his master are both in good health "and now prosper in learning."[27]
The first two letters probably come from 1527 or 1528, the last from 1528
or early 1529, suggesting a birth date for Gregory of c.1520, and a stay at
Little Marlow from about age seven to eight.

Vernon's charm is particularly visible in a letter forestalling Cromwell's
choice of a master for Gregory and suggesting her own preference for an
Oxford MA named William Ynglefield.[28] Vernon's reasons for recom-
mending him were based on his previous stay at Little Marlow with a
pupil, "to whom he gave attendance with so great diligence and virtuous
bringing up that you could not be better sped." Her teasing conclusion
deprecates her interference and suggests her fondness for Gregory: "if he

[26] *LP*, V, no. 19. I have transcribed from Green, *Letters*, II: xxii, pp. 53–56, changing Green's reading
of "foresaw" to "forsyd, i.e. forced [cared]" and "looking warily" to "looking merely," based on the
summaries in *LP*.

[27] *LP*, V, nos. 18, 17, 15.

[28] I have been unable to locate Ynglefield in *BRUO 1501–1540* or in Joseph Foster, *Alumni Oxonienses,
Vol. III: Early Series (1500–1714)*, reprint edn. (Liechtenstein, 1968).

had a master who disdained my meddling it would be great unquietness to me; for if you sent here a doctor of divinity, yet would I play the smatterer [dabbler]: but always in his well doing he [Gregory] shall do his pleasure, but otherwise not."[29]

Gregory was later taught by John Palsgrave, sometime before the approximately fourteen months he spent with his cousin Christopher Wellyfed and Nicholas Sadler under the tutelage of John Chekyng at Pembroke Hall, Cambridge. Seven letters from Chekyng to Cromwell reporting on the boys' progress survive for about fourteen months, from May to July of a following year, 1528 to 1529 according to *LP*, though 1529 to 1530 seems more likely.[30]

One letter about Gregory mentions another person who was an old friend of Cromwell's, someone for whom Cromwell had drafted petitions and to whom he had loaned £60. Thomas Somer apparently knew Margaret Vernon well enough to advise her against Cromwell's choice of master for Gregory ("he will not take the pains which would be for my pleasure"). Somer was a member of the Christian brethren, a prosperous stockfishmonger who was punished for owning a copy of William Tyndale's work and in 1532 died in prison.[31] As perhaps with Marshall, Vernon's connections seem to be not only with the minister but with a circle of his reform-minded acquaintances.

Another undated letter from about this time presents one more name from that circle. During the 1520s Cromwell kept up his business both as lawyer and moneylender, and this latter occupation was part of his early relation with Vernon. Writing to him, she says:

> Of such money as was delivered into Vaughond's hands, viz. £20, I can have no more again but £15, as he says he has delivered you £5, which I do not believe, for you told me at your last being with me that the whole sum was in his hands. Let the £5 be delivered to this bearer for my creditor, as I cannot have my bonds until the duty be paid.[32]

[29] *LP*, V, no. 17.

[30] None of John Chekyng's seven letters to Cromwell about Gregory bears a year-date. The order is probably: *LP*, IV, nos. 4314, 4433, 4560, 4837, 4916, 6219, 5757, from ?May to July fourteen months later. A letter from John Hunt to Cromwell, dated July 31, indicates that Gregory and Nicholas are now under his tutelage (*LP*, V, no. 359). Later Gregory also studied with Richard Southwell and Henry Dowes (Bindoff, *House of Commons*, 1: 727–28).

[31] Brigden, *London and the Reformation*, pp. 183–84, 196, 206, 220, 381–82 for Somer. Also Susan Brigden, "Thomas Cromwell and the 'Brethren'," in C. Cross, D. Loades, and J. J. Scarisbrick (eds.), *Law and Government under the Tudors: Essays Presented to Sir Geoffrey Elton* (Cambridge, 1988), pp. 31–49.

[32] *LP*, V, no. 18, dated 1531 by *LP*.

G. R. Elton says that Stephen Vaughn entered Cromwell's service probably in 1524

> and remained in it even after his own affairs took him to Antwerp ... Every time he returned to England he busied himself on Cromwell's behalf: in 1528, for instance, he looked after his master's London house while Cromwell was at Oxford ... and in 1529 he did likewise ... their relations were closer and more equal than this master–servant situation might suggest.[33]

Two more of Vernon's letters invoke Cromwell's banking services: in one she asks if he will loan her £40 until Whitsuntide, to enable her to buy a neighbor's crop and cattle. Though the price is £47, a cash payment of £40 will be accepted, and the prioress, anticipating a profit of 20 marks by Michaelmas, offers another neighbor, one Grinder, as security for the loan.[34] In her next letter Vernon acknowledges Cromwell's assent, reaffirming the terms he requires: "two sufficient securities" – the neighbor and the London goldsmith previously mentioned, John Lewis, at the sign of the Portcullis in Cheapside.[35] Though the *LP* editor places the first letter in 1529 and the second in 1531, they are clearly only a few days apart and come from the period of Gregory's stay at Little Marlow, around 1527 or 1528. These are business letters, and not the least of their interest is what they reveal about both correspondents: for Cromwell, the sort of bread-and-butter work that supported him in the years before his rise and for Vernon, the entrepreneurial initiative of a successful administrator.

That administrative competence is shown again at the visitation of Little Marlow on October 10, 1530 by Bishop of Lincoln John Longland.[36] The house consisted of only five women besides the prioress.[37] Vernon testified at this time that Wilcocks, the house steward, did not perform his office for the benefit of the monastery but for his own benefit, and that he kept the court rolls and rent rolls and would not release them.[38] She also noted a dispute over possession of a property called nuns' mill. Given the presentation of these serious matters, it is somewhat disappointing that Bishop Longland registered only the trifling criticism of

[33] G. R. Elton, *Reform and Renewal: Thomas Cromwell and the Common Weal* (Cambridge, 1973), pp. 38–46. Merriman, *Life and Letters*, p. 52, puts their first connection in 1523.
[34] *LP*, IV (iii), no. 5971; Green, *Letters*, II: xxiii, pp. 56–57.
[35] *LP*, V, no. 16.
[36] A. Hamilton Thompson (ed.), *Visitations in the Diocese of Lincoln 1517–1531*, 3 vols., Lincoln Record Society 33, 35, 37 (Hereford, 1940, 1944, 1947), III: 7–8.
[37] Since only three are called "domina" and only four gave testimony, probably not all were professed.
[38] Walter Wilcokk was still steward in 1535; see Dugdale, *Monasticon*, IV: 422.

one of the nuns, Dame Katherine Pykard, who pointed out the large size – presumably fashionable – of the roll or headdress worn by the nuns beneath the veil. Feeling perhaps that legal problems like the mill lay outside his purview, Longland only commanded the prioress to change the nuns' dress.

Vernon's concern for her house's prosperity is shown again in a letter written probably about a year before Little Marlow's closure. First, however, it begins with a request that shows Vernon's connection with yet another of Cromwell's friends, Ralph Sadler, his secretary. She says she has heard "there is a little gentlewoman with master Saddlere which I would very fain have the governance and bringing up ... it were to my comfort now in mine age." Based on her status as Prioress of Sopwell in 1509/10, she might at this time have been aged about fifty-five.[39] We have seen that Little Marlow under Vernon had earlier at least one boy pupil accompanied by his master, and probably, like most female houses, it had a tradition of child boarders. Sopwell, Vernon's first house, and St. Helen's, her desired appointment, both took children.[40] Sometimes, as Vernon is proposing here, they were the particular responsibility of one member of the community and the development of affectionate bonds was natural.

The letter continues: "I hear the house my lady of Salusbery [Margaret Pole] had at Bysham is in the king's hand. If you help me to it for my money, I trust to have some pasture thereby to maintain my poor house. If it be passed by promise, please help me to some other." Based largely on her family's claim to the throne, the Countess of Salisbury was arrested in November 1538 and attainted in May 1539, at which time her property would have passed to the king, hence the editor of *LP* has placed this January 24 letter under 1539. This is impossible, however, since Malling, Vernon's last house, surrendered on October 29, 1538. The letter must have been written before the June 1536 closure of Little Marlow, since Bisham lies only a short distance away from that nunnery and since Malling, in Kent, the institution to which Vernon moved in that same year, could never have been called a "poor house." It seems likely that Vernon's letter, whose tone is contented and forward-looking, comes from a period before mid-1535, when Little Marlow was stripped of its members and, as

---

[39] Eileen Power, *Medieval English Nunneries c. 1275 to 1535* (Cambridge, 1922), p. 45, says the minimum age for superiors was twenty-one, but Bishop Hilsey's letter to Cromwell about Joan Fane, discussed in the previous chapter, implies the required age was thirty.

[40] Power, *Medieval English Nunneries*, pp. 568–81, for a list of "School Children in Nunneries."

its prioress clearly saw, of its future. Probably it should be dated January 24, 1535.[41]

In fact it was Little Marlow's small size that made its closure inevitable. At some time between August and December 1535 Vernon wrote to Cromwell informing him that the king's visitors, who were there to check on the presence of religious under the age of twenty-four, had come and gone, and had discharged three nuns: Dame Katherine (presumably Pykard, who had complained in 1530) and the two "young women that were last professed."[42] The record of their 1528 ceremony remains in Longland's register, along with a copy of the form of profession spoken on that day by one of them, Constance Hall (who was also listed in the 1530 visitation).[43]

This was indeed a blow – even the two youngest nuns would have been at Little Marlow for at least seven years – and effectively destroyed the community since, as the prioress says, "there shall be none left here but myself and this [one] poor maiden." She leaves the disposition of her fate and her house's entirely to Cromwell, suggesting:

> if it will please your goodness to take this poor house into your own hands, either for yourself or for mine own [blank] your son, I would be glad with all my heart to give it into your mastership's hands … trusting … that you will so provide for us, that we shall have such honest living that we shall not be driven by necessity neither to beg nor to fall to no other inconvenience.

But although this plea might have been penned at the incipient closure of their houses by any number of desperate heads (and was), the note of personal friendship is strongly invoked as well. The letter opens "with my most humble thanks for the great cost made on me and my poor maiden at my last being with your mastership." The prioress and her young nun companion have been privately entertained by the king's minister. This was not the first time; an early undated letter, perhaps 1529, asks when Cromwell will be "in these parts," that is, near Little Marlow, located in what we would now think of as London's extreme outer circle around thirty-five miles from the capital. Alternatively, she can see him at his house (presumably his well-known London residence opposite the Austin friars), "she coming on one day and going home the next," as she requires

---

[41] *LP*, XIV (i), no. 130. The dating is further complicated by the letter's address to the Lord Privy Seal, a title Cromwell did not receive until July 1536, in which case only January 1537 or 1538 would be possible.

[42] *LP*, IX, no. 1166, BL Cotton Cleopatra E.IV. f. 55. Wright, *Suppression*, XXII, pp. 55–56; Green, *Letters*, II: lxxiii, pp. 181–82; Cook, *Letters*, XLII, p. 79.

[43] *VCH Buckinghamshire*, II: 359.

his counsel in several matters. That she intended to stay with Cromwell seems a distinct possibility.[44]

Little Marlow was closed under the Act of 1536 on June 27 of that year.[45] The site and lands were granted soon after, in 1536–37, to one Elizabeth Restwold.[46] A letter on June 23, a few days before the closure, from William Cavendish, one of Cromwell's principal agents in the dissolution of the monasteries, tells his master that "we have been at the priory of Little Marlow and have dissolved it" and that "my lady takes her discharge like a wise woman ... she trusts entirely to you for some reasonable pension" and he recommends "either this or her promotion to some other house of religion."[47] But a letter from the prioress a week later, on July 1, 1536,[48] suggests that Vernon's apparent calm involved some dissembling and exposes the truth of her situation in its devastating uncertainty. Parted from Little Marlow, she writes from Stepney (where, coincidentally, Cromwell had a house):

> I have divers times been at the Rolls to have spoken with your mastership, but by reason of the great number of suitors, and also for lack of friendship within your mastership's house, I am kept back; so that I cannot come to your presence to solicit my cause ... Sir my request is to desire you to call to remembrance your good and comfortable promises made both unto me and unto my friends, whereunto I have ever hitherto trusted; beseeching your goodness to open unto me some part of your determination what thing you mind that I shall have, or else to help me to some reasonable living, so that I may not continue this long suit.
>
> For I have but singly provided for myself to maintain it withal, because your mastership commanded me that I should nothing embezzle or take away,[49] but leave the house as wealthy as I could, which commandment I followed: I hope all shall be for the best. I pray our lord put in your heart to make provision for me according to his holy will and pleasure and wholly to rule your mastership by his Spirit. Amen.

[44] *LP*, IV (iii), no. 5972.

[45] Sibyl Jack, "Dissolution Dates for Monasteries Dissolved under the Act of 1536," *Bulletin of the Institute of Historical Research* 43 (1970), 161–81, citing SC 6/Henry VIII/234.

[46] Dugdale, *Monasticon*, IV: 420, note b. Little Marlow was eventually given toward the royal re-foundation of the nearby house of Bisham.

[47] *LP*, X, no. 1188.

[48] The text says "the day after St. Paul's" and it has been calendared by *LP*, at January 26, 1535. The feast of the conversion of St. Paul is indeed January 25, but the commemoration is June 30, hence the letter was written on July 1, 1536. *LP*, VIII, no. 108. Green, *Letters*, II: lxxiv, pp. 183–84; Cook, *Letters*, XLIII, p. 80.

[49] It looks as though Cromwell gave this message to others. A letter to him from Edward Lee, Archbishop of York, says that "according to your request made to me in your letters," Lee has taken various measures to warn all monasteries under the value of £200 that they shall nothing "embezzle or alien." Wright, *Suppression*, p. 123.

The contrast between the two pleading letters could hardly be greater. A year earlier in 1535 after the king's visitors dismissed her three nuns from Little Marlow she was able to write "trusting, and nothing doubting, in your goodness that you will ... provide for us." In 1536, without prospects and without a permanent base, she beseeches "your goodness to open unto me some part of your determination [decision] what thing you mind [intend] that I shall have." Even the conventional religious epistolary closure has become more terse, though both letters invoke the evangelicals' particular patron, the Holy Spirit. Earlier she commanded a rhetoric of complement and of surrender: "I offer myself and all mine unto your most high and prudent wisdom, as unto him that is mine only refuge and comfort in this world, beseeching God of his goodness to put in you his holy spirit, that you may do all things to his laud and glory." After she left Little Marlow she simply implores: "I hope all shall be for the best. I pray our lord put in your heart to make provision for me according to his holy will and pleasure, and wholly to rule your mastership by his Spirit. Amen." Not elaborate, and a closure explicitly drafted in the form of prayer.

But Cromwell had not forgotten her. Three months later, sometime before September 24, 1536, she was abbess of the major Kentish house of Malling, as we can see by a letter of that date from Sir Thomas Willoughby to Cromwell. He asks Cromwell to write the Abbess of Malling, unnamed, on behalf of Elizabeth Rede, Malling's former abbess, asking for a retirement chamber at the house, as had been granted in the past, and for certain plate Rede's father had given her.[50] The headship had changed, but there is no record of a vote nor of any of the usual steps in the election process, and how or why Abbess Rede resigned is invisible to us.

A year and a half earlier, in spring 1535, a ferocious competition for the stewardship of Malling had begun, as two of Abbess Rede's brothers-in-law, Sir Edward Wotton and Sir Thomas Willoughby, together with Sir Thomas Wyatt and Cromwell's nephew Richard, presented themselves, or were presented, as candidates, with both Cromwell and the king hovering in the background. Abbess Rede's letters on the subject might be read as amazed or annoyed, but her assessment of the situation is never less than direct. She told Wotton, for instance, that "she might have bestowed the office upon divers which would much better have shifted therewith" than

50 *LP*, XI, no. 490.

he.[51] Her mysterious resignation in 1536 has been attributed to Cromwell's displeasure at her failure to appoint his nephew,[52] but it is striking that the resignation occurred just at the moment of Margaret Vernon's obvious need. Vernon had received a great favor indeed: Little Marlow had been valued at some £23, while Malling was worth over £300. In addition, Vernon became an abbess, not a prioress. This elevation in status was of course not lost on her: we remember her earlier letter negotiating for St. Helen's Bishopsgate in which she told Cromwell that to be his prioress would be "more comfort" to her than to be made Abbess of Shaftesbury. Now she was not Cromwell's prioress, but his abbess.

Peter Clark has stressed the power of Cromwell's influence in Kent, observing that as the king's chief minister, he had excellent entrée into local magnate politics and even positing the development in the county of a Cromwellian party, "linked by patronage, religious reform, and sometimes kinship."[53] Certainly he knew well all of the earlier contenders for stewardship: Wotton, Neville, Willoughby, and Wyatt, besides his nephew. At least the first two seem to have shared his religious position, while inconclusive marriage negotiations between Neville's daughter Margaret and Cromwell's son Gregory occurred in the mid-1530s. Wyatt and Neville would subsequently be contenders for Malling at its dissolution. Given his long friendship with Vernon, it seems that the disposition of Malling involved, for Cromwell, a choice among intimates.

A few everyday letters survive from Vernon's last period of rule. She sent (or delayed sending) several fees, and Cromwell's accounts show receipts for various sums: in June 1537, £30 "by her chaplain" and in May 1538, 10 marks, again "by Sir Rowlande, her priest."[54] A letter from her on April 22, 1537 asks for Cromwell's support for Master Chutts, her understeward, who wishes to become bailiff of Rye and will let her dispose of his Malling position as she likes.[55]

By the following spring, in April 1538, she knew from Cromwell, and from a variety of suitors, of Malling's coming dissolution. Like the former

[51] *LP*, VIII, no. 349. For a more detailed account, see Mary C. Erler, "The Abbess of Malling's Gift Manuscript (1520)," in Felicity Riddy (ed.), *Prestige, Authority and Power in Late Medieval Manuscripts and Texts* (York, 2000), pp. 147–57.

[52] C. R. Councer, "The Dissolution of the Kentish Monasteries," *Archaeologia Cantiana* 47 (1935), 126–43.

[53] Peter Clark, *English Provincial Society from the Reformation to the Revolution: Religion, Politics, and Society in Kent 1500–1640* (Cranbury, NJ, 1977), pp. 50–52.

[54] *LP*, XIV (ii), no. 782.

[55] The position was in the gift of "Master Thynne, clerk controller," that is, William Thynne, courtier and editor of Chaucer (d. 1546).

Abbess of Malling Elizabeth Rede (who was still living at the abbey), she too was the subject of very explicit pressures for her endorsement, which she reveals in two letters. At that point it appeared likely that she would be able to control events, and the first letter is remarkable for its display of confidence. Writing on Good Friday, April 19, 1538, she refers to an earlier conversation with Cromwell. She tells Cromwell she is surprised to hear that Master Stathum negotiates for her house, considering she desired the contrary, after speaking with Cromwell. She then says that when she heard Sir Thomas Neville desired it, "she said she would rather Stathum had it then that it should go to another who would not inhabit there." In other words, she appears to have been resigned to having Malling go to a lay owner and to have preferred one who would live there. But after she spoke with Cromwell, the letter continues, she "desired him [Neville] to make no suit therein, trusting to enjoy it during her life." This can only have been a possibility extended by Cromwell – or even something stronger than a possibility. She concludes by begging favor, for "unless all shall be dissolved, she would like to keep it according to Cromwell's promise."[56]

That she did not regard this promise as certain is shown by another, later April letter, which says, "On Easter eve I sent you a letter [presumably the Good Friday letter] and had no answer. If you pleased to quiet me with your letters I were much bound to your Lordship."[57] She was referring to the last sentence of her previous message, the tentatively expressed wish to keep Malling (based on their previous conversation), and is asking for a re-affirmation of that possibility. Perhaps Cromwell did reassure her that Malling might endure – in April 1538 that might not have been out of the question – since among his remembrances, calendared under 1538, is a note saying: "To send to my lady of Malling."[58]

Again, however, her oscillation between confidence and doubt can be seen, since two months later, on Midsummer Day (June 24) she told Cromwell that Mistress Stathum had visited, telling the abbess that Cromwell had counseled her "to win my goodwill for the resignation of my house and promised her your favor in the same." This opportunistic, slightly comic intervention was the work of Hugh Latimer, the reforming preacher and Bishop of Worcester. Earlier, in November 1537, Latimer had written to Cromwell describing "a faint weariness over all my body" which Mistress Stathum, his "good nurse," had addressed: "seeing what case I was

[56] *LP*, XIII (i), nos. 80–88.
[57] *LP*, XIII (i), no. 875.
[58] *LP*, XIII (i), no. 879.

in, hath fetched me home ... and doth pymper me up with all diligence."
Latimer's persistence in pressing the cause of his friend was remarkable.
He wrote Cromwell again in May and twice in June 1538, reminding him
with flat-footed tact, "I doubt not but that you will of yourself remember
my nurse."[59]

After Mistress Stathum's visit, the abbess's letter continues, "Now of late
came a servant of Master Wyatt for my goodwill, saying likewise that he
had obtained a promise from you of the same, and had also compounded
with the king, who had granted him his favorable letters."[60] Three days
earlier Thomas Wyatt, who had just returned to England from diplomatic
service abroad, had written Cromwell: "I recommend to you my matter
of Malling, in which I found the king so well disposed that I trust it is in
your hands."[61] Wyatt's servant's account of the situation, conveyed to the
abbess, is somewhat more assured than Wyatt's letter to Cromwell, a letter that probably represents more closely what the king actually said, and
that may have consisted merely of referral to Cromwell. The contradictory
claims, Vernon concludes, "doth not a little maze me" and she begs to
know "what answer I may make to all men."

And then there is silence for four months, until on October 29, 1538,
Malling surrendered.[62] About the same moment (*LP* calendars the letter at
October 28, but it seems to be undated),[63] the abbess wrote Cromwell with
a proposal. Among the various stratagems employed by dissolution-era
heads, offers of payment to be allowed to remain were not uncommon.
Vernon's proposal was quite different: accompanying or slightly preceding Malling's surrender, it acknowledged the inevitability of dissolution
and offered a plan that would have saved the royal administration from
the long-term pension payments that became standard. She asked permission to sell one of Malling's manors (Great Cornard, Suffolk and Essex,
whose yearly rent she cites as £40, though the *Valor* says it was worth £62
plus) "to provide for her sisters instead of their pensions, pay off her servants, and buy for herself a living with such of her friends as will take her."
(Presumably all these would be lump-sum payments.)

If this solution was not liked, she offered an alternative: £4 pension for
each of the nuns (the average female pension was £2) and £50 for herself
(roughly similar to the pensions received by Katherine Bulkeley, Morpheta

[59] Latimer, *Sermons and Remains*, II: letters XXV, XXX, XXXI, XXXII.
[60] *LP*, XIII (i), no. 1251.
[61] *LP*, XIII (i), no. 1228.
[62] *LP*, XIII (ii), no. 717.
[63] *LP*, XIII (ii), no. 716.

Kingsmill, and Joan Fane, all of whose houses, like hers, were valued at over £300). An experienced administrator, she employed the legal terminology that would secure the payments: "with a clause of distress [holding property, presumably Malling's, as security for payment of a debt], without any replevy of the same for non-payment of our said pensions at the day and feasts" – that is, without legal remedy (replevin) to recover the property for non-payment of the pensions. The terms she suggested, in other words, would be advantageous to central administration and would not be especially favorable to the nuns.

Sibyl Jack has pointed out that hindsight gives us a tremendous advantage in assessing the various courses of action taken by nuns and monks at the dissolution: "The story has too often been told as if it must have been clear to the religious from the outset exactly what the options were, and what would be their best line of conduct."[64] Though we may regard Vernon's proposal as doomed it probably did not appear so either to her or to Cromwell. Inventive, energetic, knowledgeable, daring, the letter constituted a strong attempt to wring the most for herself and her nuns out of the confused final moment.

One more undated letter comes from this time. A brief note tells Cromwell that she has received his letter "and perceives it is the king's pleasure that she should come to Cromwell. She trusts he will consider her age and unableness to journey so far in one day, and promises to be with him on Friday" – perhaps November 1, 1538, since the surrender day, on October 29, was a Tuesday.[65]

Cromwell had been thinking of her: not only did he write her (the letter does not survive) but his remembrances contain the following note: "touching my lady of Malling for her pension and her sisters,"[66] which the *LP* cataloguer has placed just before a document dated November 1, 1538. So it seems likely that she did go to London and that the two discussed her proposal. The award of the Malling pensions was made about a month later, on December 7. The abbess did not get quite what she asked for. Her pension was £40 instead of £50; the amounts granted the listed nuns are not given. A 1539 rental annotated in what Dugdale identified as Archbishop Cranmer's hand (it was he to whom Malling finally went) attempts to arrive at a yearly profit figure for the abbey: "Item to ix or x nones after iiij li a piece" but both the numbers and the pensions are approximate ("after"). The pension list printed by Dugdale from Hasted's

---

[64] Sibyl Jack, "The Last Days of the Smaller Monasteries in England," *JEH* 21 (1970), 97.
[65] *LP*, XIII (ii), no. 718.   [66] *LP*, XIII (ii), no. 736.

History of Kent (II: 217) shows eleven names: six received £3 6s. 8d. each, while five received £2 3s. 4d.[67]

We know indirectly that Margaret Vernon was pleased – although her pleasure is registered before the pensions were announced. On November 16, 1538, Hugh Latimer, who was then in London, wrote to his friend Cromwell. The letter's last sentence passes on a message from the Abbess of Malling who "desires him to thank Cromwell for his goodness." Latimer's message suggests that Vernon knew her pension amount a little more than two weeks after Malling's closure. Did Latimer know what the abbess was referring to? The Malling pensions would not yet have been public knowledge, though Latimer might have gotten a sense of the situation from either Cromwell or Vernon. Even if Latimer did not know the particulars of Cromwell's goodness to Vernon, the impression that these three persons knew each other is strongly conveyed.

The abbess drew her pension from 1539 to 1546 (I have not been able to trace her beyond the reign of Henry VIII) and thus she far outlived Cromwell. For the first two years her payment was dispensed together with that of Rose Moreton (Martyn), the most junior of the Malling nuns, and hence it is likely that they lived together. Once, but only once, Vernon's pension was collected by someone else: in 1540 by John Cocks, salter. Since Cocks collected at the same time for Richard Bowerman, Abbot of St. Albans, it may be that Vernon returned to the place where we first saw her.[68] She may have been laicized: D. S. Chambers notes that capacities, or dispensations, were much rarer for nuns than for monks or friars, though these licenses allowed nuns to live without the habit. After the middle of 1537, in fact, only three nuns are listed as receiving capacities. Two of them were Rose Moreton and Margaret Vernon.[69]

The usual regrets about paucity of material documenting women's lives are not relevant here. Vernon's twenty-one letters to Cromwell over about a dozen years outline a powerful and attractive personality. They display a friendship that began when she and Cromwell were both ambitious and rising persons and that evolved as Cromwell moved upward, into a relationship of patronage reminiscent of that between royals and their long-serving staffs, where an inequality in power does not preclude an undeniable intimacy. She relied on him, she asked him for favors, but she also paid him and socialized with him, suggesting a relationship of some

[67] Dugdale, *Monasticon*, III: 382–86.
[68] *LP*, XVI, no. 745.
[69] D. S. Chambers, *Faculty Office Registers 1534–1549* (Oxford, 1966), p. xlii.

complexity. Despite the difference in status, she was able to express her anxieties about his conduct of her affairs.

Except perhaps for the invocation of the Holy Spirit, her letters do not reveal her beliefs, but her casual mentions of Cromwell's intimates, all of whom shared his interest in reform – Thomas Somer, Stephen Vaughan, Ralph Sadler, Hugh Latimer, perhaps William Marshall – suggest that she too knew these men and found their perspectives congenial. Perhaps more central in her life is her successful administrative work – an interest she shared with Cromwell. Indeed, we might see her as exercising, in a restricted and female sphere, the same talents Cromwell displayed in his masterful supervision of an entire country. Her early formation at the two women's houses dependent on St. Albans, Sopwell and Pré, would have given her an understanding of the political dimension of institutional religious life and may have been instructive in the development of her administrative skills, so prominent later. These skills marked her remarkable rise, a rise that has enough of the classic elements to allow us to speak of her career – membership in a circle of like-minded contemporaries and regular advancement thanks to a combination of personal qualities and substantial patronage. The personal sympathy that encouraged Cromwell to entrust his son to her and the openness to reform that eased his sponsorship of her were likewise elements in the progress of the woman we are justified in calling Cromwell's abbess.

CHAPTER FIVE

"Refugee Reformation"
The effects of exile

The flight to the Low Countries of English intellectuals and religious started as early as 1534, in response to the Act of Supremacy. Because this early movement included remnants of Thomas More's circle – Rastells, Clements, Ropers – it has drawn some attention. The exodus accelerated with the dissolution of the monasteries in the second half of the 1530s and with the ascent of Edward VI in 1547.[1] After the five years of Mary's reign, a second period of exile began with Elizabeth's accession, when in the 1560s and 1570s the controversial writings produced by English exiles living abroad made the exchange between England and the continent somewhat more visible.

Throughout these years, roughly between the mid-1530s and 1570s, one result of England's religious upheaval was to position some English religious and scholars physically closer to their continental peers.[2] The contacts, indeed the friendships, that developed abroad point to ways in which English religious thought may have been both reinforced in some long-established patterns and turned in fresh directions. Diarmaid MacCulloch has urged that the Reformation be viewed as an international movement, its English history essentially a part of this larger reality.[3]

The term "refugee Reformation" is Mark Greengrass's, derived from Heiko Oberman's work. Greengrass calls the refugee Reformation "one of the major catalysts of European cultural exchange resulting from religious change in early modern Europe." "Two Sixteenth-Century Religious Minorities and Their Scribal Networks," in H. Schilling and I. G. Toth (eds.), *Cultural Exchange in Early Modern Europe, Vol. 1: Religious and Cultural Exchange in Europe, 1400–1700* (Cambridge, 2006), p. 317.

[1] "The purging of distinguished Catholics from the university [after 1550] had the unforeseen effect of establishing what was to become the chief centre of scholarly opposition to the policies of the government of Elizabeth, in a community of learned Catholics in exile at Louvain." James McConica, "The Catholic Experience in Tudor Oxford," in Thomas M. McCoog (ed.), *The Reckoned Expense: Edmund Campion and the Early English Jesuits: Essays in Celebration of the First Centenary of Campion Hall, Oxford (1896–1996)* (Woodbridge, 1996), p. 45.

[2] Peter Marshall, *Religious Identities in Henry VIII's England* (Aldershot, 2006), p. 229, gives a list of 127 English religious exiles between 1533 and 1546.

[3] Diarmaid MacCulloch, "Protestantism in Mainland Europe: New Directions," *Renaissance Quarterly* 59.3 (2006), 700.

Sixteenth-century Catholicism too was an international movement, one
that sought to re-invent traditional religion,[4] especially after the Council
of Trent (1545), and it may be that the most accurate way to view the
English exiles is as privileged conduits for European theological and devotional thought, colporteurs for ideas that were planted subsequently with
varying success at home in Elizabethan and Jacobean England.

In 1557 William Peryn, an Oxford graduate and a Dominican, published in London a book he called *Spirituall Exercyses*.[5] Peryn had been a
notable conservative preacher under Henry VIII and had gone abroad,
probably after the Act of Supremacy in 1534.[6] The two nuns to whom he
dedicated the book, Katherine Palmer of Syon and Dorothy Clement, a
Poor Clare, were the best-known female members of the Louvain diaspora. Peryn's book was heavily influenced both by Ignatian and by Low
Countries spirituality, and the opportunity to make such ideas available
in English, for English nuns, was the fruit of religious exile with its consequent direct exposure to continental writing and thought.

Louvain was, of course, a natural home for English intellectuals and religious, partly due to the 1517 foundation at the university of its Collegium
Trilingue (Greek, Hebrew, Latin), though the university had had a reforming emphasis from early on, perhaps due to the influence of the Brethren
of the Commmon Life.[7] The city had in 1525 a population of 19,000,
reduced by plague to 14,000 in 1565; it was home to two dozen male and
female convents with nearly a thousand religious.[8] Still, the English exile
community was substantial, even in comparison to these numbers. On
March 8, 1566 the English exiles gathered there sent a petition to the pope

---

[4] "In a sense, the Reformation in this period was less about the creation of a confessional divide …
than about a range of responses to a single reformist impulse." Lucy E. C. Wooding, *Rethinking
Catholicism in Reformation England* (Oxford, 2000), p. 14.

[5] *STC* 19784. The Huntington Library copy (viewed on EEBO) has "Wlyam Peryn" written on the
title page. A MS copy of the book survives; it was "sold at the sale of the Trentham Hall Library [the
Marquis of Stafford] in November 1906 and presented to the church [St. Bartholomew the Great]
by a member of the Restoration Committee." E. A. Webb, *The Records of St. Bartholomew's Priory
and of the Church and Parish of St. Bartholomew the Great, West Smithfield*, 2 vols. (Oxford, 1921), 1:
283. This member was the Rev. E. S. Dewick, according to a pencil note on the MS's first flyleaf. It
is currently LMA MS 20845 and is dated 1597 in what appears to be the hand of the scribe, which
might suggest some relation to the printed edition by Peter le Chandelier in 1598, printed at Caen,
STC 19785.

[6] A. B. Emden, *A Survey of Dominicans in England Based on the Ordination Lists in Episcopal Registers
(1268–1538)*, Dissertationes Historicae Fasciculus 18 (Rome, 1967), pp. 422–23, with several inaccur-
acies; also *BRUO 1501–1540*, p. 444.

[7] Henri de Vocht, *History of the Foundation and the Rise of the Collegium Trilingue Lovaniense, 1517–
1550*, 4 vols. (Louvain, 1955), 1: 76–78.

[8] Craig Harline, *The Burdens of Sister Margaret: Inside a Seventeenth-Century Convent*, abridged edn.
(New Haven, 2001), p. 12.

for financial support that gives an idea of the diaspora's size: "In Louvain and in the vicinity we are about 200 … priests, religious, monks, scholars, and one elderly man and another elderly man with wife and family."[9]

Ten or fifteen years earlier, however, the numbers would have been considerably smaller and the English nuns would have included only Dorothy Clement, her younger sister Margaret Clement, Margaret's mentor, the important but little-known nun Elizabeth Woodford[10] (the last two at the Augustinian convent of St. Ursula's, Louvain), and six Syon women at the Brigittine house at Termonde, twenty miles northwest of Louvain. Katherine Palmer has been considered their leader. Peryn's preface to *Spirituall Exercyses* is dated the last of December 1555; in that year the total number of English female religious abroad, all at or near Louvain, was nine. In this community the book's dedicatees, Katherine Palmer and Dorothy Clement, were central figures.

In writing the book for them, as its author says, "to satisfy your most earnest and most importune desire," Peryn was providing a traditional service. The clerical spiritual director who supplies texts, often through translation, for the spiritual guidance of women in his care is a figure as old as Ælfric. In this case the material is of particular interest, since it reflects the European currents in which Peryn, and more recently the two nuns, had been immersed.

In his preface Peryn points out that the first text in his book is an adaptation of Nicholas van Ess's *Exercitia theologiae mysticae*.[11] This Latin work was published in 1548, the same year that Ignatius Loyola's *Spiritual Exercises* first appeared. Peryn's editor believes van Ess, and hence Peryn, was indebted to the Ignatian method,[12] and indeed Peryn's translation has been called the first appearance in English of Ignatian spirituality.[13] Van Ess knew well several early followers of Ignatius; he had lived with the first German Jesuit Peter Canisius (1521–87) when both were students, and Canisius had introduced him to another member of the order, Peter Fevre

[9] Printed and translated in Ginevra Crosignani *et al.* (eds.), *Recusancy and Conformity in Early Modern England: Manuscript and Printed Sources in Translation* (Rome, 2010), p. 59. Christian Coppens, *Reading in Exile: The Libraries of John Ramridge (d. 1568), Thomas Harding (d. 1572) and Henry Joliffe (d. 1573), Recusants in Louvain*, Libri Pertinentes no. 2 (Cambridge, 1993), p. xi.

[10] Her life is outlined in Appendix 5.

[11] See Albert Ampe, "Eschius (Esschius, Van Esche, Van Essche, Van Es) Nicholas, vers 1507–78," *Dictionnaire de Spiritualité Ascetique et Mystique* (Paris, 1960), IV: 1060–66. A Latin biography written soon after his death was reprinted by de Ram, *Venerabilis N. Eschis vita et opuscula ascetica* (Louvain, 1858), cited in James Brodrick, SJ, *Saint Peter Canisius S.J. 1521–1597* (London, 1935), pp. 11–19 (p. 12, n. 1).

[12] Claire Kirchberger, *Spiritual Exercises of a Dominican Friar* (New York, 1929), p. xix.

[13] William Wizeman, *The Theology and Spirituality of Mary Tudor's Church* (Aldershot, 2006), p. 211.

or Faber, with whom van Ess had made the Ignatian spiritual exercises in 1543.[14] Van Ess had been chaplain of a beguinage at Diest, twenty miles from Louvain, hence was practiced in the care of female souls, but he had both founded and reformed other religious houses as well, both male and female.[15] A letter of 1545 from van Ess asks Canisius for contributions for the Diest beguines who were van Ess's responsibility.[16] He had intimate connections with the Carthusian house of St. Barbara at Cologne, where in fact he had a personal cell. The Cologne Carthusians' long-established interest in spiritual writing, often strongly mystical, was demonstrated in the sixteenth century by their publication of works by Johannes Tauler (1290–1361), Hendrik Herp (†1478), and Jan van Ruysbroeck (1293–1381). Peter Canisius in fact edited Tauler's sermons in 1543 and five years later one of Canisius's friends, the Cologne Carthusian Lawrence Surius, produced a Latin edition of Tauler's sermons that acquired "genuine international status."[17] Van Ess himself translated into Latin a classic work of Netherlandish spirituality, the *Margarita Evangelica* (*The Pearl of the Gospel*),[18] published by the Cologne Carthusians in 1535; Queen Mary Tudor owned a copy.[19] This house's sponsorship of the beguine mystic Marie van Hout (Marie d'Oisterwijk) and their publication of her writing – writing known to Syon – has been recently studied.[20] Van Ess was Marie's mentor, the founder of her beguinage of Bethlehem.[21] Canisius too was part of a circle that venerated Marie, calling her "mater noster."[22]

This was the spiritual and devotional milieu out of which Peryn's book sprang – Jesuit, Carthusian, strongly mystical, female-influenced. Van Ess's work, the opening text in Peryn's book, comes from the first years of Ignatian presence in the Low Countries and thus represents a particularly recent form of European devotional writing.

[14] Ampe, *Dictionnaire de Spiritualité*, IV: cols. 1060–62.

[15] Ampe, *Dictionnaire de Spiritualité*, IV: col. 1060.

[16] Brodrick, *Saint Peter Canisius*, pp. 11–17, 27, 63–64.

[17] *Johannes Tauler, Sermons*, trans. Maria Shrady (New York, 1985), p. xiii.

[18] "The *Pearl* was a great summation of Rhineland mysticism, and also an anthology. Whole sections from the works of other authors, especially from Ruysbroeck and … Harphius were inserted into it." Carlos Eire, "Early Modern Catholic Piety in Translation," in Peter Burke and R. Po-chia Hsia (eds.), *Cultural Translation in Early Modern Europe* (Cambridge, 2007), pp. 83–100 (p. 90).

[19] T. A. Birrell, *English Monarchs and Their Books from Henry VII to Charles II, The Panizzi Lectures 1986* (London, 1987), pp. 21–22.

[20] Alexandra Barratt, *Anne Bulkeley and Her Book: Fashioning Female Piety in Early Tudor England – A Study of London, British Library, MS Harley 494* (Turnhout, 2009), pp. 19–21, 103–04, 218–19.

[21] "In 1539 [van Ess] bought a house with land for nine poor honest virgins … in Oisterwijk; mystic Mary van Hout, with whom Nicholas had been acquainted for some time, and women of her 'circle', were presumably the first inhabitants." Walter Simons, *Cities of Ladies: Beguine Communities in the Medieval Low Countries, 1200–1565* (Philadelphia, 2001), pp. 293–94.

[22] Albert Ampe, "Marie d'Oisterwijk, beguine, †1547," *Dictionnaire de Spiritualité*, XII: 519–20.

Two additional texts follow: the source for "Ten gostly lettes and losses in the way of perfeccyon" remains unidentified, but the last work, called by Peryn "Certaine steppes or stayres general to know how much thou doest profite and grow in the loue of god," is a partial translation of Hendrik Herp's *Een Spieghel der Volcomenheit* (*A Mirror of Perfection*). Herp was at first rector of the Brethren of the Common Life at Delft (1445) and later became a Franciscan. He studied in Louvain, was provincial of the Cologne Franciscan province, and died as the guardian of the friars' convent at Mechelin (1478). This major work, written in Dutch and strongly influenced by Ruysbroeck, was translated into Latin in 1509 by Cologne Carthusian Peter Blomevenna and into various vernaculars soon afterward, thus making widely available a spirituality that Herp's editor calls characteristic both of Franciscanism and of the Devotio Moderna.[23] Peryn's translation covers part four of Herp's *Mirror*, addressed to those expert in mysticism. Having earlier treated preparation for the spiritual life, the spiritual active life, and the spiritual contemplative life, Herp turns here to the most advanced level, "superessential" union with God, outlining nine stages or steps.

Syon had known this important continental author before its dissolution. J. T. Rhodes has pointed out that Syon monk William Bonde's *Pylgrimage of Perfection* (1527, 1531) refers to "mayster Harpe" on the flood of joy experienced by the contemplative.[24] The immediate source for Peryn's translation may have been a 1538 compilation of Herp's spiritual works published in Latin at Cologne, in which the *Mirror* appears as the second work, titled *Directorium aureum contemplativorum*.

Herp's time in Louvain and his consequent local reputation made it natural that the English exiles would have read him while living there, particularly Dorothy Clement, who in exile became a member of a Flemish Franciscan house. Katherine Palmer, as a nun of Syon who was likely to have read Bonde's *Pylgrimage* when it first appeared in 1527, may have known Herp's work even earlier since the Syon catalog shows a copy of his *Speculum aureum decem praeceptorum Dei* (Basel 1496), as well as a copy of his sermons.[25] John Ramridge, an English priest murdered in 1568 on the

---

[23] Rik van Nieuwenhove, "Hendrik Herp, *A Mirror of Perfection, Part 4*," in Rik van Nieuwenhove *et al.* (eds.), *Late Medieval Mysticism of the Low Countries* (New York, 2008), pp. 144–64.

[24] J. T. Rhodes, "Religious Instruction at Syon in the Early Sixteenth Century," in James Hogg (ed.), *Studies in St. Birgitta and the Brigittine Order*, 2 vols. (Salzburg, 1993), II: 154, 164, discussing *Pylgrimage* ff. 289v–90. Rhodes says Bonde is citing Herp's *Directorium aureum contemplativorum* and *Tractatulus de effusione cordis*.

[25] Vincent Gillespie (ed.), *Syon Abbey, with the Libraries of the Carthusians*, ed. A. I. Doyle, Corpus of British Mediaeval Library Catalogues 9 (London, 2001), no. 1184.

road while traveling to visit the Syon nuns in Mechelin, owned a copy of Herp's *Directorium* published at Cologne in 1564. A complete list survives of Ramridge's remarkable library, sold after his death. His editor suggests that the library may have constituted "the supply of reading for a broader circle, probably other recusants and perhaps, young priests and religious in training."[26] He adds that "leading figures among the English immigrants made use of his books," hence it is possible that Ramridge shared his copy of Herp with Syon. Living abroad, the community had certainly read Herp by 1571, in which year, Rhodes has discovered, Katherine Palmer commissioned Herp's *Directorium* to be copied for her nuns by an English secular priest, Edmund Hargat.[27]

Even though Peryn's book was so much a product of its moment, it had a substantial afterlife. A. G. Dickens noticed that it was part of the York martyr Margaret Clitheroe's reading in the 1580s.[28] Dickens also suggested that the devotional writing of the man he calls "the last medieval Englishman," Robert Parkyn, might be indebted to Peryn and, through him, van Ess, particularly in the use of ejaculations or aspirations with which Peryn ends each chapter. Parkyn too recommends these prayers, "like darts, full of godly affection, which we cast, as it were, at God, as when we say O good Jesu, O gentle Jesu ... Go to, good Lord, vouchsafe to shoot my heart through with the dart of thy love."[29] Augustine Baker, the seventeenth-century mystic and spiritual director for the Benedictine nuns of Cambrai, read and recommended Peryn's book, calling it by its subtitle, *The Waie to Perfection*.[30] Thus Peryn's effort, which presented together two powerful elements from a European devotional tradition – the new Ignatian spirituality (van

---

[26] Coppens, *Reading in Exile*, no. 337 and p. 34.
[27] Rhodes, "Religious Instruction," p. 164. The priest (here called Edmund Hargot) is listed in Aidan Bellenger, *English and Welsh Priests, 1558–1800* (Bath, 1984), p. 68, where his place of training is given as Louvain, his date of ordination (uncertain) as 1570.
[28] A. G. Dickens, *Tudor Treatises*, Yorkshire Record Series 125 (Wakefield, 1959), p. 22, citing John Mush's life of Clitheroe.
[29] A. G. Dickens, "The Last Medieval Englishman," in Peter Brooks (ed.), *Christian Spirituality, Essays in Honour of Gordon Rupp* (London, 1975), p. 162. The quotation is from Parkyn's *Brief Rule for ... a Christian Life*.
[30] Several of Baker's book lists are printed by John Clark, *Father Augustine Baker: Directions for Contemplation – Book H* (Salzburg, 2000). These lists include Downside MS 26559 (Baker MS 2), pp. 79–81, dated 1645, where the second item is "Doctor Perin"; and Yale, Beinecke MS Osborne b. 268, pp. 82–89, item 20, "The Waie to Perfection by Doctor Perin. All" (i.e. entirely recommended). Also in a list of printed books, p. 86, "Doctor Perin." See also J. T. Rhodes, "Dom Augustine Baker's Reading Lists," *Downside Review* 111 (July 1993), 157–73. Baker knew Herp's writing as well.

Ess) and the earlier but still powerful Devotio Moderna influenced by Ruysbroeck (Herp) – had a substantial afterlife for English readers both at home and abroad. Intended at the time of its composition to provide spiritual direction for exiled English nuns, then subsequently published at home in England under Queen Mary at a time when that exile appeared to be reversed, Peryn's *Spirituall Exercyses* continued to be read in the seventeenth century, as the institution of female religious life moved permanently out of England.

William Peryn

Much of what is known about Peryn comes from Anthony Wood, who says that when young he

> did spend some time ... among the ... Black Fryers, in their coll. at Oxon, of which order he was a most zealous member. Afterwards retiring to the house of that order in London, lived there, and became a violent preacher against such that were called heretics, especially about the time when K. Hen. 8 renounced the pope's power in England [presumably the Act of Supremacy, 1534], for which his zeal, he was forced to leave the nation for some years.[31]

He was at home again in 1543, when he supplicated B. Th. at Oxford in May. In that year he is recorded as priest of a St. Paul's chantry commemorating Bishop of London Fulk Basset (d. 1259) and his brother Philip, chief justiciar. The cathedral had about fifty chantries under the general oversight of the dean and chapter. The dean at this time was John Incent (1540–45). Before his consecration as Bishop of London in 1540, Edmund Bonner had been appointed a canon and a prebendary of Paul's in 1537, and it is possible that Peryn owed the chantry position, with its modest salary of about £6 annually, to Bonner.[32] It has been suggested that Peryn returned from abroad in order to be appointed as one of Bishop Bonner's chaplains,[33] and indeed he did dedicate to Bonner his 1546 *Thre Godlye and Notable Sermons, of the Sacrament of Thaulter*, calling the bishop "his

---

[31] Philip Bliss (ed.), Anthony Wood, *Athenae Oxonienses (1813–1820)* (Hildesheim, reprint edn., 1969), I: 248–49. Joseph Foster, *Alumni Oxonienses, Vol. III: Early Series (1500–1714)* (Liechtenstein, reprint edn., 1968), p. 1148.

[32] *BRUO 1501–1540*, p. 444; *L&MCC*, pp. xxix–xxx, 56.

[33] Richard Rex, "The Friars in the English Reformation," in Peter Marshall and Alec Ryrie (eds.), *The Beginnings of English Protestantism* (Cambridge, 2002), p. 55.

special good lorde and mayster" (*STC* 19785.5–6), though no record of his appointment survives. Peryn's sermons, preached at St. Anthony's Hospital, which was connected with the parish of St. Benet Fink (John Bale calls Peryn "Father Finke"),[34] certainly were part of Bonner's effort to mount a public defense of conservative theology.[35] Centered on the eucharist, they anticipated Bonner's own 1549 sermon on transubstantiation that was responsible for the bishop's imprisonment in the Marshalsea throughout the reign of Edward.

Before Bonner's notorious sermon, however, Peryn had recanted one of his own, delivered on April 23, 1547 (St. George's Day) at St. Andrew Undershaft parish in London. On June 19 in the same pulpit he apologized for his April statement that it was good to worship the pictures of Christ and the saints. "Now he said he had been deceived, and was sorry that he had taught such doctrine."[36] It is likely that some pressure was brought to bear: Edward VI had been crowned just four months earlier, on February 13, 1547, and the progress of reform had been vigorously implemented.

Peryn must subsequently have gone abroad again, since Kirchberger discovered a record of him in May 1553, when the Acta of the Dominican general chapter in Rome transferred "father Wilelmum ex provincia Angliae" to the Louvain house.[37] Such back and forth movement was satirized by the radical poet Robert Crowley in his *One and Thirty Epigrammes*, published in 1550. Peryn was prominent enough to have been Crowley's specific target, though the lines may be intended more generally.

---

[34] John Bale, *Select Works of John Bale D. D. Bishop of Ossory*, ed. Henry Christmas (Cambridge, 1849), p. 154.

[35] J. W. Blench, *Preaching in England in the Late Fifteenth and Sixteenth Centuries: A Study of English Sermons 1450–c.1600* (New York, 1964), speaks of Peryn's "ornate style" and calls him a "representative of the Old Learning," who "stresses faith as against sense and reason"; pp. 19, 141, 157, 165, 249.

[36] John Stow, edited by Edmund Howes, *The Annales or Generall Chronicle of England* (1615), p. 594, and followed by John Strype, *Ecclesiastical Memorials Relating Chiefly to Religion, and the Reformation of It, and the Emergencies of the Church of England, under King Henry VII, King Edward VI and Queen Mary I*, 6 vols. (Oxford, 1822), II, pt. 1: 61, who adds "But in Queen Mary's reign they both [Peryn and Nicholas Sander] appeared in the pulpits open defenders again of that and the like renounced doctrines." The rector of St. Andrew Undershaft at the time was John Standish, a conservative who, like Peryn, had preached in support of transubstantiation and had been appointed by Bishop Bonner on September 3, 1543. Susan Brigden says that although in Henry's reign Standish was "a conservative champion … with each successive regime … he adroitly found favour." *London and the Reformation* (Oxford, 1989), p. 577.

[37] Kirchberger, *Spiritual Exercises*, p. xviii.

An obstinate papist,
That was sometime a friar
Had of his friar's coat
So great a desire,
That he stole out of England
And went to Louvain,
And got his friar's coat
On his fool's back again.[38]

His contemporary John Howes believed Peryn was deeply involved in the London struggle over monastic property around 1553, along with Greenwich Observant Franciscan William Peto, the two friars undertaking an attempt to block the foundation of Christ's Hospital school and to re-install the Franciscans in their onetime London headquarters, the Greyfriars. Howes says "the friars made great friends and great means to be restored to that house because it stood whole and was not spoiled as other houses were." He adds that trifling resistance to the new institution came from "poor friars which had been friars in the house before … [but] they only depended upon Perin and Peto."[39]

Two anonymous friars are mentioned in a letter of Cardinal Pole, written early in 1555 and quoted thus by Anstruther: "On 3 February, the queen ordered the lord chancellor [Stephen Gardiner] to summon two friars of St. Dominic, one of whom is at Brussels and the other at Louvain." Anstruther identifies these Dominicans as Richard Hargrave at Brussels and William Peryn at Louvain, commenting, "they duly responded to the queen's commands and returned to England."[40]

Though the effort to restore the London Franciscan house failed, Peryn's own Dominican house was one of the six re-established by Queen Mary. This was effected formally at Easter 1556 (April 5), according to Charles Wriothesley,[41] in the buildings of St. Bartholomew's, Smithfield, which had been given to Mary on December 17, 1555 by their owner Sir Richard

---

[38] Robert Crowley, *Select Works of Robert Crowley*, ed. by J. M. Cowper, EETS ES 15 (London, 1872), pp. 45–46.

[39] William Lempriere (ed.), *John Howes' MS., 1582* (London, 1904), p. 23. Howes says the restoration of the Franciscans was prevented by an Italian Dominican who burst into tears when he saw the poor children of Christ's Hospital. Thomas F. Mayer identifies the Dominican as Juan de Villagarcia, in *Reginald Pole, Prince and Prophet* (Cambridge, 2000), p. 286.

[40] Godfrey Anstruther, *A Hundred Homeless Years: English Dominicans 1558–1658* (London, 1958), pp. 3–4, citing Archivio Vaticano, Fondo Pio, 136, f. 192. This letter does not appear in Thomas F. Mayer (ed.), *The Correspondence of Reginald Pole*, 4 vols. (Aldershot, 2002–08).

[41] Charles Wriothesley, *A Chronicle of England during the Reigns of the Tudors, from A.D. 1485 to 1559*, 2 vols. (Westminster, 1875–77), II: 134.

Rich.[42] As the new community's head, Peryn preached at St. Paul's on that day. The community may have gathered earlier, as David Loades says, "[a]t some time during the summer of 1555 a group of Dominicans had also been established at St. Bartholomew's Smithfield."[43] Although chronicler Henry Machyn calls the Dominicans at St. Bart's "the first house that was set up by queen Mary's time,"[44] even if we accept Loades's dating of summer 1555, the Dominicans would still have been preceded by the Greenwich Observant Friars on Palm Sunday 1555. The re-foundation date of 1553 given by A. F. Pollard in the old *DNB* ("William Peryn") and followed by A. B. Emden, is clearly too early, especially since Mary reigned only from July 1553.[45]

The preface to Peryn's *Spirituall Exercyses* is dated the last of December 1555, when he was almost surely in England, though the book did not appear until 1557. Machyn mentions two sermons Peryn gave at the cathedral, on February 8, 1556 (Sir Thomas Sampson's penance for bigamy) and November 26 (the funeral of Mistress Heys, a mercer's wife), and one at St. Mary le Bow on April 4, 1557.[46] After its 1556 re-establishment, Blackfriars had resumed one of its traditional functions as an elevated secular apartment house and an anonymous account of the funeral of one of its inhabitants, Lord John Bray, gives an intriguing glimpse of Peryn's preaching. Bray died at the Blackfriars on November 18, 1557. On November 23 the body was taken by barge to Chelsea parish church where Peryn, as Prior of the Blackfriars, preached the funeral sermon on the text "Scio quia resurget in resurrection in novissimo die." The chronicler summarizes: "whereupon he [Peryn] declared how Christ raised Lazarus from death, saying how he was a gentleman given to chivalry for the wealth of his country, and so he said that noble man which there lay dead was [Bray], in whose commendation among many other things, he finished his sermon."[47] This is the last mention of Peryn. He died just four months

[42] Webb, *St. Bartholomew's,* I: 280–85.
[43] David M. Loades, *The Reign of Mary Tudor* (New York, 1979), pp. 353–54, giving no reference.
[44] Henry Machyn, *A London Provisioner's Chronicle, 1550–1563 by Henry Machyn,* ed. Richard W. Bailey *et al.,* online: http://quod.lib.umich.edu/m/machyn (listed under August 2, 1558).
[45] According to Pollard, Peryn "returned in 1553, when he was made prior of the Dominican house of St. Bartholomew in Smithfield, the first of Mary's religious establishments" (*DNB* XV, 931), and he wrongly refers to St. Mary Undershaft (for St. Andrew), an error followed by *ODNB* and *BRUO 1501–1540.*
[46] Machyn, *Chronicle,* dates as indicated.
[47] Anstruther, *A Hundred Homeless Years,* p. x, mentions Peryn's sermon, citing the funeral account "copied from the original in the Herald's College," in Thomas Faulkner, *An Historical and Topographical Description of Chelsea and Its Environs,* 2 vols. (Chelsea, 1829), I: 204–06, from which the quotation is taken.

after Elizabeth's accession, fortunately before the Syon community and the nuns of Dartford, Dominicans like himself, were forced to move abroad once again, on May 25, 1559. Machyn records his burial on August 22, 1558, at St. Bartholomew's.[48]

Dorothy Clement

The first of Peryn's two dedicatees, Dorothy Clement, is overshadowed by her younger sister Margaret, who was elected prioress of the important Louvain nunnery of St. Ursula's. Two sources give some details of their lives: Margaret's biography was written in 1626, fifteen years after her death, by a younger nun of her house, Elizabeth Shirley (the "Life"),[49] while sometime after 1659 a later, anonymous nun composed a history of the house's first half-century (the "Chronicle").[50]

Dorothy and Margaret were the daughters of physician and Greek scholar John Clement and mathematician and classicist Margaret Giggs, both protégés of Thomas More; they were married in 1526.[51] The number of their children is unclear. The "Life" calls Margaret the youngest of eleven;[52] presumably many died, since the "Chronicle" says "To this man [John Clement] had Almighty God left one only son ... but four daughters ... and two of his daughters he espoused to Christ, in Louvain, the one, called Dorothy, in the Order of Poor Clares, the other, named

---

[48] Machyn, *Chronicle*, dates as indicated.

[49] For Shirley's life of Margaret Clement see Nicky Hallett (ed.), London, *English Convents in Exile 1600–1800, Part 1, Vol. III: Life Writing*, Aldershot, 2012.) John Morris produced a synthesis from two MS sources, which he titled "The Life of Our Reverend Old Mother Margaret Clement, partly from the original manuscript life by Sister Elizabeth Shirley and partly from the manuscript chronicle of St. Monica's." Morris printed his synthesis in *The Troubles of Our Catholic Forefathers Related by Themselves*, 1st ser., vol. 1 (London, 1872). In addition, Elizabeth's Shirley's "Life" was given a careful summary (again, using the "Chronicle" as well) by C. S. Durrant, *A Link between Flemish Mystics and English Martyrs* (New York, 1925), pp. 183–210. In presenting the Shirley life, Morris, Durrant, and Hamilton (see note 50 below) made different selections. A short summary of Margaret Clement's life appears as well in Joseph Gillow, *Biographical Dictionary of English Catholics*, 5 vols. (London, 1885), 1: 500–01. The original MS of the "Life" is held at the priory of Our Blessed Lady of Nazareth in Bruges, according to Betty Travitsky, "Bibliography of English Women Writers 1500–1640," online: www.itergateway.org/mrts/earlywomen/index.cfm?action=showwriter&id=599 (under "Elizabeth Shirley"). I have quoted from a typescript transcription of the original manuscript, held at the Priory of Our Lady of Good Counsel, Sayers Common, West Sussex. I thank Dr. Caroline Bowden, Department of History, Queen Mary College, University of London, for giving me a copy.

[50] The "Chronicle" was edited by Adam Hamilton, *The Chronicle of the English Augustinian Canonesses Regular of the Lateran, at St. Monica's in Louvain*, 2 vols. (Edinburgh, 1904–06).

[51] Hamilton, *Chronicle*, 1: 5, though the *DNB*, followed by *ODNB*, says c.1530.

[52] Morris, *Troubles*, p. 31.

Margaret ... at St. Ursula's."[53] The birth of the Clements's youngest child, Margaret, can be dated 1539 by the "Chronicle" account of her election as prioress in 1569 when she was "not above thirty."[54] She entered St. Ursula's in April 1551 as a student, aged twelve;[55] if her older sister Dorothy were eighteen in that year, when she entered religious life, Dorothy would have been born c.1532.[56]

The Clement family emigrated from England sometime in "King Edward the Sixth's days" and were "the first family that came over to these Low Countries, with all their household and children."[57] The Clements's son Thomas is recorded as matriculated at Louvain on July 20, 1547,[58] six months after Henry VIII's death, but the rest of the family may have come later. A. W. Reed connects the family emigration with the required use of the first prayer book of Edward VI, announced on June 9, 1549. John Clement left England in July, his wife Margaret in October, and daughter Winifred and her husband William Rastell in December of that year.[59] The Clement family first lived at Bruges, then moved to Mechelin, and by 1551 to Louvain.

Dorothy's choice to become a Franciscan is somewhat surprising. John Moorman lists two Louvain houses of Clarisses, one founded "soon after 1490," the other founded in 1516.[60] In either case Dorothy would have

---

[53] Hamilton, *Chronicle*, I: 25. Hamilton provides a Clement pedigree that lists six children (in no particular order, Thomas, Bridget, Helen, Winifred, Dorothy, and Margaret; vol. I, no page). De Vocht, *History*, IV: 425, calls Winifred the eldest daughter. "She was born at the end of 1526 or early in 1527 and had married in 1544; unfortunately she fell ill and died in Louvain on 17 July 1553."

[54] Hamilton, *Chronicle*, I: 29.

[55] Using the "Life" and the "Chronicle" together, Margaret Clement's life can be outlined as follows: 1539, date of birth; 1551, placement at St. Ursula's, age twelve; October 11, 1557, profession, age eighteen; 1569, election as prioress, age thirty; 1607, golden jubilee, age sixty-eight; May 20, 1611, death, age seventy-two.

[56] "Dorothy, being of sufficient years to make election of her state, according to her desire, they dedicated unto God in the Order of St. Clare ... Margaret, being as yet but young, they placed [at St. Ursula's] that she might learn there the form of good life and religious conversation." Hamilton, *Chronicle*, I: 26.

[57] Hamilton, *Chronicle*, I: 29.

[58] De Vocht, *History*, I: 425, citing Louvain University's *Liber IV Institutatorium: Feb. 1529–Aug. 1569*, p. 228.

[59] A. W. Reed, "John Clement and His Books," *The Library* 4th ser., 6 (1926), 329–39. An eleventh-century MS in Greek of Josephus's *De bello Judaico*, books 9–14, belonged to Winifred Clement Rastell. At her death in 1553 it passed to her father John and then to her brother Thomas; it is now Leiden UL MS Bibl. Publ.Gr.16J. Alan Coates, *English Medieval Books: The Reading Abbey Collections from Foundation to Dispersal* (Oxford, 1999), p. 142.

[60] John R. H. Moorman, *Medieval Franciscan Houses*, 2 vols. (St. Bonaventure, NY, 1983), II: 609, citing J. M. R. Fonseca, *Annales Minorum*, ed. L. Wadding, 3rd edn., 17 vols. (Rome, 1931–35), XIV: 570 and 16: 36. E. de Moreau, *Histoire de l'Eglise en Belgique*, 6 vols. (Brussels, 1945–52), "Repertoire des Chapitres, Abbayes, Prieures et Convents," I: 488, lists only the 1516 foundation.

been the only Englishwoman in a Flemish community. It is possible that her ownership inscription in a copy of the 1494 *Scale of Perfection* may have commemorated her profession day: "Thys boke belongeth vnto syster dorothe clement," written in a Tudor italic hand, not especially regular.[61] Coincidentally, Katherine Palmer also owned a copy of the *Scale* from the same Wynkyn de Worde edition. It bears an *ex dono* inscription: "Katehrin [sic] Palmer ... Dedit hunc librum in Ihu Christi dilectione Antonio bolney pia mater Katherina Palmere Anno dni M.D.xlvj."[62]

The next mention of Dorothy Clement comes a quarter-century later, in two wills that offer glimpses of the Louvain exile community at that time. In 1572 the will of Thomas Harding, former Regius Professor of Hebrew at Oxford, the teacher of Lady Jane Grey, and an important Catholic controversialist, left Elizabeth Woodford, Margaret Clement, and Dorothy Clement each four dalders, while the Clarisse house and St. Ursula's, Margaret Clement's house, received 20s. each for mass and dirige. In the following year, 1573, Henry Joliffe, a former chaplain to Queen Mary, bequeathed 20s. to Dorothy Clement and 40s. to the nuns of her house for prayers. He gave St. Ursula's £3 6s. Flemish, while Katherine Palmer and her sisters of Mechelin were left £6.[63] Finally, we are given one glimpse of the Clement sisters living together. Margaret Clement's "Life" speaks of the famine that afflicted Louvain about 1578, noting that Prioress Margaret herself "went abroad and begged," and that at this time Dorothy, her sister, came to St. Ursula's.[64] The account says that

> [Margaret Clement] had also a sister elder then herself which was a religious in the poor Clares. This sister being enforced through the poverty of the time to leave her monastery, as the rest of the religious did, she desired to come to St. Ursula's to live with her sister till the times were better which her superiors lightly granted knowing the fame of our Reverend Mother and so she lived there holding her own order of their ceremonies. She would say sometimes to her sister that though their order had outward show of more strictness, yet our order did go beyond in true discipline of mortified religion.

What the "Life" tells us about Margaret's spirituality may be suggestive for Dorothy's as well, since the Louvain exile milieu even in the 1560s

---

[61] New York, Pierpont Morgan Library, Ch.L.f.1804; *STC* 14042.
[62] CUL Inc. 3.J.I.2 (3534).
[63] Coppens, *Reading in Exile*, pp. 165, 213.
[64] Typescript "Life" chapter 5, not in Morris. De Vocht, *History*, p. 427, dates this move 1606, probably wrongly since Dorothy would then have been aged about seventy-five. The *ODNB* account of John Clement, which says that Dorothy became a Poor Clare in 1571, is incorrect.

and 1570s was not large. Margaret Clement's first spiritual director was Adriaan Adriaensens, SJ (1520–80), the earliest superior of the Jesuit college in Louvain. A Jesuit presence in the city is attested from 1542, when the *Chronicon* of Juan de Polanco, SJ, notes that "[o]urs gathered at Louvain toward the beginning of autumn. Pursuing the study of philosophy that they had begun at Paris, they laid the foundations for [our] college at Louvain."[65] In 1551 Ignatius named Adriaensens the superior of that community, later the Jesuit college. At Louvain, Adriaensens wrote a catechism in Dutch (1550)[66] and a little spiritual work, *Dry suyberlijcke Tractaetkens* (1557), translated into Latin at Cologne and Arras. He was a popular confessor and spiritual director,[67] although a historian of the order calls him "the gloomy rector" and alludes to "frequent uncomplimentary mentions of this professed father in the correspondence of the period."[68]

Later, presumably after Adriaensen's death in 1580, "Dr. Jansonius" became Margaret Clement's spiritual director. Professor of theology at the University of Louvain, a member of the secular clergy, and the Archbishop's official visitor to St. Ursula's, he is not to be confused with the man Durrant calls "his more famous disciple, Cornelius Jansenius of Ypres [1585–1636], author of the *Augustinus*."[69] This posthumously published work on Augustine's theology of grace (1640) was attacked by the Louvain Jesuits, initiating a controversy in which the Jesuits continued to be involved throughout the century.[70] The relation of Jesuit spirituality to that of English nuns exiled on the continent would subsequently become a source of conflict,[71] but here we might simply notice the early connection, probably from the 1560s, between the Jesuits and St. Ursula's.

---

[65] Juan de Polanco, *Year by Year with the Early Jesuits (1532–1556): Selections from the "Chronicon" of Juan de Polanco, S.J.*, trans. John Patrick Donnelly, SJ (St. Louis, 2009), p. 16.

[66] John W. O'Malley, *The First Jesuits* (Cambridge, MA, 1993), p. 120.

[67] Alain Deneef and Xavier Dusausoit, "Quelques Iesuites Insignes," in *Les Jesuites Belges 1542–1992: 450 ans Le Compagnie de Jesus dans les provinces belgiques* (Brussels, 1992), p. 321.

[68] James Brodrick, SJ, *The Progress of the Jesuits (1556–79)* (New York, 1947), pp. 147, 185–87. Elsewhere, Brodrick says of Adriaensens that he "belonged to the school of those whose principle is, We have a law and according to that law he ought to die," pp. 89–90.

[69] Durrant, *Link*, pp. 200–01.

[70] Dirk Aerts, *Leuven in Books, Books in Leuven: The Oldest University of the Low Countries and its Library* (Leuven, 1999), pp. 65, 88–89.

[71] See Nancy Bradley Warren, *The Embodied Word, Female Spirituality, Contested Orthodoxies, and English Religious Cultures, 1350–1700* (Notre Dame, 2010), p. 64.

Katherine Palmer

Based on an early account of Syon's peregrinations composed by Robert Parsons, SJ, about 1594, it has been generally accepted that one group of Syon monks and nuns went abroad, to the Brigittine house of Maria Troon (Mary's Throne) at Termonde or Dendermonde, near Louvain. The account says that

> In this time [the reigns of Henry VIII and Edward VI] our Lord inspired one of the principal of these religious women, called Katherine Palmer, to join herself with other sisters of the same monastery of Sion, and so to leave England, and go to the city of Dermond in Flanders, to live in a monastery of the same Order of St. Bridget, where they continued some years, being received with great love and charity by the Abbess and Religious of that place, rejoicing much to have reserved there some relics of the famous monastery of Sion.[72]

The historian of Syon John Rory Fletcher believed that the move to Termonde led by Katherine Palmer took place in 1539; he cited as evidence a note in what he described only as "Syon Records": "July 28, 1539, Fr. John Branston died the year we left England."[73] Peter Cunich has recently observed, however, that the Augmentation Office pension records show Katherine Palmer received her quarterly pension payments fairly regularly until 1551.[74] (My reading of these accounts shows brief earlier absences in 1542;[75] such irregularities are found for almost all the Syon members and probably the years between 1539 and 1557 were a time of frequent movement as temporary living arrangements dissolved and re-formed.)[76]

---

[72] "A Preface, Written by Father Robert Parsons, S.J, to the History of the Wanderings of Syon …," in Adam Hamilton (ed.), *The Angel of Syon* (Edinburgh, 1905), p. 102.

[73] John Rory Fletcher, *The Story of the English Bridgettines of Syon Abbey* (South Brent, Devon, 1933), p. 37.

[74] Peter Cunich, "Palmer, Katherine (d. 1576)," *ODNB* (2008; online edn. May 2009), online: www.oxforddnb.com/view/article/96817 (accessed October 18, 2008).

[75] TNA E 315/251, ff. 12v–13. Payments were made quarterly. On April 17, 1542 Palmer collected for a half-year. Though there were many reasons for irregular collection, she might have been absent for the previous six months. On November 21, 1542 she collected her pension due at St. John Baptist (June 23) and Michaelmas (September 29) of that year, again suggesting she might have been away from April to November.

[76] For similar conclusions, see Peter Cunich, "The Brothers of Syon, 1420–1695," in E. A. Jones and Alexandra Walsham (eds.), *Syon Abbey and Its Books, Reading, Writing and Religion c. 1400–1700* (Woodbridge, 2010), pp. 70–71. A summary of Syon's movements is given in the same volume by Claire Walker, "Continuity and Isolation: The Bridgettines of Syon in the Sixteenth and Seventeenth Centuries," pp. 157–58.

Evidence from Termonde shows that a Syon group did come to Maria Troon by ones and twos, but not until four years after the January 1546 death of Syon abbess Agnes Jordan and the dispersal of the living community she had headed at Denham, Buckinghamshire. The house chronicle of Termonde, begun by Abbess Marie van Oss (1466–1507) and continued after her death, shows the arrival of Syon members in 1550 and 1552. Katherine Palmer came first, on the feast of John the Baptist (June 24) 1550; then, on the feast of St. Augustine (August 28) 1550, Margery Covert and Dorothy Slight arrived. Anthony Little and John Massey came also in 1550, without a month-date. Two years later, the account puzzlingly says on the feast of St. Margaret (July 20) *and* St. Anne (July 26) 1552, Mary Neville arrived, and on the eve of All Saints (October 31) 1552, Margaret Mannington and Anne Dancy came, while William Turlington also emigrated in 1552.[77] Covert, Slight, Little, Massey, and Neville had lived with Abbess Jordan, as her will makes clear.[78]

Parsons's account says that, en route to England from Rome to assume his duties as apostolic legate, Reginald Pole saw the Syon community at Termonde, in the second year of Philip and Mary's reign.[79] This accords with the date and itinerary of Pole's trip, as he himself related in a letter. He left Brussels on November 13, 1554 and went via Termonde, Ghent, Bruges, Nieuwport, and Dunkirk, to Gravelines on November 19 and arrived in London on November 24, 1554. He probably visited Maria Troon on November 13 or 14, 1554.[80]

To summarize: a Syon group of nine lived at Termonde beginning in the years 1550 to 1552 until their return to England, probably in early 1557 (the document of re-institution is dated February 23, 1557 and the ceremonial

---

[77] Ulla Sander Olsen published a summary of the chronicle from Termonde: "The Late Medieval Chronicle of Marie van Oss, Abbess of the Brigittine Monastery Maria Troon in Dendermonde, 1466–1507," in Erik Kooper (ed.), *The Medieval Chronicle: Proceedings of the 1st International Conference on the Medieval Chronicle, Dreibergen (Utrecht) 13–16 July 1996* (Amsterdam, 1999), pp. 240–50. She subsequently published an edition of the manuscript in the city archives of Cologne, Historisches Archiv der Stadt Köln [HAStK] MS Geistliche Abteilung [GA] 178: "De kroniek van Abdis Marie van Oss, Maria Troon, Dendermonde [Text edition]," in *Oudheidkundige Kring van het Land van Dendermonde. Gedenkschriften*, R. 4: 21 (Jaarboek 2002), pp. 250–332. Dr. Olsen has generously provided me with an English summary of the chronicle's entries for Syon members.

[78] TNA PCC 4 Alen (Prob 11/31/55), made October 28, 1545, about three months before her death. The will's careful provisions for the dismantling of the community's temporary home at Denham suggest that the move abroad may have been well planned.

[79] Hamilton, *Angel*, p. 102.

[80] Thomas F. Mayer (ed.), *The Correspondence of Reginald Pole, Vol. II: A Calendar, 1547–1554 – A Power in Rome* (Aldershot, 2003), no. 998, p. 379, letter dated December 1, 1554.

dedication of the new Syon took place on August 1 of that year).[81] Thus in the present state of our knowledge, we can only be sure of Katherine Palmer's Flemish life from 1550 to around 1557. Her first arrival occurred perhaps about the same time that Dorothy Clement came to the Low Countries. We do not have evidence for Syon's immediate contact with Jesuit spirituality in the 1550s, of the kind that Margaret Clement's life provides later, but Jesuit Robert Parsons's sympathetic account of Syon's wanderings on the continent, composed after 1596, is probably only the most visible evidence of a variety of such contacts.[82]

Reading before and after the dissolution

Syon had earlier provided a conduit through which continental spiritual writing flowed to England – perhaps especially what has been called the Rheno-Flemish mystical tradition[83]. Hence much of the reading that was opened to religious in exile after the dissolution was not entirely unfamiliar. The Franciscan David of Augsberg's (†1271) *Formula Noviciorum*, a guide for the young religious both to external behavior and internal disposition that circulated widely in the Low Countries among followers of the Devotio Moderna, was copied as well for Syon (and perhaps translated) by its dissolution-era brother Thomas Prestius (†1543).[84] The founder of the Modern Devotion Geert Grote translated the work of his influential predecessor Heinrich Suso (†1366), the *Horologium aeternae sapientiae*, into Middle Dutch, where it received the same wide readership as did its version circulating in England, *The Treatise of the Seven Points of True Love and Everlasting Wisdom* (copies were owned by the female religious houses of Ankerwyke, Campsey, and Dartford).[85] No copy of the *Seven Points* survives from Syon, but the house owned three copies of the

[81] Peter Cunich counts the group as ten, rather than nine: "Palmer, Katherine (d. 1576)," *ODNB* (October 2008; online edn. May 2009), online: www.oxforddnb.com/view/article/96817 (accessed June 4, 2009). The document of re-institution is calendared, most recently, in Thomas F. Mayer (ed.), *The Correspondence of Reginald Pole, Vol. III: A Calendar, 1555–1558 – Restoring the English Church* (Aldershot, 2004), pp. 374–75. The date of the re-institution comes from Henry Machyn's diary.

[82] Ann M. Hutchison, "Syon Abbey Preserved: Some Historians of Syon," in Jones and Walsham (eds.), *Syon Abbey*, pp. 240–41.

[83] Eire, "Catholic Piety," p. 86.

[84] Wybren Scheepsma says it "circulated widely" in Modern Devout circles. *Medieval Religious Women in the Low Countries: The Modern Devotion, the Canonesses of Windesheim, and Their Writings* (Woodbridge, 2004), p. 18. David N. Bell, *What Nuns Read: Books and Libraries in Medieval English Nunneries* (Kalamazoo, MI, 1995), pp. 200–01.

[85] Bell, *What Nuns Read*, p. 105 (Ankerwyke), p. 123 (Campsey), p. 132 (Dartford).

Latin text.[86] And of course the *Imitation of Christ*, a central text for the Devotio Moderna, found a similar endorsement at Syon.

By the time of the dissolution, these staples of the Modern Devotion had been confirmed as spiritual classics. The work of the Low Countries Franciscan Hendrik Herp (†1478) was more recent, though no less popular. Like Suso and Tauler, he had been engaged in the *cura monialium*, and his work too had been known at Syon before the dissolution. In addition to Herp's use by Syon author William Bonde, Syon owned printed copies both of Herp's sermons (Speyer, after January 17, 1484) and his *Speculum aureum* (either Mainz 1474 or Basel 1496).[87] (The *Speculum aureum* is the same work as Herp's *Directorium*, the text from which Peryn translated excerpts in his *Spirituall Exercyses*.)

Syon's connections with the Cologne Carthusians, perhaps through Sheen, their neighboring Carthusian house, seem to have preceded the dissolution as well. In the Syon-associated devotional miscellany London, BL MS Harley 494, the inclusion of a five-wounds devotion composed by the Cologne-sponsored mystic Marie d'Oisterwijk, taken probably from the 1532 printed edition of her work in Latin, dates the miscellany between 1532 and 1539, and demonstrates that Syon was familiar in the last years of its life with the most recent German/Low Countries devotional and mystical writing.[88] Alexandra Barratt has also suggested that another Syon manuscript, London, Lambeth Palace MS 546, shows German influence, since it contains the sayings of St. Albert the Great of Cologne, by Ruysbroeck, and the story of the stigmatic Magdalena Beutler of Freiburg (1407–58) and the revelation to her of the *Golden Litany*.[89] Recently Alexandra da Costa has pointed out that Syon monk John Fewterer's *Myrrour or Glasse of Christes Passion* is a direct translation of a work by Nuremberg physician Ulrich Pinder, published in 1506 and 1519.[90]

Broadly speaking, then, Syon was familiar with many forms of continental spirituality before the dissolution. Physical presence on the continent after the dissolution, however, must have intensified that familiarity as, for instance, when the English nuns read Herp in Peryn's translation, on the highest stage of mysticism, "Certaine steppes or styres" marking

[86] Gillespie, *Syon Abbey*, nos. SS1P 806, SS1.823b, SS1.945f.
[87] Gillespie, *Syon Abbey*, nos. 1184, 1331. A copy of the *Speculum Aureum* was taken by London Carthusian Thomas Goldwin on loan to Mount Grace, Yorkshire, in 1519/20; see Doyle no. C.7 in Gillespie, *Syon Abbey*, pp. 627–29.
[88] Barratt, *Anne Bulkeley*, pp. 218–19.
[89] Barratt, *Anne Bulkeley*, p. 101.
[90] Alexandra da Costa, "John Fewterer's *Myrrour or Glasse of Christes Passion* and Ulrich Pinder's *Speculum passionis domini nostri*," *Notes and Queries* 56 (2009), 27–29.

the ascent to perfection. Besides the inclusion in the *Spirituall Exercyses* of this separate work by Herp, Kirchberger points out that Peryn's "Fourth Exercise" is a translation of Herp's treatise on mortifications from his *Theologia mystica* (Book I, Part II) which had appeared in van Ess's book.[91] It is likely, too, that familiarity with Tauler, the great Dominican mystic of the Passion, came while abroad, after the publication by the Cologne Carthusian Laurence Surius of the 1548 Latin edition of his work, a copy of which Katherine Palmer owned. It has two inscriptions: "ad usum sororis Katherine palmere" and "vsui sororis Katherine Palmer."[92]

Peryn's *Spirituall Exercyses* is in fact suffused with the mysticism of union, while at the same time it is firmly structured by times and days. In this way it represents (like its source, van Ess's book) a fusion of traditional Flemish spirituality with Ignatian,[93] while the deep devotion to the Passion found everywhere in Peryn's book comes from both these traditions. In particular, the use of the imagination and deliberate stimulation of the emotions can be seen in the last exercise of Peryn's book, where a willed and practiced move toward union with God is set out. First one envisions oneself as Mary Magdalene and imaginatively wipes Christ's feet with tears. Here the will and understanding must be stirred up "not without some labour." In the conclusion of the exercise, however, one is to approach the heart of Christ "and enter therein as into an infinite sea … forgetting clean and leaving out of thy mind all things created … deeply drown, hide, and transform thyself wholly into … everlasting love … And thou shalt desire to be swallowed up and clean consumed by that infinite goodness and also to consume it into thyself."[94] Van Ess's may be the intelligence responsible for this synthesis of routine practice and transcendence, but it was Peryn's adaptation, made for his exiled female co-religionists, that brought these features into an English devotional and mystical ambit in the sixteenth and seventeenth centuries.

[91] Kirchberger, *Spiritual Exercises*, p. 35, n.1. "Peryn had the original before him and corrects and amplifies the version made by van Ess."

[92] Ann M. Hutchison, "What the Nuns Read," *Mediaeval Studies* 57 (1995), 212. The book is part of the Syon Collection now at University of Exeter Library Special Collections.

[93] Wizeman, *Mary Tudor's Church*, provides a detailed comparison of Peryn with Ignatius, pp. 207–16.

[94] Kirchberger, *Spiritual Exercises*, pp. 96–97.

CHAPTER SIX

Richard Whitford's last work, 1541

Richard Whitford of Syon was the most popular English religious author of the sixteenth century. His gift for shaping moral and spiritual guidance to fit lay lives took his *Werke for Housholders* through nine editions between 1530 and 1537. During the religiously fraught decade of the 1530s he produced a torrent of printed editions that made him the spokesperson for a newly emphatic lay spirituality. He has been characterized as representing the last moment of traditional English Catholicism, yet that perspective is provided by hindsight, and for contemporaries it is likely that his spiritual guidance, in its many considerations of lay life, represented a modern accommodation of traditional religious direction.

It is possible to see Whitford in another way as well. The recognition afforded his spiritual writing has somewhat elided the extent to which that writing was intended as a response to heresy and was part of a program of reform within the church.[1] In 1522, Martin Luther's *On the Abrogation of the Private Mass* investigated the connected subjects of the eucharist, priesthood, and life in religion, or broadly, monasticism. Published about a decade later, Whitford's 1532 *Pype of Perfection* offers a response to the last of these topics: "We have of late seen divers works in Latin sent out openly in print against all manner of religion [i.e. forms of religious life]. For the great heretic Luther with all his disciples does deprave and utterly condemn all manner of religion except only (as they call it) the religion of Christ" (*STC* 25421, A3).

In writing this affirmation of religious life, whose value and character was so central an issue in the 1520s and 1530s, Whitford joined a number of other voices whose responses outline an internal defense of the institution of monasticism. Whitford's connections with the London and Sheen Carthusians are well known (in *Pype* he cites these two houses as examples

---

[1] This is the thesis of P. G. Caraman's essay, "An English Monastic Reformer of the Sixteenth Century," *Clergy Review* 28.1 (1947), 1–16.

of the religious life well lived). Those English houses' sixteenth-century connections with their German Carthusian counterparts has been established, principally through an August 1532 letter from London prior John Houghton to Cologne vicar Theodoric (Dirk) Loher, asking for various books that house was currently engaged in publishing, including ten copies of all the works of Dionysius Carthusiensis.[2]

Since the opening of the sixteenth century the Cologne charterhouse of St. Barbara had been engaged in a massive defensive program of writing and publishing that replied to heresy but, more broadly, presented an approach to belief that was both conservative and renewed.[3] The mystical works in which their house had always been particularly interested seemed to them "most effective for strengthening the faithful and for combating heretics" and while they were "fully engaged in the battle of words against heretics ... they continued to emphasize the need for inner reform."[4] Perhaps the most remarkable member of that house was the prolific late-fifteenth-century writer Denys Rykiel or Dionysius Carthusiensis (1402–71).[5] His treatise on religious life, *De vita canonicorum*, sharply condemned current abuses while offering an inspiring vision of that life's possibilities. It was published around 1510 at Cologne, then around 1514 at Paris.[6] At Cologne in 1532 it appeared for the third time as part of a heroic editorial project managed by Theodoric Loher and six other Cologne Carthusians that ran from 1521 to 1538 and was designed to publish all of Denys's writing.[7] Around 1533 an English translation of

---

[2] Summarized in E. Margaret Thompson, *The Carthusian Order in England* (London, 1930), pp. 329–30 and printed in L. Hendricks, *The London Charterhouse, Its Monks and Martyrs* (London, 1889), pp. 366–68.

[3] Carlos Eire, "Early Modern Catholic Piety in Translation," in Peter Burke and R. Po-chia Hsia (eds.), *Cultural Translation in Early Modern Europe* (Cambridge, 2007), pp. 83–100.

[4] Sigrun Haude, *In the Shadow of "Savage Wolves": Anabaptist Munster and the German Reformation during the 1530s* (Boston, Leiden, Cologne, 2000), p. 62, and see Sigrun Haude, "The Silent Monks Speak Up: The Changing Identity of the Carthusians in the Fifteenth and Sixteenth Centuries," *Archiv für Reformationgeschicte* 86 (1995), 124–40. "Le souci d'une vie religieuse irréprochable fondeé sur l'exercice de la théologie mystique ... explique aussi l'intérêt que les chartreux portaient aux monastères reformés"; Gérard Chaix, "Sainte-Barbe, Cologne, et l'empire du xviᵉ siècle," *Analecta Cartusiana* 83.3, *Die Kartäuser in Österreich* (1980–81), 101.

[5] *Dictionnaire de Spiritualité Ascetique et Mystique* (Paris, 1937), III: 434. The modern edition of his work in forty-four volumes is *Doctoris ecstatic D. Dionysii cartusiana Opera Omnia...* (Montreuil, 1896–1901; Tournai, 1902–13; Parkminster, 1935).

[6] See: http://istc.bl.uk, Dionysius Carthusiensis, nos. 12, 13.

[7] *Dionysii Cartusiensis Opera Selecta*, ed. Kent Emery, Corpus Christianorum Continuatio Medievalis, vols. CXXI and CXXI(A) (Turnhout, 1991), I: 30, speaks of the extraordinary efforts of Theodoric Loher, "who in the years 1521–38 obtained the mss and funds for the publication of 57 of Denys's works in different formats and by different printers." Three of Denys's works were dedicated to English figures: *Enarrationes in quatuor Evangelistes* to Henry VIII in March 14, 1532; a

this work appeared, *The Lyfe of Prestes* (*STC* 6894), probably made by an English Carthusian. Like Whitford's *Pype of Perfection* published about a year earlier, *The Lyfe of Prestes* was concerned with the renewal of a religious life that had become stale and lax. In its preface, addressing what he calls negligence, Denys says he will treat "the good conversation and living of religious persons or regulars … the state of whom (alas the more pity) is fallen to great ruin and decay" (A 4v).

Denys's work and to a lesser extent Whitford's were efforts from within to produce a reforming ecclesiology. There were other contributions: another member of the Cologne house, Johannes Justus Lanspergius (like Denys, well known for his spiritual and devotional writings) published two pamphlets in 1528 and 1529 on the monastic life. Written in German to insure wide distribution, *A Clear Instance of What Constitutes True Evangelical Religion* and *A Dialogue on the Monastic State* were controversial pieces, the first demonstrating the historic validity of monastic life, the second, its orthodox place in a scheme of salvation.[8]

In England the most notable contribution on this subject was John Fisher's. His principal anti-Lutheran work, the *Confutation of Luther's Assertion*, was published in Antwerp on January 2, 1523, but it is in two smaller Latin works, published in Cologne, 1525, that Fisher countered Luther's writing on priesthood and monasticism most specifically: *Defense of the Sacred Priesthood* and *Defense of the Royal Assertion*.[9] Fisher gave two English sermons as well, one in 1521 and one in 1526, that treated this matter among others, and his defense of priesthood to the Reformation parliament of 1529 is well known. The Commons had called the clergy vicious, ravenous, and insatiable; Fisher asked, "What, are all of this sort?" and accused them of endeavoring "to bring [priests] into contempt and hatred of the laity." Reminding them of the trouble Hus and Luther brought to Bohemia and Germany, Fisher prophesied that if obedience were withdrawn, "government of the Turk" would ensue, all due to lack of faith.[10]

The relations among this group of writings have not been traced, but it seems likely that Whitford understood himself to be part of a collective

---

commentary on the wisdom books to Thomas Cromwell on June 24, 1533; and a commentary on the seven canonical epistles to Nicholas West, Bishop of Ely. Chaix, "Sainte-Barbe," 99.

[8] *Eyn schone vnderrichtung* … and *Red vnd antwardt vom closterlichen Stand*. See Jon Derek Halvorson, "Religio and Reformation: Johannes Justus Lansperger … and the Sixteenth-Century Religious Question," PhD dissertation (Loyola University, 2008).

[9] Edward Surtz, *The Works and Days of John Fisher* (Cambridge, MA, 1967), p. 325. Richard Rex, "The English Campaign against Luther in the 1520s," *Transactions of the Royal Historical Society* 39 (1989), 85–106 (95); Richard Rex, *The Theology of John Fisher* (Cambridge, 1991), pp. 134–35.

[10] Stanford E. Lehmberg, *The Reformation Parliament 1529–1536* (Cambridge, 1970), p. 87.

response. Certainly his introduction to *Pype* places the work as a combative reply: "[h]ere is somewhat spoken in our common tongue, that all you may know all their false and subtle deceits" [A1v]. Considered as an answer to the question of whether monasticism was any longer valid, *Pype* offers a statement by one of the most prominent of English monks, at a level less elevated than Fisher's, but one that utilizes the perspective of an experienced spiritual director. After Luther, the church in England, as elsewhere, struggled to define what it meant to be a religious. Lanspergius's two tracts, it has been suggested, allow us to recover the monastic voice speaking on this question.[11] Whitford's *Pype* provides that voice in English.

A partial chronology of Whitford's writing

Whitford's last work, *Dyuers Holy Instrucyons and Teachynges Very Necessary for the Helth of Mannes Soule*, is full of surprises.[12] Its very existence is startling, since Syon had been dissolved on November 25, 1539, around two years before the book was published in 1541. Yet the end of English institutional religious life and the closure of his own monastery did not mean the end of Whitford's writing and publishing. For whom was he writing in *Dyuers Instrucyons*? What can its four texts, each preceded by one of Whitford's characteristically personal introductions, tell us about his perspective and his intentions? These introductions, in their presentation of authorial preoccupations and their incidental recovery of a milieu, recall the work of Osbern Bokenham about a century earlier and, like Bokenham's prologues, allow some insight into the author's life and concerns.

Before considering Whitford's last work, however, an examination of the unusual patterns thrown up by his career may be useful. Based on the February 14, 1511 date of his will, made before entering religious life,[13] it seems likely that he entered Syon in that year. The trajectory of his subsequent writing and publishing is not straightforward since the frequent gaps between the composition of his works and their publication have not

---

[11] Halvorson, "Religio," p. 8.

[12] *STC* 25420, it survives in four copies: BL, CUL, Folger, Syon Abbey (now University of Exeter). A facsimile of the Syon copy has been published as *Richard Whytford, Vol. II*, ed. Veronica Lawrence, *Salzburg Studies in English Literature: Elizabethan and Renaissance Studies* 92.18 (Salzburg, 1991). This copy was owned by sixteenth-century book collector Myles Blomefylde, whose name or initials appear in five places.

[13] James Hogg (ed.), *Richard Whitford's The Pype or Tonne of the Lyfe of Perfection*, 5 vols., Salzburg Studies in English Literature: Elizabethan and Renaissance Studies 89 (Salzburg, 1979–89), V: appendix 3.

been evaluated. In particular, the concentration of much of that writing in
the first decade of his life as a monk, accomplished under and for Abbess
Elizabeth Gibbs who died on August 30, 1518, has not been registered,
though its extent suggests the existence of what may have been an abbatial
program of formation directed toward her Syon nuns.

Whitford's probable first work at Syon, for instance, *A Dayly Exercyse and
Experyence of Dethe*, though dateable about 1513 was not published until
1534, about two decades later. Another instruction, his work on patience,
was probably composed a little after *Dethe*, around 1514, but was not published until 1541, in his last book. His translation of the Augustinian rule
may have come next. Whitford's first published work, it was issued in 1525
in two parts. In the preface to the second part (his own and Hugh of
St. Victor's commentary on the rule) he says he completed the first part,
the rule proper, seven years ago, hence in 1518. That Whitford thanks the
nuns who "sent" him their old version of the rule for amendment suggests
that he was not addressing Syon nuns whom he would have seen daily,
but another unknown women's house, and consequently, that he did not
translate the Augustinian rule for Syon. As to this work's genesis, it is a
remarkable coincidence that a year before Whitford finished his translation of the Augustinian rule in 1518, Richard Fox, Bishop of Winchester,
had published in 1517 his English translation of the Benedictine rule, made
for the four houses of nuns in his diocese. Fox and Whitford knew each
other; according to William Roper's life of Thomas More, Whitford had
been Fox's chaplain around 1507, before entering Syon.[14]

One more of Whitford's writings can probably be assigned to his first
years as a monk. *Pype of Perfection*, his apologia for the religious life
described above, was not published until 1532, but its title page verso notes
that "this work was written years ago and now thought necessary to be sent
forth because of these newfangled persons" who "deprave all religions,"
that is, all forms of institutional religious life. The text is headed "A work
of the three vows of religion contrary unto the great heretics Lutherans."
Yet, elsewhere in it, the author says, "And yet you know well, I am but as a
novice in religion myself, more meet to learn than to teach religion" [A2].
(*Pype* is addressed to "good devout religious daughter" and "your sisters.")
Because of the subtitle, "a work of the three vows," Caraman has suggested
that *Pype* was originally intended to follow Whitford's 1525 publication of

---

[14] The time was before the death of Henry VII in 1509. E. V. Hitchcock (ed.), *The Life and Death of
Sir Thomas More*, EETS OS 186 (London and Oxford, 1932), p. 16. "The death of the king not long
after ensuing."

the Augustinian rule and its commentary and to discuss further the vows of poverty, chastity, and obedience.[15] After the spread of Lutheran writing in the 1520s, however, revision has turned what was previously a meditation on the religious life into its later form, a defense of it.

(Even Whitford's *Werke for Housholders* may come from early in his writing life and, indeed, from before his *c.*1513 work on death, since in his 1537 edition of *Dethe* he twice mentions *Werke* (e.g. "making a cross with a holy candle … after the manner that you have in your book for householders" [D3v]).[16] *Werke*, which is strikingly free of patristic or classical allusions, might possibly have been composed before Whitford's Syon entry, reflecting his experiences at Cambridge and in Bishop Fox's household.)[17]

These works, *Dethe* (*c.*1513), *Pacience* (*c.*1514), the Augustinian *Rule* (*c.*1518), and *Pype* (*c.*1525) – even perhaps his *Werke for Housholders* – were all published after a lapse of years and can be assigned to Whitford's early period of authorship. In his final publication, *Dyuers Holy Instrucyons* (*STC* 25420), the 1541 volume, two of its four pieces come from this early time, its first and last items. The first is the book of patience; the concluding item, a short piece from an *ad populum* sermon ("On Detraction") was composed in the past as well, as Whitford explains, though it is impossible to suggest a date. The two central items in the book, however, a translation of a recently acquired anonymous Latin tract on hindrances to perfection and a translation of the popular pseudo-Isidorian *Counsels*, had both been recently completed.

After Syon's closure: last work

In 1539 the Syon community was physically scattered, as groups of three or four found lodging with family or friends, their membership and their locale changing frequently. It has traditionally been suggested that at this time Whitford was living in London with Charles Blount, fifth Baron Mountjoy, but there is no firm evidence of his whereabouts and we are left to wonder about the circumstances under which Whitford put together

---

[15] Caraman, "English Monastic Reformer," 4. Though Caraman does not sugest this, *Pype* might have been written even earlier, after Whitford completed his translation of the rule alone, in 1518, and before his subsequent presentation in 1525 of his own and Hugh of St. Victor's commentary on the rule.

[16] Hogg, *Richard Whytford's Pype*, I, pt. 2: 142.

[17] Hogg, "Richard Whytford," in James Hogg (ed.), *Studies in St. Birgitta and the Brigittine Order*, 2 vols. (Salzburg, 1993), II: 261.

(and to some extent composed) his last work. What *Dyuers Instrucyons* does show is the continuation of some form of community life, since in the prefaces to three of its four texts Whitford tells us that their impetus came from the suggestion of another Brigittine brother. This person both provided Whitford with new material and pointed out thematic correspondences between Whitford's older work and his current projects. Deeply familiar with Whitford's previous writing, this man was able to suggest relationships between that earlier work and present possibilities and thus to create for Whitford in 1541 an unexpected extension of his long-sustained authorial and spiritual roles.

Dyuers Instrucyons opens with two prefaces. In the first, a preliminary to the whole work, Whitford explains why he has provided a table of contents for each text and has included his own name. He recounts how in an earlier publication his essay, *A Dayly Exercyse and Experyence of Dethe*, although named in the table of contents, was omitted and the work of another man substituted. Whitford had recorded this same complaint earlier, in 1537, in his preface to another collection of his works published by John Wayland (*STC* 25413.5). What he called then a "much vicious and faulty" edition has not been identified.

Following this caution a second example of the dangers of anonymous publication is provided, this time an English work of Luther that Whitford saw, published without the author's name. In 1541 it was probably *A Boke Made by a Certayne Great Clerke agaynst the Newe Idole and Olde Deuyll*, printed in 1534 (*STC* 16962), in which Luther attacked the papacy and in particular its practices with regard to canonization.[18] This anxiety about anonymous publication recurs frequently in Whitford's prefaces and is addressed long before the printing mishap. In the preface to his second publication, the 1526 Syon *Martiloge*, Whitford for the first time sounds the caution against anonymous authorship that would be so often repeated in his subsequent works: "Another cause why I do so set forth my name is that I have heard of divers works that been sold in print as fatherless children without authors, that be not only the less regarded because they be without authors but also be suspected as not holding and keeping the right path of Christianity" (*STC* 17532, preface, no sig.).

More surprising is the sounding of another note of continuity. In inveighing against the anonymous Lutheran work, Whitford says it was

---

[18] Other works of Luther published in English before 1541 are *A Very Excellent and Swete Exposition vpon the Two & Twentye* [23rd] *Psalme* (1537; *STC* 16999) and *An Exposition vpon the Songe … Called Magnificat* (1538; *STC* 16979.7).

"against the kings honour, because he hath by his noble work condemned him [Luther] for an heretic" [A2]. Of course Henry's *Assertio septem sacramentorum aduersus M. Lutherum*, published in 1521 (*STC* 13078), no longer represented the king's position twenty years later, yet for Whitford the invocation of royal authority continued to be powerful after two decades. Like the author of the *Greyfriars Chronicle* whose religious house Henry had also closed, Whitford's self-presentation is a loyalist one.

Whitford's second preface explains that the initial work offered in *Dyuers Instrucyons*, the *Boke of Pacience*, is an early Whitford composition here printed for the first time. It thus constitutes something of a discovery for contemporary readers, who presumably would be pleased to have a new work by this popular author. Whitford situates it within his long career, telling the reader that "I wrote this work many years ago (as I said of the work of death) & by like occasion." In Whitford's work on death, first published c.1534 (*STC* 25413.7), he noted it had been written more than twenty years earlier, at the request of then-abbess of Syon Elizabeth Gibbs and had been stimulated by "the oft calling upon and remembrance of certain of her devout sisters." *Dethe's* composition more than twenty years earlier might then be about 1513. That *Pacience* followed the work on death is demonstrated by a reference in it which says, "How that every craft is learned: we showed you in your draught of death" (*STC* 25420 [F 2v]). *Pacience* might thus be dated around 1514 and the two works might represent Whitford's first compositions after his c.1511 Syon entrance. (*Dethe* has a surprising later addition, a preface inserted, Whitford says, "when I had written up this little work ready to the printing," that is, around 1534. A "wise and well-learned man" then suggested that since in it Whitford had discussed the subject of "rapts or trances," he might do well to warn readers against easy belief in visionaries, "for many of them have destroyed full many men that were full holy and devout," but innocent. This may refer to the Nun of Kent, Elizabeth Barton, executed April 20, 1534 with Hugh Rich, head of the Greenwich Observant friars and Henry Gold, rector of St. Mary Aldermary, London. The Syon community had been divided in its assessment of the nun, but this passage suggests Whitford's lack of sympathy for her visions.)[19]

Although in his work on patience Whitford quotes liberally from St. Cyprian's treatise *De bono patientiae*, this is not a translation and is much longer than Cyprian's text (about 23,000 words versus about 7,500

---

[19] Alan Neame, *The Holy Maid of Kent: The Life of Elizabeth Barton, 1506–1534* (London, 1971), pp. 198–99.

words).[20] Why Cyprian? Speaking of Erasmus "and many other humanist editors and translators," Carlos Eire says their focus was "recovery of the devotional life of the early church, not the search for theological precisions" and this may have been Whitford's motive as well.[21] In addition, what William Wizeman says about the reliance on patristic sources in the Marian church of the 1550s is relevant here too: use of the Fathers demonstrated the continuity of theological positions. Both Cyprian and Chrysostom, used by Whitford, were among those most frequently cited between 1553 and 1558.[22]

We cannot say whether Whitford revised *Pacience* for publication in 1541. As far as it is possible to tell, it seems not to reflect the turbulence of the 1530s in which Syon was involved: the executions of Elizabeth Barton, Thomas More and John Fisher, the Carthusians, and Richard Reynolds, in 1534/35. Though it was not printed before 1541, it may, however, have circulated in manuscript at Syon and have been part of some continuing interest in Cyprian there. John Fewterer of Syon owned a large volume of Cyprian's work, including *De bono patientiae*, printed in Paris in 1512, which Whitford might have consulted.[23] Much later Sir Thomas Elyot translated Cyprian's sermon on mortality, dedicating its editions in 1534 and 1539 to his half-sister Susan Kyngeston, a vowess at Syon, and remembering two other half-sisters, nuns of the community there (*STC* 6157, 6158).[24]

Pacience is a work of twenty chapters; Whitford's table of contents, which is organized by topic, lists the virtue's definition, behavior, and fruits and benefits, both secular and religious. J. T. Rhodes notes that this work's humanistic character is emphasized by an unusually varied selection of authorities: Prudentius's *Psychomachia*, Solon, Cato, Seneca, plus English proverbs and stories from *Vitas Patrum*.[25] The text contains an interesting sidelight on life at Syon: speaking of the importance of patience, Whitford says:

---

[20] *Patrologia Latinae* (Paris, 1891), IV: cols. 645–62. *The Ante-Nicene Fathers*, ed. and trans. Alexander Roberts and James Donaldson (Buffalo, 1886), V: 484–91.
[21] Eire, "Early Modern Catholic Piety," p. 89.
[22] William Wizeman, *The Theology and Spirituality of Mary Tudor's Church* (Aldershot, 2006), pp. 67–68.
[23] Vincent Gillespie (ed.), *Syon Abbey, with the Libraries of the Carthusians*, ed. A. I. Doyle, Corpus of British Medieval Library Catalogues 9 (London, 2001), no. 861.
[24] Mary C. Erler, *Women, Reading, and Piety in Late Medieval England* (Cambridge, 2002), pp. 87–89.
[25] J. T. Rhodes, "Private Devotion in England on the Eve of the Reformation," PhD dissertation (University of Durham 1975), p. 184.

And but late two manner of persons in divers countries dwelling, and making suit at London at the law for lands, came hither unto the pardon and asked counsel, which persons notwithstanding did not follow the counsel, unto the time that they had spent more than the lands were worth after 24 years purchase, and yet in the end were fain to follow the same counsel that first was given unto them. (*STC* 25420 [C iv])

Whitford is probably referring to the feast of St. Peter ad Vincula on August 1, when the Pardon of Syon was available to large crowds visiting the monastery – along with spiritual and secular counseling, it seems. Though the date of *Patience*'s composition was long past, its publication in 1541 was of course relevant to Whitford's current situation. His self-identification was clearly added after the dissolution: "Amen. Pray of your charity for a late brother of Syon R. Whitforde."

Whitford's second text in this compilation is titled *A Worke of Dyuers Impediments and Lettes of Perfection*. His preface says that "but late" he published a little work on the life of perfection (*Pype of Perfection*'s only edition appeared in 1532). When "here now" one of his brothers brought him "a treatise or little draft in Latin of an uncertain author which he found by chance," Whitford thought it would "frame well" with *Pype*. Hence he translated it and added many things he thought useful ("convenient").

Whitford's source has not so far been identified, but it seems likely to have been a small Latin book whose full title is *Enchiridion vitae spiritualis ad perfectionem instituens quo novem impedimenta quae in via dei progredi cupientibus occurrent*. It was published anonymously at Cologne in 1530 by Petrus Buschius.[26] In 1536 it appeared again, attached to a text of Cologne Carthusian John Justus Lanspergius's *Pharetra divini amoris* (*Arrows of Divine Love*), a collection of prayers and devotions in which Lanspergius, like Ignatius later, recommends the use of ejaculatory prayers or aspirations.[27] It is possible that this later edition was the one Whitford used but whether or not that is so, the text's association here with a work by

[26] J. Benzing, *Die Buchdrucker des 16. und 17. Jahrhunderet in deutschen Sprachgebiet* (Frankfurt, 1963), p. 225.

[27] *Pharetra divini amoris* ... Antwerp, apud Martinum Caesarem ... [February 1536] ... auctore Iohanne Lanspergio, recens elucubrate, numquam primum typis excusam. Item, enchiridion vitae spiritualis ad perfectionem instituens quo novem quae in via dei progredi cupientibus occurrent, aperiuntur. 16° (World Catalogue: OCLC 69004048). *Pharetra* had been published earlier by de Keyser in Antwerp, 1532, and by J. Gennep in Cologne, 1533, but without the *Enchiridion*. John Ramridge, a Louvain recusant, owned a copy of the Gennep edition. Christian Coppens (ed.), *Reading in Exile: The Libraries of John Ramridge (d. 1568), Thomas Harding (d. 1572) and Henry Joliffe (d. 1573), Recusants in Louvain*, Libri Pertinentes no. 2 (Cambridge, 1993), p. 66.

Lanspergius demonstrates the spiritual milieu from which this little work came.

The Cologne charterhouse has been called "a fountainhead of the religious life of [the city] and the surrounding region,"[28] particularly because of its sponsorship of printed mystical texts. As early as 1509 they had published Hendrik Herp's *Mirror of Perfection* translated into Latin by Prior Peter Blomevenna (1466–1536),[29] and their publishing in the 1530s has been noted above. Whitford's translation of the *Impedimenta* suggests the ties between Syon and the spirituality represented by the Cologne charterhouse. Alexandra Barratt has recently shown that the writing of a German mystic, Marie d'Oisterwijk, which was published in 1532 by the Cologne house, was known at Syon and she has suggested that in the 1530s, as earlier, the mysticism of German and Dutch writers was being transmitted to England via the reading community constituted by the London and Sheen Carthusians together with the Brigittines.[30] The influence of this Rheno-Flemish devotional tradition has been visible earlier in this book, in Simon Appulby's translation (see Chapter 1) and in William Peryn's book (see Chapter 5) as well as in Whitford's work.

The third item in Whitford's compilation, the counsels of St. Isidore, was a popular medieval text, its source the spurious *Monita* or *Consilia Isadori*.[31] Whitford knew it was not Isidore's work, since he twice says in his preface that it is "attributed to St. Isidore." He also notes its episodic quality, describing it as "rather called and taken for notes gathered than for any work digested and ordered"; indeed it consists of short paragraphs organized by topic headings: "of evil thoughts," "of superfluous feeding," "of the company and presence of the contrary sex" (in Whitford's headings). Whitford's endorsement of it might seem a bit dismissive: "If you read them and note them well you shall, I doubt not, be edified thereby."

[28] Richard B. Marks, *The Medieval Monastic Library of the Charterhouse of St. Barbara in Cologne*, 2 vols., Analecta Carthusiana 21, 22 (Salzburg, 1974), I: 40; see also Louis Cognet, *Post-Reformation Spirituality* (New York, 1959), p. 16.

[29] *Dictionnaire de Spiritualité Ascetique et Mystique* (Paris, 1937), I: cols. 1738–39.

[30] Alexandra Barratt, *Anne Bulkeley and Her Book: Fashioning Female Piety in Early Tudor England – A Study of London, British Library, MS Harley 494* (Turnhout, 2009), pp. 218–19, discussing BL MS Harley 494. Barratt also suggests German influence on another Syon-associated MS, Lambeth Palace MS 546, which contains the sayings of St. Albert the Great of Cologne, by Ruysbroeck, and the story of the revelation of the Golden Litany to the stigmatic Magdalena Beutler of Freiburg (1407–58), p. 101.

[31] Robert Raymo, "Works of Religious and Philosophical Instruction," in Albert E. Hartung (ed.), *A Manual of the Writings in Middle English 1050–1500* (New Haven, CT, 1986), VII: cols. 2253–378, 2467–582.

As he announced in 1525 in his first printed work, the *Rule of Saynt Augustyne*, Whitford consistently rejects a literal approach to translation. Here he says he has translated "more after the sense and meaning of the author than after the letter" and he has supplemented the text rather than reducing it. The manuscript version of the *Counsels* in BL MS Harley 1706, printed by Horstmann,[32] provides thirty-seven items and Whitford follows these headings, except that he adds a long original final section, on alms.

What is surprising, however, is Whitford's failure to acknowledge the many circulating versions of this work. He translated the *Counsels*, he says, because "a devout brother of ours instantly requiring forced me to translate the matter" (A3). Yet P. S. Jolliffe lists fourteen surviving manuscripts,[33] among them the well-known nuns' manuscript BL MS Harley 1706, associated with Barking.[34] In addition Horstmann notes that in the early days of English printing the *Counsels* were published in Latin by William Machlinia at the end of his *Speculum Christiani* (c.1486, Duff 415, *STC* 26012). Closer in time to Whitford's 1541 book, a short anonymous English translation of the *Counsels* was printed by Thomas Berthelet in 1534, 1539, and 1544.[35] It provided only the first eleven of the thirty-seven topics treated in MS Harley 1706. Given all this activity, and particularly the editions of 1534 and 1539, it is surprising both that Whitford's Syon brother thought a new translation necessary and that Whitford agreed.

The final piece in Whitford's book, on detraction, he calls a "draught," a term suggesting brevity, and indeed it is only a little under 2,000 words (see Appendix 6). Whitford describes it as "a piece of a sermon that I spoke unto the people years ago." (That Whitford was able to provide the printer with a text from years past suggests that he had been able to take away personal notes and manuscripts at Syon's closure.) It constitutes a rarity, since almost no Syon sermons survive.[36] This lack is the more remarkable since

---

[32] C. Horstmann (ed.), *Yorkshire Writers: Richard Rolle of Hampole, an English Father of the Church, and His Followers*, 2 vols. (London, 1895–96), II: 367–74.

[33] P. S. Jolliffe, *A Check-List of Middle English Prose Writings of Spiritual Guidance* (Toronto, 1974), pp. 110–11.

[34] A. I. Doyle, "Books Connected with the Vere Family and Barking Abbey," *Transactions of the Essex Archaeological Society* n.s. 25 (1958), 222–43.

[35] *STC* 14270, 14270.5, 14271. It was attributed to Thomas Lupset in Thomas Berthelet's 1546 collected works of Lupset. The author's modern editor does not believe the work is Lupset's; see John Archer Gee (ed.), *The Life and Works of Thomas Lupset* (New Haven, CT, 1928), pp. 168–69.

[36] Susan Powell, "Preaching at Syon Abbey," *Leeds Studies in English* n.s. 31 (2000), 229–67 (233, 241), mentions a sermon on Syon pardons composed by Simon Wynter, in BL Harley MS 2521, and the "Hamus Caritatis" (hook of love) on the Ten Commandments of the Old Testament and two precepts of the New Testament, printed by Caxton in his second edition of Mirk's *Festial* (1491). "Seven Syon brethren are recorded in the index to the Syon *Registrum* as having their sermons

the corpus of sermons composed by Syon brothers must originally have been large. The Brigittine rule specified that its priests should undertake an active preaching ministry, part of the order's vocation as a new vineyard designed to amend the slackness of existing religious orders. Sermons to the people on every Sunday and on specified feasts were mandated. At the Brigittine motherhouse of Vadstena this necessitated public preaching on almost 100 days each year.[37] A huge body of sermons survives from Vadstena, around 5,000 of them, written by members of the order. Those public sermons were perhaps an hour in length, or slightly longer, and might be delivered outdoors on the great pilgrimage days like the feast of St. Peter ad Vincula mentioned above.

The excerpt printed from Whitford's *ad populum* sermon is at root an injunction to charity and, as such, suitable for a general audience. It comes from the third of St. John Chrysostom's "Homilies on the Statutes," twenty-one sermons addressed to the people of Antioch in the year 387. It translates a self-contained section of that homily and in Chrysostom's work, this excursus on speaking well of others constitutes something of a tangent to the homily's main thrust. Whitford presents faithfully the entirety of this section (in its modern edition, sections 12–17 of the Greek Father's sermon),[38] taking care to make Chrysostom's references contemporary ones. Where Chrysostom advises that the slanderer "hast struck at the common welfare of the Church for … the reproach is fastened on the Christian community,"[39] Whitford observes that the backbiter hurts "all other of his faculty and manner of living & oft times of his country, as if he backbite a soldier, a merchant or a priest, the hearers will … grudge … against all soldiers, all merchants, and all priests, & likewise of the countries. As northern men, southern men, Welshmen, Irish men, Scots or Frenchmen" (Appendix 6 [Y 2v]). That Whitford originally used Chrysostom in a sermon setting that was not only pastoral but broadly popular, rather than in a more private manner (individual spiritual direction) or a more restricted one (printed publication, as here), shows his reliance on the Fathers as widely relevant to the contemporary care of souls.

---

preserved in the library"; Gillespie, *Syon Abbey*, p. xxxiii. (That the sermon might have been delivered before Whitford entered Syon, while he was a fellow of Queens, is possible but less likely.)

[37] Roger Andersson and Stephen Borgehammar, "The Preaching of the Bridgettine Friars at Vadstena Abbey (ca. 1380–1515)," *Revue Mabillon* n.s. 8 (1997), 209–36 (221).

[38] St. John Chrysostom, "The Homilies on the Statutes," trans. W. R. W. Stephens, in Philip Schaff (ed.), *A Select Library of the Nicene and Post-Nicene Fathers, Vol. IX: St. Chrysostom – On the Priesthood, Ascetic Treatises, Select Homilies and Letters, Homilies on the Statutes* (Grand Rapids, MI, 1956), IX: 359–61.

[39] St. John Chrysostom, "Homilies," p. 359.

And indeed Chrysostom was the most famous preacher of his age, for his "great natural facility of speech ... as well as [his] popular way of presenting and illustrating [his thoughts] and his whole-hearted earnestness and conviction."[40] Hence his sermons give a most appropriate model for the hugely popular public Syon occasions and it might be possible to think of Whitford as a latter-day Chrysostom.

The inclusion of this little piece, like the two preceding ones, we also owe to Whitford's Syon brother, who suggested that the sermon contained some points of similarity with the preceding Isidorian *Counsels*. The paragraph on backbiting in the manuscript version of the *Counsels* is spare and general but in his version Whitford has expanded it considerably (T3v–T4v) with a homely comparison of backbiting to horse stealing, where physical restitution can easily be made. How is it possible, though, to restore a reputation? Whitford says the sinner must tell everyone he spoke to that he committed the sin of backbiting (not specifying whether the matter was true or false) and must require each person to relay that information to those he told. Presentation of the sermon fragment "On Detraction" was probably due to logistical considerations, since the preceding text, the *Counsels*, ends on Y1v, and another short text was needed to fill out the Y gathering. Nonetheless there is some thematic connection between the third and fourth pieces in Whitford's book, and in its powerful recommendations to charity "Detraction" makes an appropriate finale for the book.

Thus three of the book's four items – everything except its first tract, on patience – were suggested by this anonymous Syon brother, who either brought Whitford a work to translate (*Impedimentes and Lettes*), requested a translation of another work (Isidore's *Counsels*), or pointed out the similarity between that work and a sermon of Whitford's from the past. This man – if it is a single person – may have been the lay brother John Massey, whose name appears grouped with Whitford's in the pension payment list dated the last of June 1541, the year Whitford's last book was published.[41] Since earlier payments to Massey do not show him with Whitford,[42] their period together can only have begun in mid-1541, between April and June

---

[40] Chrysostom Baur, "St. John Chrysostom," *Catholic Encyclopaedia* (New York, 1912), VIII: 452–57. One of the first Vadstena friars, Johannes Giorderi (1379–84) was known as a second Chrysostom; Andersson and Borgehammar, "Preaching," 236.

[41] TNA E 315/250.

[42] Massey appears on July 6, 1540 in a group of seven including John Stewkyn and most from the Agnes Jordan group, later in Michaelmas quarter 1540 with Stewkyn, Dorothy and Alice Bettenham, and Bridget Fitzherbert (both E 315/249), and also on April 7, 1541 with Anthony Sutton and Elizabeth Knottisforde (E 315/250).

(see below). Hence the suggestion that John Massey was Whitford's helper depends on whether Whitford could have translated both *Impedimentes and Lettes* (about 9,500 words) and Isadore's *Counsels* (about 11,000 words) and seen the book through the printing process in approximately the latter half of 1541.[43]

Massey was one of the members of Syon who later went to Dendermonde, in his case in 1550 as the house chronicle shows.[44] The English pension accounts agree with this departure date, since on October 31, 1552 Massey was paid his pension for one year and one quarter, due at Christmas last (1551), that is, for all of 1551 and the last quarter of 1550, making it possible that he had been away since autumn 1550 (TNA E 315/261). Massey had been left 40s. in Abbess Jordan's 1545 will, to which he had been a witness, but the bequest is not placed with the legacies to the other Syon members who lived at Denham. Instead it is listed with the remembrances to servants, making it seem unlikely that Massey was a permanent member of the Denham group.[45] Peter Cunich says, "John Massey had proven particularly versatile in the years of survival between 1539 and 1553. He appears to have moved around frequently between the various households … he was, perhaps, a reliable and resourceful trouble-shooter who went wherever he was most needed."[46]

At the dissolution, Massey was not a young man: the Dendermonde chronicle says that when he arrived there in 1550 he was forty years professed. He thus would have entered Syon at about the same time as Whitford did, around 1511 or 1510, and since twenty-five was the minimum age for profession, he would have been born about 1485, or earlier, and been about seventy-one when he died at Dendermonde on April 6, 1556. Thus, whatever their respective ages, Massey and Whitford were contemporaries in religion. Cunich has outlined in some detail the responsibilities of the lay brothers: to serve mass and assist the priests at divine service and to attend to the monastery's physical care.[47] To what extent

[43] I am much indebted to Peter Cunich, Dept. of History, University of Hong Kong, for his advice on this point.
[44] Ulla Sander Olsen (ed.), "De kroniek van Abdis Marie van Oss, Maria Troon, Dendermonde [Text edition]," in *Oudheidkundige Kring van het Land van Dendermonde. Gedenkschriften*, R.4:21 (Jaarboek 2002), pp. 250–332.
[45] TNA PCC 4 Alen (Prob 11/31/55).
[46] Peter Cunich, "The Brothers of Syon, 1420–1695," in E. A. Jones and Alexandra Walsham (eds.), *Syon Abbey and Its Books: Reading, Writing, and Religion c. 1400–1700* (Woodbridge, 2010), pp. 39–81 (p. 71).
[47] Cunich, "Brothers of Syon," pp. 52–53.

they could read Latin is a question; certainly the brother who helped Whitford with his last book was Latinate.

Although Whitford's first publications in the 1520s were single texts, from the early 1530s he – or his publishers – had evolved a successful formula of presentation: the compilation. Offering together a group of several texts, more or less closely related, seems to have been a conscious strategy on the part of a man well aware of the advantages of printing. (The title page of his 1525 *Rule* says, "[t]he translator doth advise and counsel all the disciples of this rule to bear always one of these books upon them, since they are so portable and may be had for so small a price.")

This last work, in 1541, continues that format by presenting four texts whose connections, despite protestations, are more the product of authorial convenience than of thematic coherence. As he had done earlier, Whitford makes available in print part of his voluminous manuscript oeuvre, again with a substantial gap between composition and publication. At the same time, he brings new work forward quickly. Two of the elements in the book come from the past, the first and final items, while the two works in between are relatively current.

There is no striking resonance with recent events – the dissolution of the monasteries and the dispersal of the Syon community. Peter Marshall has noted the powerful grounding of "the habit of loyalty" in the social elites, both clerical and lay, at this time, and how "from 1529 onwards, changes came incrementally, and did not always seem irreversible."[48] Indeed, Whitford seems not to have experienced these political events as constituting an end. With the benefit of hindsight, we understand the last years of the 1530s differently. But Whitford's publication in 1541 of *Dyuers Holy Instrucyons* indicates his continuing involvement in the work of spiritual direction, despite the disruption that events had produced. He died in the following year: his pension (for the first quarter of 1542) was paid for the last time on April 5, 1542. An inscription in a sixteenth-century hand in the Lambeth Palace copy of his *Pype of Perfection* reads: "obijt an*n*o d*o*mini 1542," and the Syon Martyrology lists his death on September 16, giving no year.[49] Like every English citizen in these years, he was involved in a process, one whose resolution was by no means visible. While it lasted, he would continue to write and advise, as he had always done. His last book, two years after the closure of his house, demonstrates the continuity of

---

[48] Peter Marshall, *Reformation England 1480–1642* (London, 2003), p. 56.
[49] Hogg, *Pype*, I, pt. I: 48–49.

his intellectual interests, the preservation of some semblance of monastic community, and, it seems, the expectation of a continuing audience.

Coda

One more work, like this late-published volume, may just possibly have been the product of Whitford's last years. A piece that never saw publication, it is titled *A Looking Glace for the Religious*. It survives only in a single manuscript, Syon MS 18 now at the University of Exeter, and is written in an italic hand, probably of the seventeenth century.[50] The handwritten "Register of Syon Manuscripts" describes it as follows: "The preface containing the argument of this book. At the end is written 'Farewell, and pray for me your wretched brother. Amen'." The register adds: "N.B. Query has been raised whether this is a translation of Richard Whytford, and in his own handwriting. If so, it would be the earliest English translation known."

James Hogg noted that *A Looking Glace* is a translation of Ludovicus Blosius's first work, printed at Louvain in 1538. It was titled *Speculum Monachorum, a Dacryanus ordinis Sancti Benedicti Abbate conscriptum*,[51] and was addressed to a perhaps fictitious monk named Odo, in response to his request for a spiritual mirror or looking glass. A treatise on perfection in religious life, it appealed to lay readers as well. Its modern editor, who provides the English translation published in Paris in 1679, calls it a classic of monastic literature.[52] Comparison of this seventeenth-century translation with the text of Syon MS 18 shows that each is an independent translation from Blosius's Latin. Each reproduces Blosius faithfully, without cutting or supplementing. Blosius closes with the injunction "farewell and pray for me" while Syon MS 18 adds "your wretched brother" – the basis for speculation about Whitford's authorship. The Syon MS is not an author's autograph, rather it copies a source, either a manuscript or, perhaps, a lost printed text.

---

[50] It has been edited by Veronica Lawrence, *Richard Whytford: A Looking Glace for the Religious*, Salzburg Studies in English Literature: Elizabethan and Renaissance Studies 92.18, 3 vols. (Salzburg, 1979), I. Vol. III is a photographic reproduction of the MS: *Syon Abbey MS 18, A Looking Glace for the Religious, Presented by James Hogg*. See also Veronica Lawrence, "Syon MS 18 and the Medieval English Mystical Tradition," in Marion Glasscoe (ed.), *The Medieval Mystical Tradition in England, Exeter Symposium V, 1992* (Woodbridge, 1992), pp. 145–62 (p. 153).

[51] Hogg, *Pype of Perfection*, I, pt. I: 62.

[52] Roger Hudleston (ed.), *A Mirror for Monks (Speculum Monachorum) by Ludovicus Blosius* (New York, 1926), p. xvi.

The career of this Flemish abbot and author (1506–66) was devoted to the renewal of religious life. Eire calls him "a great Renaissance synthesizer" and notes his promotion by the Cologne Carthusians."[53] After the publication of his reforming ideas in the *Speculum Monachorum* of 1538, in the following year Blosius issued his Statutes of Reform for the Benedictine order, which received papal approval in 1545.[54] Whitford shared this concern for a purified religious life; indeed it might be considered the central focus of his writing, together with his concern to develop a lay spirituality of parallel strength and sophistication. Starting with his translation of the rule of St. Augustine published in 1525 and progressing to his *Pype of Perfection* in 1532, a work whose purpose is both to glorify the religious life and to defend it from current attacks, Whitford was in the forefront of English thinking on the worth and the place of traditional monasticism in modern society. Presenting Blosius's contemporary writing on this subject would have appealed to Whitford – if the translation is his work – as perhaps extending and commenting upon the same subjects he had treated six years earlier in *Pype*. If Whitford were the translator, he might have produced the work in his last year at the monastery or at any time during Syon's diaspora, before his death in 1542. The translation of Blosius's vision of a renewed monasticism, one that harmonized with Whitford's own desires, would thus have been made at almost the last moments of English religious life.

---

[53] Eire, "Early Modern Catholic Piety," p. 91; and see J. T. Rhodes, "Abbot Blosius and Father Baker," in Geoffrey Scott (ed.), *Dom Augustine Baker 1575–1641* (Leominster, 2012), pp. 133–52.

[54] Eire, "Early Modern Catholic Piety," p. xiv.

Anchorites of All Hallows London Wall parish, 1402–1537

Margaret Burre (†1402)	Her will, LMA: DL/AL/C/002/MS09051/001, f. 97v
	Executors: Sir John Banbury, rector, and churchwardens John Surman, carpenter, and Nicholas Bedewell, whitetawyer (his will, as above, f. 314v)
Unknown	
1457/58	4 marks from Bishop of London to All Hallows anchoress (Welch, p. 4)
1459/60	Two gifts of the anchor to the church, 6s. 8d. and 4d. (Welch, p. 7)
1461, October 15	Gift of Margaret Bedewell to anchor of a towel "of werk" and a silver spoon to celebrate a trental (her will: LMA: DL/C/B/004/MS09171/005, f. 333)
1462, June 10	Gift of John Stede to anchor, 5d. (his will: as above, f. 331v)
1465	Gift of Wm Gregory, former Mayor of London, to anchorite, 6s. 8d. (Welch, p. xxix)
1466, November 19	Gift of Margaret Prate to anchor, a towel of diaper four rods in length; asks burial before the door of the anchor's house (her will: as above, f. 393v)
1469/70	Gift of the anchor "to the church work," 3s. 4d. (Welch, p. 9)
1474, February 13	Gift of John Emlyn, upholder, xij d. to anchorite, vi d. to anchoress (*CPMR 1458–1482*, vi:135)
1474/75	Gift of the anchor toward making the new "bolles of laton of ye beme," 2s. 8d. (Welch, p. 14)
William Lucas, priest (before 1478–86)	
1477/78	Gift of the anchor, 20s. (Welch, p. 20)
1478	Papal permission for fifteen-month trip to Rome and "divers other holy places." He is said to have been enclosed at All Hallows "for several years." (Clay, p. 80, quoting *CPL*, xiii.625)
1479/80	William Lucas sues Richard West, merchant tailor, to recover parish money he lent to West (TNA C1/66/66–69, Welch, pp. xxx–xxxi)
1480	Gift of Anne, Duchess of Buckingham, to anchor, 6s. 8d. for twenty masses and twenty diriges (her will: PCC 2 Logge [Prob. 11/7, ff. 14v–15v]). Parish accounts record receipt of the money (Welch, p. 22)

1482/85	Gifts of the anchor to the church at three separate times, 3s. 4d. twice, 8d. once (Welch, pp. 28–29)
1484, August 27	Thomas Sunnyff, tiler, asks to be buried "byfore the wyndowe of the Ancris Chapell in the parish of Alhalowen in the wall of London" (his will, PCC 9 Logge [Prob. 11/7, ff. 69v–70])
1485, September 13	Gift of John Skirwith, master of Leathersellers' Company 1476–77 and 1483–84, to the anchor for a trental, 10s. (his will: PCC 23 Logge [Prob. 11/7, ff. 176r–v])
1486, June 15	Papal indult to William de Lucasa, anchorite, to choose a confessor (*CPL*, xv.417)
1486, July 28	Papal indulgence for contributors to parish (*CPL*, xv.63)
1486, November 6–1487, June 24	Received of the executors of Sir Wm Lucas, the old anchor, for the great bell, 3s. 4d. (Welch, p. 33)
	Received of Harry, clerke, "that we strayned in our hands because that he had so litill of the executours of the seid Anckor for his wages," 18d. (Welch, p. 33)
	Paid "in sute of plee agaynst the executours of syr William lukas somtyme Her Ancker," xv s. xj d. (Welch, p. 35)
1487	William Lucas's name entered under "dead priests" in bede roll of the Fraternity of Clerks (LMA: CLC/L/PB/C/001/MS04889; James, II: 421)
1488, June 24–1492, March 27	"ffor ye beriying off ser jon ye hanckorys pryst iij s iiijd" (Welch, p. 36)
Robert Lynton(?) (d. 1487?)	
1486, November 6–1487, June 24	Received for the burying of the "nve Ancker," 6s. 8d. (Welch, p. 34)
	Received from the executors of the "seid Ancker of sich goodes that he gave to the chyrch," 53s. 4d.
1488, May 10	Commission from John Morton, Archbishop of Canterbury, to administer goods of Robt Lynton, anchor of London Wall, who died intestate (Morton's register 1, no. 297)
Unknown	
1488, June 24–1492, March 27	Received for the anchor from Doctor Jane, 26s. 8d. (Welch, p. 36; Clay, p. 81, who calls it "the episcopal annuity," transmitted by the archdeacon)
Giles (1491)	Gift of Richard Bodley, warden of the Grocers' Company, his two best gold rings and £6 13s. 4d. (Collis, p. 35; his will PCC 1 Doggett [Prob. 11/9, ff. 5v–6])
Unknown	
1495, March 25–1496, September 29	Received of the anchor "for beryyng of ser john mother xx d" (Welch, p. 40)
	Received of the anchor "for ye guttar making," 6s. 8d. (Welch, p. 40)
1500	Gift of Jane, Viscountess Lisle, 13s. 4d. to anchor, same to anchoress (Collis, p. 36, quoting *Sede Vacante Wills*, pp. 130–31)
1500–01	"Item a grett paxe wyth iij Images off sylver by the gyfftt of the Anker" (Welch, p. 68)

1509–11	"Item Reste In Master Anker hands In Redy money for the church xxv s" (Welch, p. 51)
Simon Appulby (1513–37)	
1513, June 26	Simon Appulby's installation (Fitzjames Register, Guildhall MS 9531/9, f. 41; Clay, p. 82)
1513–28	Received of the anchor "Syr Symon of the Gaynes of A stande of ale whiche he gave to the cherche iiij s vj d ob" (Welch, p. 52)
	Paid to the anchor's servant for plastering the church wall, 4d. (Welch, p. 53)
1514	First edition of *Fruyte of Redempcyon*
1517	Second edition
1520–21	Anchor's gift of a chalice weighing 8 oz. (Welch, p. 68)
1528–29	Received of the anchor "of the gift of divers men and women of their devotion at divers times," 9s. 3d. (Welch, p. 56)
	Received of the anchor for scaffold poles, 8s. (Welch, p. 57)
	Master Anchor's name in parish "loan list" for 32s. and in a separate list of those contributing to the new aisle, the same amount. The parish gives him 8s. in partial repayment of 40s. (Welch, pp. 58–59)
1530	Third edition of *Fruyte of Redempcyon*
1531	Fourth edition
1532	Fifth edition
1532, February 24	Holy Trinity priory suppressed. Alderman John Champneys requests from mayor and aldermen the next voidance after decease of anchorite; granted (COL/CA/01/01 [*Repertory* 8], f. 214v; Clay, p. 84)
1537, June 6	Simon Appulby's will (Foxford, f. 252v)
1538	Anchorhouse given to city swordbearer (COL/CA/01/01 [*Repertory* 10], ff. 20v, 36v, 37v; Clay, p. 84)

Sources

Clay: Rotha Mary Clay, "Further Studies on Medieval Recluses," *Journal of the British Archaeological Association* 3rd ser., 16 (1953)

Collis: Jennifer Mary Collis, "The Anchorites of London in the Late Middle Ages," MA thesis (University of London, 1992)

CPL: W. H. Bliss *et al.* (eds.), *Calendar of Entries in the Papal Registers Relating to Great Britain and Ireland: Papal Letters, vol. XV, 1484–1492* (London, Public Record Office, 1893)

CPMR: Philip E. Jones (ed.), *Calendar of Plea and Memoranda Rolls Preserved among the Archives of the Corporation of the City of London at the Guildhall A.D. 1458–1482*, 6 vols. (Cambridge, 1961)

Darlington: Ida Darlington (ed.), *London Consistory Court Wills 1492–1527*, London Record Society 3 (London, 1967)

Foxford: C. A. McLaren (ed.), "An Edition of Foxford, a Vicars'-General Book of the Diocese of London 1521–1539, ff. 161–268," M.Phil. thesis (librarianship) (University of London, 1973). From LMA: MS DL/C/330

James: N. W. James and V. A. James (eds.), *The Bede Roll of the Fraternity of St. Nicholas*, 2 vols., London Record Society 39 (London, 2004)

LMA: London Metropolitan Archives

Morton's register: Christopher Harper-Bill (ed.), *The Register of John Morton, Archbishop of Canterbury 1486–1500*, vol. I, Canterbury and York Society 75 (Leeds, 1987)

Sede Vacante Wills: C. Everleigh Woodruff (ed.), *Sede Vacante Wills: A Calendar of Wills Proved before the Commissary of the Prior and Chapter of Christ Church, Canterbury*, vol. III (Canterbury, 1914)

Welch: Charles Welch (ed.), *The Churchwardens' Accounts of the Parish of All Hallows, London Wall* (London, 1912)

Will of Simon Appulby

LMA: DL/C/330, fols. 252v–253. Reprinted with permission (and modernized) from C. A. McLaren, "An Edition of Foxford, a Vicars'-General Book of the Diocese of London 1521–1539, fols. 161–268," M.Phil. thesis (librarianship and archive administration) (University of London, 1973), no. 649.

In the name of God Amen. The 6th day of June the year of our lord God 1537 and the 29th year of the reign of our sovereign lord King Henry the VIIIth, I Simond Appulby, priest, anchor in the house or anchorage adjoining to the parish church of Allhallows in the wall of London, being of good and perfect memory, laud and praise be unto almighty God, make, ordain and dispose this my present testament and last will in manner and form following, that is to wit: First, I commend my soul unto almighty God my maker, my savior and redeemer, and my body to be buried within the tomb already set and made within the anchorage aforesaid. Item, I will that the priests of Pappy come and be at my burial to whom I bequeath, so coming, twenty pence; and in likewise I bequeath to the brotherhood of the clerks coming to my burial, after the custom and manner by them used, twenty pence. Item, I bequeath to 14 children bearing 14 tapers at my said burial, which I have already provided and bought, two shillings fourpence, that is to say to every of them same [sic] 14 children for their labors twopence. Item, I bequeath other two shillings fourpence unto fourteen poor people dwelling within the said parish of Allhallows, that is to say to every of them twopence. Also I will that there be expended at the time of my burial in buns, cheese and ale to and for the company being at my burial eight shillings and fourpence. Item, I will that at the month day next after my decease there be expended at the discretion of mine executor and overseer undernamed five shillings. Moreover my very mind and will is that all such books and vestments as now be within the chapel of the said anchorage shall there perpetually remain to the use of the anchor which after my decease shall supply the same room, so that the same room of an anchor there be supplied within one year and a day next after my decease; otherwise and without that so be, I will that all the same books and vestments shall be put to such use as shall seem good to mine executor. The residue of all my goods whatsoever they be, the goods which I by my writing late gave unto John Drynkmylke except, and my burial in form abovesaid done, I will shall be disposed in deeds of pity and charity by mine executor undernamed as to his discretion shall seem best. And of this my present testament and last will I make and ordain mine executor John Davell, citizen and wax chandler of London. And I bequeath unto the same John for his labor in the premises three shillings and fourpence. And the overseer of the same my testament I make and ordain Thomas Hygson, citizen and fletcher of London. And I bequeath unto the same Thomas for his labor in that behalf three shillings and fourpence. These being witness ..."[1]

---

[1] Entry unfinished, followed by note "Probatum fuit suprascriptum testamentum coram magistro Barrett."

Letters of Katherine Bulkeley, Morpheta Kingsmill, and Joan Fane

The text is taken most often from Mary Anne Everett Wood Green (ed.), *Letters of Royal and Illustrious Ladies of Great Britain*, 3 vols. (London, 1846) or from other nineteenth-century collections; otherwise the *Letters and Papers* summary is provided.

Katherine Bulkeley to Thomas Cromwell

1. October 6 [1536?], *LP*, XI, no. 570; Green, *Letters*, III: xxxiii.

Pleaseth it your honour,

After my most humble duty, with immortal thanks for all your great goodness showed unto me, to be advertised that I have sent by this bearer your old fee of 40s. and your new fee of other 40s., due both at Michaelmas last. I am ashamed of them, that they be so little, but I beseech you to accept them, seeing my power is no better; for if it were, truly you should have more. And if it may please your honour to send me the same two convent seals, I shall make them both in one to your lordship, and to your son, Master Gregory, and to the longer liver of you both; for gladly would I do you some pleasure, if I wist how, God knoweth my heart.

In declaration whereof, for lack of better stuff, I do send you a dish of old apples, whereof some be a twelvemonth old, and some two year old, beseeching you to accept them and to license me to set open a back gate of this monastery which hath been shut ever since the king's visitation, for the which I have great displeasure of my neighbours. For indeed it is very nocive [hurtful] for them, especially the winter time, for by reason thereof they be fain to go two mile about, as this bearer can more at large declare to your honour, as knoweth our Lord, who ever preserve you to His pleasure. Amen.

At Godstow, the 6th day of October,
Your most bounden beadwoman,
Katherine Bulkeley, Abbess there

2. March 7 [1538?], *LP*, XIII (i), no. 441; Green, *Letters*, III: xxxii.

My most humble commendations premised, with my most entire
thanks for all your goodness done unto me: whereas you have of nothing brought me to all that I have by your mere [utter] goodness, never
deserved of me in any part. It is so, my good lord, that the stewardship
of this monastery is now void by the death of Master Welch, which had
it; and is of so small value, being but 40s. fee by the year, that I dare not
be so bold so to desire your lordship to take so small a thing. But if it
would please you not to be offended therewith, both my poor sisters
and I do most heartily beseech you to accept it, which were greatly
to our comfort. It is more honest than profitable, for you shall have
at your commandment twenty or thirty men to do the king service
thereby, as Master Welch had to the north.[1] I can make it no better than
it is, but if it were a 1000*l.*, your good lordship should have it with all
my heart and prayers. And in case it will not stand with your pleasure
to accept it, yet I beseech you point it to whom it shall please you. A
under steward we have, which is a honest man, permanent with us, and
hath his patent thereof for his life, which is and ever must be, at the
high steward's beck and commandment. As knoweth our Lord Jesus,
who ever preserve your honour, daily to increase to his pleasure. Amen.

At Godstow, the 7th day of March,
By your most bounden beadwoman,
Katherine Bulkeley, Abbess of Godstow

3. March 12 [1538?], *LP*, XIII (i), no. 492; Ellis, III: cccxliv; Cook, *Letters*,
XCIX. Text from Ellis.

My most especial good Lord: after my most humble duty and
immortal thanks for your infinite goodness toward me, these be to
advertise your honour that whereas the last week I was informed by
the Dean of the Arches's letters[2] that you are so good lord unto me
as to accept this little office of the stewardship of this monastery, I
am so bold as to send unto your honour herewith the patent thereof

---

[1] The northern risings of 1536/37 in which, it seems, Godstow fought for the king.
[2] Dr. Richard Gwent, an Oxford-educated doctor of canon and civil law, became Dean of the Arches
in 1532. His connection with Godstow came early: *ODNB* says in 1524 the convent appointed him
to the vicarage of St. Giles, Oxford, which he resigned.

under our convent seal for term of your life, beseeching your honour to accept the same, though it be but small. For if it were a thousand times better you should have it with all my heart and prayers, as knows our savior Christ, who ever preserve you in honour duly to increase to his pleasure. Amen.

At Godstow, the 12 day of March,
Your most bounden beadwoman,
Katherine Bulkeley, Abbess there

4. June 26 [1538?], *LP*, XIII (i), no. 1262.

I send your Lordship a couple of Banbury cheeses and pray God reward you for staying the mayor and commonality of Oxford from entering upon the commons which I and my tenants have held this 400 years. I trust at the King's next coming to Woodstock, to see you here. I beg you will stay the commission which the mayor did labour to you, for it would be great hindrance to the poor tenants to attend on the Commissioners during harvest. Defer it till the beginning of next year, if not till your coming. [*LP* summary]

5. November 5, 1538, *LP*, XIII (ii), no. 758; Wright, *Suppression*, CXII; Cook, *Letters*, CXXXVI. Text from Wright.

Pleaseth it your honour with my most humble duty to be advertised that where it hath pleased your lordship to be the very mean to the King's majesty for my preferment most unworthy to be abbess of this the king's monastery of Godstow, in the which office I trust I have done the best in my power to the maintenance of God's true honour, with all truth and obedience to the king's majesty, and was never moved nor desired by any creature in the King's behalf or in your lordship's name to surrender and give up the house, nor was never minded nor intended so to do otherwise than at the King's gracious commandment or yours, to the which I do and have ever done and will submit myself most humbly and obediently, and I trust to God that I have never offended God's laws, neither the King's whereby that this poor monastery ought to be suppressed.

And this notwithstanding, my good lord, so it is that Doctor London,[3] which as your lordship doth well know was against my

---

[3] John London (1486–1544), Oxford canon lawyer, warden of New College, King's visitor in the diocese of London, whose religious position was variously assessed. His notarial mark carried the motto, "Gratia dei sum id quod sum." Died in the Fleet for his activities in the prebendaries plot.

promotion and hath ever since born me great malice and grudge, like my mortal enemy, is suddenly come unto me with a great rout with him, and here doth threaten me and my sisters, saying that he hath the King's commission to suppress the house, spite of my teeth. And when he saw that I was content that he should do all things according to his commission, and showed him plain that I would never surrender to his hand, being my ancient enemy, now he begins to entreat me and to inveigle my sisters one by one otherwise than ever I heard tell that any of the King's subjects hath been handled, and here tarries and continues to my great cost and charge, and will not take my answer that I will not surrender till I know the king's gracious commandment or your good lordship's.

Therefore I do most humbly beseech you to continue my good lord, as you ever have been, and to direct your honorable letters to remove him hence; and whensoever the King's gracious commandment or yours shall come unto me, you shall find me most ready and obedient to follow the same. And notwithstanding that Doctor London, like an untrue man, hath informed your lordship that I am a spoiler and a waster, your good lordship shall know that the contrary is true, for I have not alienated one halporthe [halfpenny] of the goods of this monastery, moveable or unmovable, but have rather increased the same, nor never made lease of any farm or piece of ground belonging to this house other than hath been in times past always set under convent seal for the wealth of the house.

And therefore my very trust is that I shall find the King as gracious lord unto me as he is to all other his subjects, seeing I have not offended and am and will be most obedient to his most gracious commandment at all times, with the grace of almighty Jesus, who ever preserve you in honour long to endure to his pleasure. Amen.

At Godstow the 5th day of November,
Your most bounden beadwoman,
Katherine Bulkeley, abbess there

6. November 26 [1538?], *LP*, XIII (ii), no. 911; Green, *Letters*, III: xxxiv; Ellis, III: cccxlv; Cook, *Letters*, CXXXVIII.

My most singular good lord,

After my most humble duty, these be specially to thank you for that it pleaseth you to direct your letters for the stay of Doctor London, which was here ready to suppress this poor house against my will and all my sisters, and had done it in deed if you had not so speedily sent contrary commandment, for the which your goodness you shall be well assured, as I am already most bounden, of a poor maiden's prayer during my life, seeing I have no other riches to recompense you withal.

And where it pleased you to direct your letters since that time to me and my sisters for the preferment of Master Doctor Owen[4] to our domains and stock, these be to certify your lordship that we have accomplished the same with all favor and gentleness, as I trust he will report and give your lordship thanks therefor. For no man living, under the King, could have had it of us with our good wills, saving your lordship. And therefore, as my very trust and comfort is in you, I beseech you to continue my good lord, as I trust you shall never have cause to the contrary, for your lordship shall be well assured that there is neither pope nor purgatory, image nor pilgrimage, nor praying to dead saints, used or regarded amongst us; but all superstitious ceremonies set apart, the very honour of God and the truth of his holy words, as far as the frail nature of women may attain unto, is most tenderly followed and regarded with us, not doubting but this garment and fashion of life doth nothing prevail toward our justifying before God. By whom, for his sweet son Jesus' sake, we only trust to be justified and saved, who ever preserve your honour to his pleasure. Amen.

At Godstow, this 26 day of November,
Your most bounden beadwoman,
Katherine Bulkeley, Abbess there

November 17, 1539, surrender of Godstow.

Morpheta Kingsmill to Thomas Wriothesley

January 1 [1538?], *LP*, XIII (i), no. 8.

It pleased your mastership to labour for the advowson of the prebend of Myddelton for Doctor Legh[5] to which we agreed. Now that it is void by the death of Doctor Fawnes[6] we understand that Master

---

[4] George Owen was physician to Henry VIII; he received his bachelor's and doctor's degrees in medicine from Oxford in 1525 and 1528. He attended the birth of Edward VI and was rewarded by the king with many grants of lands and houses in Oxford and nearby. In March 1540 he bought Godstow abbey for £558. See *ODNB*.

[5] Rowland Lee (*c.*1487–1543), Bishop of Coventry and Lichfield in 1534, friend of Cromwell. See *ODNB*.

[6] For John Fawne, DD, see *AC*, I (xxii), 525.

Cooke[7] pretends [claims] a title to it. If it were known how he came by it and "two seals more" against our wills it would sound to his shame. We opened this matter before you, Master Chancellor[8] and Master Parys,[9] the bishop of Winchester's treasurer. Please speak to Master Cooke that he will not pursue his suit. If he will not, I and my sisters desire your mastership to show my Lord Privy Seal how the matter stands, and how Master Cooke has beguiled us. May it please his lordship and you that Doctor Legh may enjoy our gift, whose learning and excellent qualities may profit us and our monastery, and not such as may buy it of Master Cooke, who, we hear, has sold it to two or three already. "Pleasith it your mastership" to ponder how he has vexed our monastery with his "seals." [*LP* summary]

November 21, 1539, surrender of Wherwell.

Joan Fane to Thomas Cromwell

September 9 [1538?], Green, *Letters*, III: xxxix; Cook, *Letters*, XC.

Jesus

Right honourable and my singular good lord,

In my most humble and obedient manner I have me recommended unto your good lordship, advertising your good lordship that I have received your gentle and loving letter touching the delivery of one Bridget Browning, one of my religious company, as yet not professed in the sight of the world, but only in heart to God, who was brought to my monastery long time past, only by the great labour, means, and request made by her mother to the late prioress of the said monastery now deceased,[10] to the intent she should be a religious woman and recluse, and nothing at the desire nor request of the said late prioress, neither by her provocation, neither yet by her nor me detained or kept against her friends' minds, contrary to any statute, decree, or ordinance, in that behalf provided but that the said late prioress, I, and my sisters, have always been ready to permit and suffer the said Bridget to depart to her said mother at her free

---

[7] The quarrelsome and self-promoting John Cooke was Principal Registrar for at least six bishops of Winchester – Richard Fox, Thomas Wolsey, Stephen Gardiner, John Ponet, John White, and Robert Horne – from 1524 to sometime after 1564.

[8] Edmund Stuarde, a conservative, was Chancellor of the Bishop of Winchester 1531–51, 1553–57.

[9] Philip Parys, Stephen Gardiner's Treasurer.

[10] Elizabeth Cressener was Prioress of Dartford from *c.*1487 to 1537.

will and liberty. Which to do she always, being very sore prefixed in her outward mind, and also as it should seem in her heart to my said religion, hath refused and denied. Wherefore it may please your good lordship that she may come to your lordship's presence, and that the effects of her heart and mind may be by your good lordship tenderly accepted and heard, and farther, she to be remitted as it shall appertain to your good lordship's great wisdom and authority. Wherein your good lordship shall bind me and all other my sisters to be your lordship's daily oratrices. As knoweth our Lord God, who ever have your good lordship in his tuition and governance.

Written at Dartford the 9th day of September, by your lordship's poor and faithful oratrice,
Joanna Vane, Prioress

Between April 1 and October 18, 1539, surrender of Dartford.

Letters of Margaret Vernon to Thomas Cromwell

A suggested chronology*

Date	*Letters and Papers*	Contents
At Little Marlow:		
1. ?Spring 1522–28	*LP*, IV (iii), no. 5971 (*LP* dates 1529)(SP 1/55/175)	Request for £40 loan
2. Same	*LP*, V, no. 16 (*LP* dates 1531)	Securities for loan
3. ?1522-28, or any time	*LP*, IV (iii), no. 5972 (*LP* dates 1531)(SP 1/55/176)	Request for advice
4. ?1527, ?1528,	*LP*, V, no. 17 (*LP* dates 1529)(SP 1/65/40)	?Gregory's master
5. Same	*LP*, V, no. 18 (*LP* dates 1531)	Gregory at Little Marlow
6. Between August 22 and early December 1528	*LP*, IV (iii), no. 5970 (*LP* dates 1529)(SP 1/55/173–74)	?Prioress of St. Helen's
7. Same	*LP*, V, no. 15 (*LP* dates 1531)	?Prioress of St. Helen's; Gregory at Little Marlow
8. Same	*LP*, V, no. 20 (*LP* dates 1531)	?Prioress of St. Helen's (addressed to Cromwell "of the council")
9. After November 29, 1530	*LP*, V, no. 19 (*LP* dates 1531)	?Prioress of St. Helen's
10. 1531–32	*LP*, V, no. 21 (*LP* dates 1531)	How is Gregory?
11. ?1531 or any time	*LP*, V, no. 22 (*LP* dates 1531)	Restrain Mr. Grantham
12. January 24 [?1535]	*LP*, XIV (i), no. 130 (*LP* dates 1539)	"Little gentlewoman," M. Pole's house
13. August–December 1535	*LP*, IX, no. 1166 (*LP* dates thus)	Visitors discharged three nuns
[June 27, 1536, Little Marlow dissolved]		
14. Day after St. Paul [June 30 1536]	*LP*, VIII, no. 108 (*LP* dates January 26, 1535)	Haven't been able to see you

(cont.)

Date	*Letters and Papers*	Contents
At Malling:		
15. St. George's eve [April 22 1537]	*LP*, XII (i), no. 999	Support Mr Chutts bailiff of Rye
16. April 6 [1538]	*LP*, XIII (i), no. 692	Can't make payment now
17. Good Friday [April 19 1538]	*LP*, XIII (i), no. 808	Stathum and Neville want Malling; Cromwell has promised she can keep it
18. After April [19 1538]	*LP*, XIII (i), no. 875	Sending 100 m; ?answer to Easter eve letter
19. Midsummer Day [June 24 1538]	*LP*, XIII (i), no. 1251	Stathum and Wyatt want Malling
20. [October 28, 1538] [October 29, 1538, Malling dissolved]	*LP*, XIII (ii), no. 716	Financial proposal
21. [November 1, 1538]	*LP*, XIII (ii), no. 718	Will come as summoned

* The first eleven letters are entirely undated.

Letters of Margaret Vernon

Where available, the text is taken from Mary Anne Everett Wood Green (ed.), *Letters of Royal and Illustrious Ladies of Great Britain*, 3 vols., London, 1846; otherwise the *Letters and Papers* summary is provided.

1. ?Spring 1522–28, *LP*, IV (iii), no. 5971; Green, *Letters*, II: xxiii.

> Jesus
> Right worshipful sir,
>   With all my heart I commend me unto you, thanking you of your kindness always showed unto me, which I am not able to deserve but only with my prayer, of the which you shall be always assured during my life.
>   Pleaseth it you to understand that one of my neighbors removing to another farm will sell both corn upon the ground and also his cattle, for the which is offered £47 upon days of payment, and for ready money I shall have it for £40, so it be paid by Sunday or Monday next. Sir, in this bargain by Michaelmas I doubt not but

there would be twenty marks gained. Wherefore I beseech you to be so good unto me at this time to spare me the said sum of £40 until Whitsuntide, at what time I am assured to make ready your money with malt and wheat and for the assurance of the same you shall have my house bound by convent seal and, if farther need be, my neighbor Grynder shall be bound for the same.

Thus I am bold to write unto you at this time for the profit of my house, trusting that of your goodness you will help, and in your so doing you shall farther bind me to be your beadwoman during my life, with the grace of our Lord, who ever preserve you.

By your,
Margaret Vernon

2. ?Spring 1522–28, *LP*, V, no. 16.

I thank you for your great kindness. My woman informs me that you will be so good as to lend me £40 till Whitsuntide if I obtain two sufficient sureties. My neighbor Grynder and John Lewis, goldsmith, living at the sign of the Portcullis in Cheapside, will attend you on Wednesday next. [*LP* summary]

3. ?1522–28, or anytime, *LP*, IV (iii), no. 5972.

Begs to know when he will be in these parts, or when she can see him at his own house, she coming on one day and going home the next, as she requires his counsel on several matters. [*LP* summary]

4. ?1527, ?1528, *LP*, V, no. 17; Green, *Letters*, II: xxiv.

Right worshipful sir,

With all my heart I recommend me unto you, desiring you to send me word how you have done for the priest that you promised me, and if you be not provided already, I doubt not but I shall have one which shall be as good for your purpose as you can desire, for of him I have had the proof already. It fortuned so upon a three years past I was destitute of a priest, and then I sent to Oxford to a friend of mine, which sent to me the same man, and he brought with him a gentleman's child to whom he gave attendance with so great diligence and good virtuous bringing up, that in no place I think you cannot be better sped. And to give you knowledge what I have done in the furtherance of the same, I sent to him this week, and his answer is that he will purchase license for a year and farther he cannot promise, for he is a master of art and fellow of Lincoln College in Oxford, whose name is William Inglefield.[1]

Good master Cromwell, let me know your pleasure in this case shortly, for I would that your child should lose no more time. I think the gentleman that you promised should be much to your charge, and yet perchance in every thing not so well for your child as this man shall. And farther to show you, as I perceive by Master Somer,[2] he is such a man that will not take the pain that should be for my pleasure, which is this – good master Cromwell, if it like you to call unto your remembrance, you have promised me that I should have the governance of your child till he be twelve years of age, and at that time I doubt not with God's grace but he shall speak for himself if any wrong be offered unto him, whereas yet he cannot but by my maintenance, and if he should have such a master which would disdain if I meddled, then it would be to me great unquietness, for I assure you if you sent hither a doctor of divinity yet will I play the smatterer [interferer], but always in his well doing to him he shall have his pleasure, and otherwise not. As our Lord knoweth, whom I beseech to preserve you ever to his pleasure.

By your own,
Margaret Vernon

5. ?1527, ?1528, *LP*, V, no. 18; Green, *Letters*, II: xxv.

Jesus
  Right worshipful sir,
  With all my heart I recommend me unto you, certifying you that your son is in good health and is a very good scholar, and can construe his Pater Noster, Ave, and Creed. I doubt not but at your coming next to me you shall like him very well.
  Furthermore, pleaseth it you to understand that of such money as was delivered unto Vaughan's[3] hands, which was the sum of £20, I can have no more again but £15. His answer is that he hath delivered

---

[1] Not in *BRUO 1501–1540*, nor in Joseph Foster, *Alumni Oxonienses, Vol. III: Early Series (1500–1714)* (Liechtenstein, reprint edn., 1968). Not the son or grandson of Sir Thomas Englefield (1455–1514), Speaker of the House.

[2] Thomas Somer, a London stockfishmonger and member of the Christian Brethren and friend of Cromwell in the 1520s.

[3] Stephen Vaughn, Cromwell's friend and employee, was known to him "at least as early as 1523" and was employed by him in 1526. R. B. Merriman (ed.), *The Life and Letters of Thomas Cromwell*, 2 vols. (Oxford, 1968), I:52.

£5 to you, which I do not believe, for you showed me at your last being with me that the whole sum remained in his hands. Wherefore I right heartily desire you to be so good master unto me as to cause him to deliver the said £5 to this bearer, for he must pay it to my creditor, for I cannot have my bonds until the duty be all paid. And thus I take my leave of you at this time, praying our Lord to send you always as well to fare as your own heart can desire.

By your own assured beadwoman,

Margaret Vernon

6. [Between August 22 and early December 1528], *LP*, IV (iii), no. 5970; Green, *Letters*, II: xxi.

Sir,

Pleaseth it you to understand that there is a goldsmith in this town named Lewys, and he showeth me that Master More hath made sure promise to parson Larke[4] that the subprioress of St. Helen's shall be prioress there afore Christmas day. Sir, I most humbly beseech you to be so good master unto me as to know my lord's grace's pleasure in this case, and that I may have a determined answer whereto I shall trust, that I may settle myself in quietness, the which I am far from at this hour. And farthermore, if it might like you to make the offer to my said lord's grace of such sum of money as we were at a point for, my friends thinketh that I should shortly be at an end.

Sir, I have learned that immediately after Christmas you shall ride about my lord's business and if this matter take not effect afore that time, I will never trouble you neither myself farther. Wherefore, in the honour of God, let me not be forgotten, but with diligence tender my pains, as I shall be ever your beadwoman, and surely deserve your goodness, if God make me able, whom I beseech to preserve you ever in much worship.

By your own assured,
Margaret Vernon

7. [Between August 28 and early December 1528], *LP*, V, no. 15.

I thank you for the great pains you have taken for me and beg credence for Dr. Smyth, the bearer. Your son and his master are in good

---

4 John Larke, nominated by Thomas More as vicar of his parish of Chelsea in 1530, was also vicar of London's parish of St. Etheldreda and elsewhere. He was executed for treason March 7, 1544.

health, and now prosper in learning more in one day than before in a week, by reason of Nicholas Saddelar,[5] who is of very good conditions. Master Copland[6] every morning gives each of them "a laten [Latin lesson?] the which Nicholas doth bear away, as well Gregory's lesson as his own, and maketh the same Gregory perfect against his time of rendering." The master takes such comfort that he is with them three times a day. The bearer will show you the sayings of the Chancellor of London,[7] who is my great enemy. I beseech you, put your helping hand to the matter, if my Lord's Grace intend to perform his promise. The sub-prioress and Lark have been at the court to make all the friends they can, to the great wasting of the goods of that house. [*LP* summary]

8. [Between August 22 and early December 1528], *LP*, V, no. 20.

It has come to my knowledge that divers of my friends have labored with Master Harper[8] for the house of St. Helen's, who, though he has been offered 200 marks to it, for the good reports he hears of me is better contented with me without demanding a groat rather than have the other parties with the sum aforesaid. I beg your favor in this matter, that all men may see that I am your prioress, which is more comfort to me than to be made abbess of Shaftesbury, for then my slanderous adversaries might be discouraged in speaking against me. I beseech this of you for my sake and the love you bear to your son Master Gregory. [*LP* summary]

9. After November 29, 1530 *LP*, V, no. 19; Green, *Letters*, II: xxii.

Right worshipful sir,
    In my most humble wise I commend me unto your mastership, being very glad to hear of your prosperous health, the which I pray our Lord maintain to his pleasure. Fartbermore, pleaseth it your goodness to understand that as I am informed there is certain of my friends that hath moved you for the house of St. Helen's, as master

---

[5] Nicholas Sadler cannot be the son of Cromwell's protégé Ralph Sadler, whose sons were born in the 1530s, but might possibly be the son of Sadler's wife Helen's first marriage, adopted by Sadler.
[6] Perhaps John Copland, a merchant tailor and friend of Thomas Somer, who was also a member of the Christian brethren.
[7] *LP* says "John Edmunds, STP, was chancellor of the Bishop of London from 1517 to Feb. 1529, when he resigned and was succeeded by Thomas Bage or Williams."
[8] Unidentified.

Marshall[9] one, and our simple steward[10] another. Sir, I am right sorry that either of these persons should trouble your mastership with this matter, unfeigned it was not to my knowledge. Nevertheless for so much as they have entered this matter into your mastership's ears already, I most humbly beseech you of license that I may at large show you my whole determination in this matter in writing, forsomuch as I may not speak with your mastership conveniently myself.

Sir, it is so that there is divers and many of my friends that hath written to me that I should make labour for the said house unto your mastership, showing you that the king's grace hath given it to master Harper, who saith that he is proffered for his favor two hundred marks of the king's saddler,[11] for his sister; which proffer I will never make unto him, nor no friend for me shall, for the coming in after that fashion is neither godly nor worshipful. And beside all this I must come by my lady Orell's[12] favour, which is a woman that I would least meddle with. And thus I shall not only be burdened in conscience for payment of this great sum, but also entangled and in great cumbrance to satisfy the avidity of this gentlewoman. And though I did, in my lord cardinal's days, proffer a hundred pounds for the said house, I beseech you consider for what purpose it was made. Your mastership knoweth right well that there was by my enemies so many high and slanderous words, and your mastership had made so great instant labour for me, that I shamed so much the fall thereof that I forsyd [cared] little what proffer was made; but now, I thank our Lord, that blast is ceased and I have no such singular love unto it. For now I have two eyes to see in this matter clearly: the one is the eye of my soul, that I may come without burden of conscience and by the right door, and laying away all pomp and vanity of the world, looking merely upon the maintenance and supportation of the house which I should take in charge, and cannot be performed, master Harper's pleasure and my lady Orell's accomplished. In consideration whereof I intend not willingly, nor no friend of mine shall not, trouble your mastership in this case.

9 Possibly William Marshall (†1540), the social and religious reformer. See *ODNB*.
10 Walter Wilcokk, steward of Little Marlow in 1530 and at the dissolution. See also a chancery suit between 1529 and 1532: TNA C1/658/58.
11 Sir Robert Acton (before 1497–1558), who became king's saddler sometime before September 6, 1528, MP for Southwark and client of Cromwell. See *ODNB*. His sister Joyce Acton was Prioress of Westwood, Worcestershire, at the dissolution. The earliest mention of her in Smith, *Heads*, occurs on December 10, 1532.
12 Mary, widow of Sir Lewis Orell, Kt, married to Thomas Parker and dwelling in St. Helen's close.

Yet nevertheless, according to my bounden duty I give unto your mastership my most hearty thanks, trusting to your goodness that you will remain my special good master in all other my right and reasonable pursuits, as I may be your daily beadwoman, by the grace of our Lord, whom I beseech to preserve you ever with long life to his pleasure.

By your assured oratrice,
Margaret Vernon

10. ?1531–32, *LP*, V, no. 21.

I thank you for your gentleness to the bearer. He cannot as yet pay you easily such duties as he should have done before this. I beg you to spare him till St. Andrew's Eve. Send me word how Gregory your son doth. [*LP* summary]

11. 1531, or any time, *LP*, V, no. 22.

One Master Grantham[13] has a lease from my house for a term of years, wherein are certain young woods reserved by special words, except certain underwoods. But of his extort mind he cuts down great numbers of young oaks contrary to his indentures. My lord of Lincoln[14] wrote to him to forbear but of late he has felled more than threescore oaks and laid them along the hedges. As my house is poor I cannot follow the law with him and beg you to interpose. [*LP* summary]

12. January 24 [?1535,], *LP*, XIV (i), no. 130.

I hear "there is a little gentlewoman with Master Saddlere[15] which I would very fain have to governance and bringing up." It were to my comfort now in mine age. I hear the house my lady of Salusbury[16] had at Bysham is in the king's hand. If you help me to it for my money, I trust to have some pasture thereby to maintain my poor

---

[13] Unidentified.
[14] John Longland, Bishop of Lincoln 1521–47.
[15] Ralph Sadler, Cromwell's secretary.
[16] Margaret Pole, Countess of Salisbury (1473–1541), was arrested and interrogated on treason charges in November 1538, attainted in May 1539, and executed May 7, 1541. Because her lands would have been forfeit to the crown after the attainder, the *LP* editor has placed the letter under 1539. This would be after the closure of Malling, however. Instead the letter must have been written while Vernon was still at Little Marlow, very near Bisham.

house. If it be passed by promise, please help me to some other. [*LP* summary]

13. August–December 1535, *LP*, IX, no. 1166; Green, *Letters*, II: lxxiii; Wright, *Suppression*, XXII; Ellis, III: xxlv; Cook, *Letters*, XLII.

After all due commendations had unto your good mastership, with my most humble thanks for the great cost made on me and my poor maiden at my last being with your mastership, farthermore pleaseth it you to understand that your visitors hath been here of late, who hath discharged three of my sisters. The one is dame Catherine, the other two is the young women that were last professed,[17] which is not a little to my discomfort; nevertheless I must be content with the king's pleasure.

But now as touching mine own part, I most humbly beseech you to be so special good master unto me, your poor beadwoman, as to give me your best advertisement and counsel what way shall be best for me to take, seeing there shall be none left here but myself and this poor maiden. And if it will please your goodness to take this poor house into your own hands, either for yourself or for mine own … your son, I would be glad with all my heart to give it into your mastership's hands, with that you will command me to do therein; trusting and nothing doubting in your goodness that you will so provide for us that we shall have such honest living that we shall not be driven by necessity neither to beg nor to fall to no other inconvenience. And thus I offer myself and all mine unto your most high and prudent wisdom, as unto him that is my only refuge and comfort in this world, beseeching God of his goodness to put in you his Holy Spirit that you may do all things to his laud and glory.

By your own assured beadwoman,
Margaret Vernon

June 27, 1536, Little Marlow dissolved.

14. The day after St. Paul, June 30 [1536], *LP*, VIII, no. 108; Green, *Letters*, II: lxxiv; Cook, *Letters*, XLIII.

After most humble commendations &c., pleaseth it your goodness to be advertised that I have divers times been at the Rolls to have

---

[17] Dame Catherine Pikard and Dame Constance Hill were two of the three.

spoken with your mastership but by reason of the great number of suitors, and also for lack of friendship within your mastership's house, I am kept back so that I cannot come to your presence to solicit my cause. Wherefore I most humbly beseech you to license me to write my mind at large, and that it may stand with your pleasure to command one within your house to put you in remembrance for an answer of your determination and pleasure.

Sir, my request is to desire you to call to remembrance your good and comfortable promises made both unto me and unto my friends, whereunto I have ever hitherto trusted, beseeching your goodness to open unto me some part of your determination what thing you mind that I shall have, or else to help me to some reasonable living so that I may not continue this long suit. For I have but singly provided for myself to maintain it withal, because your mastership commanded me that I should nothing embezzle or take away but leave the house as wealthy as I could, which commandment I followed: I hope all shall be for the best. I pray our Lord put in your heart to make provision for me according to his holy will and pleasure and wholly to rule your mastership by his Spirit. Amen.

Written from Stepney the day after St. Paul,
Your assured and most humble beadwoman,
Margaret Vernon
Late prioress of Little Marlow

15. April 22 [1537], *LP*, XII (i), no. 999.

In favor of Master Chutts, understeward of her house, for the bailiwick of Rey [Rye?], "the which offer hath Master Thynne,[18] clerk controller." Chutts has promised she shall do her pleasure with his office in Malling. Malling, St. George's eve [*LP* summary]

16. April 6 [1538], *LP*, XIII (i), no. 692.

I perceived by Master Doctor Lee[19] that Master Dormer[20] hath not fulfilled his promise with you, for which I am sorry. He sent me word

---

[18] William Thynne (†:546), the editor of Chaucer's collected *Works* (1532) and, by 1537, clerk controller to Henry VIII.

[19] Thomas Legh (d. 1545), a Cambridge lawyer and monastic visitor, an abrasive personality who between 1538 and 1540 assisted at over sixty-nine monastic dissolutions and "profited handsomely from being a visitor." See *ODNB*.

[20] A distant possibility might be Sir Robert Dormer, a wealthy wool merchant and grazier who from 1520 was seated at Wing, Buckinghamshire, near Vernon's former house of Little Marlow.

last term that he would see you satisfied or he left the town. But now I must trust to myself; wherefore I beg you bear with me a little, for I have paid so much since coming hither, and yet have received nothing of this half year's rent so that I cannot at this time fulfill my promise made by Master Dormer. [*LP* summary]

17. Good Friday, April [19, 1538], *LP*, XIII (i), no. 808.

Is surprised to hear Master Stathum²¹ makes labour for her house, considering she desired the contrary, after speaking with Cromwell. At the time when she heard Sir Thomas Nevell²² made labour for it, she said she would rather Stathum had it than that it should go to another who would not inhabit there. But after she spoke with Cromwell, she desired him to make no suit therein, trusting to enjoy it during her life. Begs favor, for unless all shall be dissolved, she would like to keep it according to Cromwell's promise. Has broken her day of payment, but within "this 14 nights" he shall be pleased. Good Friday, at Malling. [*LP* summary]

18. After Good Friday [see preceding letter], *LP*, XIII (i), no. 875.

I have sent by bearer £16. and one mark which makes up 100 marks, yet I acknowledge myself in your lordship's debt. On Easter eve I sent you a letter and had no answer. If you pleased to quiet me with your letters I were much bound to your Lordship. [*LP* summary]

19. Midsummer Day, June 24, [1538], *LP*, XIII (i), no. 1251.

Of late Mistress Stathum was with me, who says your Lordship commanded her to win my goodwill for the resignation of my house and promised her your favor in the same. Now of late came a servant of Master Wyett²³ for my goodwill, saying likewise that he had obtained a promise from you of the same, and had also compounded with the King, who has granted him his favorable

²¹ Master and Mistress Stathum were connections of Hugh Latimer, Bishop of Worcester and friend of Cromwell. On June 17 [1538] Latimer wrote asking Cromwell to remember Mistress Stathum's suit (*LP*, XIII (i), no. 1202). In November 1537 he had related how in response to "a faint weariness over all my body" Mrs. Stathum "doth pymper me up with all diligence" (*LP*, XII (ii), no. 1043; Wright, *Suppression* pp. 147–48, who spells it "Pasham").

²² Sir Thomas Neville (*c.*1484–1542), lawyer, Speaker of the House of Commons, and Kentishman. He offered Cromwell 500 marks for Malling after its dissolution. See Erter, "Abbess of Malling".

²³ Sir Thomas Wyatt had been made high steward of Malling in February 1535, and sheriff of Kent in 1536. He returned to England from diplomatic service in Spain in June 1538.

letters, which tidings "doth not a little maze me." I beg to know what answer I may make to all men. Malling Midsummer Day. [*LP* summary]

20. [October 28, 1538], *LP*, XIII (ii), no. 716.

"These be the requests of me, Margaret Vernon, abbess of Malling, to the right honourable lord, my lord of the Privy Seal."

First, to obtain licence to sell the manor of Cornarde, Suffolk,[24] of the yearly rent of £40., in order with the money to provide for her sisters instead of their pensions, pay off her servants, and buy for herself a living with such of her friends as will take her.

If not, she begs that each of her sisters may have £4. a year pension, and herself £50. a year out of certain lands "with a clause of distress without any replevy of the same for non-payment of our said pensions at the day and feasts." [*LP* summary]

October 29, 1538, Malling surrendered.

21. [November ?1, 1538] *LP*, XIII (ii), no. 718.

Has received his letter and perceives it is the King's pleasure that she should come to Cromwell. Trusts he will consider her "age and unableness to journey so far in one day." Will be with him on Friday. [*LP* summary]

---

[24] The *Valor* calls this manor Magna Cornard, valued at £62 plus. Dugdale, *Monasticon*, III: 385–86.

Life of Elizabeth Woodford

The life of Elizabeth Woodford belongs to a genre only beginning to be recognized: life-writing (biography or autobiography) of religious women. Historically, such lives were presented, as Woodford's is, folded into the narrative of a collective – a religious house.[1] The compiler's intention is often focused elsewhere, on the account of communal survival and growth, yet the individual histories are seen as making their important contribution to the cumulative effect of the narrative. And indeed, the anonymous nun-author of the chronicle of St. Ursula's (*c.*1626), the English nunnery in the Low Countries that gives one of the two sources for Woodford's biography, presents her subject's life as crucially important to what follows. "This being the first draught of the history which reacheth unto full fifty years from the cloister's erection, but beginneth above fifty years before ... In the year of our Lord 1548 ... Elizabeth Woodford, leaving her native soil ... came into Brabant ... and was graciously received." The modern editor of the chronicle is even more explicit: "Elizabeth Woodward ... was to be the link connecting at least four communities of English Canonesses with their sisters of the old days of Catholic England."[2]

---

[1] Nicky Hallett (ed.), *Lives of Spirit: English Carmelite Self-Writing of the Early Modern Period* (Aldershot, 2007), presents the lives of around sixty English Carmelite nuns living in Low Countries nunneries between 1619 and 1794, written by members of their communities.

[2] Adam Hamilton, *The Chronicle of the English Augustinian Canonesses Regular of the Lateran, at St. Monica's in Louvain, 1548 to 1625*, 2 vols. (Edinburgh, 1904), 1: 24. In addition to the *Chronicle*, Hamilton draws partly upon the manuscript life of Mother Margaret Clement composed by Sister Elizabeth Shirley about 1611. For Shirley's life, see now Nicky Hallett (ed.) *English Convents in Exile, 1600–1800, Volume 3: Life Writing* (London, 2012). It was partially printed in John Morris, *The Troubles of Our Catholic Forefathers Related by Themselves*, 1st ser., 2 vols. (London, 1872, 1875), 1: 27–58. The Shirley manuscript is held by the Priory of Our Blessed Lady of Nazareth in Bruges, with a typed transcription at the Priory of Our Lady of Good Counsel, Sayers Commons, West Sussex (St. Monica's MS Q 29), according to Betty Travitsky, "Bibliography of English Women Writers 1500–1640," online: www.itergateway.org/mrts/earlywomen/index. I have quoted from a copy of this transcription, for which I am indebted to Dr. Caroline Bowden, Department of History, Queen Mary College, University of London.

Elizabeth Woodford belonged to the abbey of Burnham, Buckinghamshire, not Dartford, Kent, as Henry Cole recorded in the eighteenth century,[3] and hence she was an Augustinian canoness, not a Dominican nun. She was the daughter of Sir Robert Woodford and his wife Alice Gate of Burnham parish and was professed on December 8, 1519, according to the chronicle of St. Ursula's, the English Augustinian house in Louvain that she later joined.[4] She appears among those present when Bishop John Longland visited Burnham on November 4, 1521,[5] where she is eighth out of twelve in the seniority list. She would then have been professed a little less than two years. During that visitation a slightly senior nun, Alice Collys, observed that Woodford and two others did not return to the dormitory immediately after matins, but waited longer ("diutius expectant"). When her turn to testify came, Woodford noted that laywomen visited the monastery and gossiped with nuns, "quod non est decens," and that the janitrix allowed laywomen to enter the cloister for no particular reason; that three named nuns did not eat in the refectory but in their rooms; that children slept in the nuns' dormitory; and that silence was not observed. All these matters, several of which had been mentioned at an earlier visitation in 1519, Longland ordered to be corrected. We might note that Woodford's comments were the most extensive of any recorded.

At the next visitation, made by the bishop's commissary Dr. Morgan on October 12, 1530, Woodford was listed sixth out of ten nuns. At this time her earlier complaint about seculars' access to the house was repeated by a slightly junior nun, who now mentioned that both men and women were allowed to enter the cloister and speak of secular matters ("communicantes de rebus mundania"). Woodford herself noted that the current number of ten nuns represented fewer than the founders' intention and that the house could support twelve.[6] Her testimony at each of these visitations gives the impression of extreme competence.

Burnham was surrendered nine years later, on September 19, 1539.[7] Adam Hamilton says, giving no source, that after its dissolution Elizabeth Woodward's "first place of refuge" was "her paternal home under the

[3] Henry Ellis, "Account of the Convent of English Nuns Formerly Settled at Louvain, in South Brabant: In a Letter Addressed to the President," *Archaeologia* 36 (1855), 74–77.

[4] Hamilton, *Chronicle*, I: 2.

[5] A. Hamilton Thompson (ed.), *Visitations in the Diocese of Lincoln 1517–1531*, 3 vols., Lincoln Record Society 33, 35, 37 (Hereford, 1940–47), II: 86–91. An earlier visitation on May 1519 does not give the names either of abbess or nuns.

[6] Thompson, *Visitations*, pp. 91–92.

[7] Smith, *Heads*, III: 632.

protection of her brother Thomas ... [but] she did not remain long in his household." The St. Ursula's *Chronicle* notes only that she lived with the family of John Clement, Thomas More's protégé and husband of Margaret Giggs Clement, "privately in his house." Their child Margaret Clement was born in 1539, perhaps the year Woodford came to the Clements's household, so it is probable that Woodford knew Margaret from infancy. We do not know if she taught this youngest Clement child, though it seems likely in view of their later relationship. Burnham's visitation records show that it had had child boarders, perhaps a school, and it is probable that Woodford had worked with children before.

According to the chronicle she entered St. Ursula's, Louvain, in 1548, nine years after her house's closure, although Elizabeth Shirley's "Life" of Margaret Clement says that Woodford "came out of England in king harry's days," which would have been slightly earlier, in or before January 1547.[8] St. Ursula's (founded 1387) was one of the women's communities sprung from the Windesheim movement and connected with the Devotio Moderna, hence it had a heritage of concern for return to the gospel and for a reformed mode of life. Many of these houses, like St. Ursula's, began as informal communities and later adopted the Augustinian rule.[9] Aside from the English and the Flemish houses' common use of the Augustine rule, the reasons for Woodford's choice of St. Ursula's are unknown. Probably her departure from England was connected with that of the Clement family, who also left about this time. A. W. Reed says that John Clement went abroad in July 1549 and that his wife followed in October, in response to publication of the first Edwardian prayerbook on June 9 of that year.[10] We know that the two youngest Clement children, Ursula and Margaret, were placed as students at St. Ursula's in April 1551, and the "Life" says it was on Woodford's recommendation, she "being the chiefest cause that the parents of our R[everend] M[other] Margaret Clement [caused her] to be placed in this monastery."[11] The account book of St. Ursula's shows that Woodford brought with her a small dowry "which yielded an annual revenue of thirty-three florins, still enjoyed by the Community till well on in the seventeenth century."[12]

---

[8] Typescript transcription of unpublished "Life," chapter 2.

[9] Wybren Scheepsma, *Medieval Religious Women in the Low Countries: The Modern Devotion, the Canonesses of Windesheim, and Their Writings* (Woodbridge, 2004), pp. 2–24.

[10] A. W. Reed, "John Clement and His Books," *The Library* 4th ser., 6 (1926), 329–39.

[11] Typescript transcription of unpublished "Life," chapter 2.

[12] C. S. Durrant, "A Link with a Pre-Reformation Monastery in England (Sister Elizabeth Woodford)," in *A Link between Flemish Mystics and English Martyrs* (New York, 1925), pp. 169–82 (p. 179, n. +), citing the archiepiscopal archives of Mechelin.

At St. Ursula's, Margaret Clement progressed from student to novice, and after she took the veil on October 11, 1557, Elizabeth Woodford acted informally as the young sister's mentor. The *Chronicle* reports that "being herself a very strict observer of regular discipline, [she] did well exercise our Margaret therein, and giving many mortifications, insomuch that she was accounted of the other religious in the House hard and cruel to her. And they did not keep that opinion only to themselves."[13] Sister Shirley's "Life" lets us hear the teacher's voice speaking sharply to the pupil:

> yet which grieved her most, was to hear the old English nun, sister Elizabeth whom she loved with great reverence and took all her words as coming from god. This nun I say after her common manner was always controlling her telling her in derision that she made a show outwardly of some feigned holiness which when examined was but mere hypocricy and in scorn said unto her, S[iste]r Margret you seem to be so holy that shortly we shall take your picture and set on the altar for a S[ain]t for it seemeth you would be accounted: These and such like words she must daily hear, all which she bore with exceeding great humility and patience.[14]

This seems remarkably harsh, yet it is clear that mistress's and pupil's temperaments were radically different, the former's grasp and competence challenged by the latter's remarkable simplicity, so pronounced that in her youth she was called (presumably by her family) "God almighty's fool." Elizabeth Shirley's "Life" says that as the family's youngest she was "the least esteemed of them all, being not so given to the world as the rest of the children and therefore accounted as simple."[15]

Despite these differences, it is possible to see Woodford's influence both on Clement's spirituality and on her later career as abbess. Writing about the young Clement's hesitancy to profess at St. Ursula's, her biographer says that she was dissatisfied with the spirit of the community.

> She saw good outward observances in order and manners, but it was the inward matter which she sought for, the which she herself knew not what it might be. Neither could she see it in any of the religious, but some little thereof in the superior … also in another religious which is named before who came out of England in king Harry's days.

Partial though this endorsement is, it suggests that for Margaret Clement, Elizabeth Woodward was the figure who most closely embodied a true religious spirit.[16]

---

[13] Hamilton, *Chronicle*, 1: 28.
[14] Typescript transcription of unpublished "Life," chapter 5.
[15] Typescript transcription of unpublished "Life," chapters 2 and 4.
[16] Typescript transcription of unpublished "Life," chapter 5.

Later, after Clement was elected superior of St. Ursula's, one of her first moves was to re-institute the practice of enclosure, a practice that had been neglected. Though she encountered opposition from the community, her emphasis on the practice was unremitting. She denied access to the cloister when the mother of one of her nuns was severely ill, and when the mother complained to the bishop, he merely smiled and wished he had many such superiors.[17] Surely it was Woodford's concern about violations of enclosure, shown in the Burnham visitations of 1521 and 1530, that bore fruit in her pupil's rule fifty years later.

One more record of Woodford's conversation is intriguing. She told Clement "that if ever she came into England, they should not admit of Abbesses in this Order, for the great abuses that she had seen to enter into religion thereby, and would probably be again introduced. But Prioresses were in England of far better observance of the Order."[18] She seems to be pointing to a difference in prestige or in wealth between the two religious ranks, and hence to be endorsing religious simplicity. She must have been recalling her own long-serving abbess at Burnham, Margaret Gibson, who was elected in 1507 and resigned in 1536.[19] Abbess Gibson's politics were certainly conservative: she was among those listed as having been told the visions and prophecies of Elizabeth Barton, the Nun of Kent, by the Observant friar Hugh Rich, later executed with Barton, and hence presumably she was sympathetic to the revelations.[20]

At the end of her life Woodford was remembered in the will of an exiled English cleric at Louvain. She and the two Clement sisters seem still to have constituted a recognized group of English nuns abroad. On September 7, 1572 the linguist and former Regius Professor of Hebrew at Oxford, Thomas Harding, bequeathed four dalders each "to the religious sisters in loven viz sister Elsabeth Wodforde, Margarete Clement, Dorothe Clement."[21] She died in the following month, on October 25, 1572, probably aged about seventy.[22] The impression of competence that Burnham's visitation records conveyed when she was young is confirmed by a detail

---

[17] Typescript transcription of unpublished "Life," chapter 7.
[18] Hamilton, *Chronicle*, I: 32.
[19] Smith, *Heads*, III: 632.
[20] *LP*, VI, no. 1468.
[21] Christian Coppens (ed.), *Reading in Exile: The Libraries of John Ramridge (d. 1568), Thomas Harding (d. 1572) and Henry Joliffe (d. 1573), Recusants in Louvain*, Libri Pertinentes no. 2 (Cambridge, 1993), p. 165. See also Henri de Vocht, "Thomas Harding," *English Historical Review* 35 (1920), 233–44.
[22] Hamilton, *Chronicle*, I: 31.

from the *Chronicle* toward the end of her life: "She was of so good a judgment that the Prioress of St. Ursula's would often ask her council and follow her advice in matters of moment."[23]

[23] Hamilton, *Chronicle*, I: 32.

Excerpt from Richard Whitford's sermon "On Detraction"

[Y2] This draft that followeth was a piece of a sermon that I spoke unto the people years ago, and because it was translated out of so holy a saint and so great a clerk, one of my brothers would needly have it sent forth with this foresaid work because it does agree with some articles therein contained. Take all unto the best, I pray you.

"Of Detraction," *from Dyvers holy instrucyons* (1541), (*STC* 25420), Y2–Y5v

The backbiter eateth the flesh of his brother. He gnaweth the flesh of his neighbor, whereof saint Paul says, "If ye gnaw and eat each other, beware ye be not among yourself consumed and destroyed." Thou backbiter, thou dost not fasten thy teeth in the bodily flesh of thy neighbor, but what is worse, thou hast wounded his name and fame, and over that thou hast infected and hurt thyself and many others with wounds innumerable. For the hearers be hurt and poisoned by the backbiting of the neighbor, willfully heard, and the same hearers, whether they be good persons or evil, have thereby occasion rather of evil than of good. For if they be evil, they (by the hearing of the evil of the neighbor) be more glad to do evil and to continue their sin. And if they be good persons, yet (by the hearing of that evil) [Y2v] they be tempted and moved to justify themselves and to despise their neighbor.

And yet furthermore, the backbiter hurteth not only the name or fame of him that he speaketh of, but also all others of his faculty and manner of living and oftimes of his country, as if he backbite a soldier, a merchant, or a priest, the hearers will not only grudge and take opinion against that soldier, that merchant or that priest alone, but also against all soldiers, all merchants, and all priests and likewise of the countries, as northern men, southern men, Welshmen, Irish men, Scots or Frenchmen.

And over all this, the backbiters causeth the glory of God to be blasphemed. For as by the good name and fame of every Christian the name of God is glorified, so by the evil name, is it blasphemed and dishonored. Thus the backbiter dishonoreth God, confoundeth and hurteth his neighbor, and rendreth himself guilty and worthy pain and punishment, since he medleth with maters that he hath nothing to do withal. And let no man say that he then only backbiteth when he sayth false of any person. For athough it be never so true, if it be evil and prively that he sayth, he backbiteth, he slandreth. For he showeth openly that before was done or said in private. And it (as I said) is always evil, and further (as seemeth by the words of this holy saint) to speak that thing that is openly known unto the rebuke or slander of any person is also detraction, as he putteth [Y3] example by the proud Pharisee that rebuketh the poor publican, which was openly known for a publican and yet went and departed the Pharisee, condemned in the sight of God and lost all his good works.

For if he would, or if any person will reform and correct the default of his neighbor or brother, the way and mean thereunto is not by detraction, by backbiting, by showing of his sin or trespass unto any other person, but rather by another mean, that is to say by the way of charity and brotherly compassion, remembering that they both be children of one father and both have offended and displeased him, and that he would do unto him as he would be done unto – weep for him, pray our lord for him with all thy whole heart, admonish and warn him gently, counsel him sadly, and exhort him devoutly to leave his sin and evil manners. So did saint Paul, saying unto the Corinthians after he had named many sins, I am afraid (sayeth he) lest when I come unto you almighty God will humble me that I shall mourn and wail for many that among you have done amiss. Thus should we show unto the misdoer charity, persuade him, counsel him, help to cure and amend him, and not defame nor yet vex him. Show him (as I said) his default gently, lovingly, meekly. And heartily entreat him to amend his manners and thus may we verily cure and help our brother. For so do physicians entreat the sick [Y3v] persons to take that meat or medicine that the sick is full loath to receive. So should we reform our neighbor and Christian brother, and never backbite him, nor show his sin.

Not only the speaker of detraction, but also the hearer thereof had need to beware and stop well his ears, remembering what the prophet sayeth "Detrahentem secreto proximo suo: hunc parsequebar." I did (sayeth he) pursue him that in privacy would backbite his neighbor. So should thou do, Christian, when thou hearest a backbiter. Say, if there be any person that he will justly praise: I will gladly hear, but if ye say evil by any person, I will stop mine ears, that water nor such filth shall not enter mine ears, water or any wet in the ears much annoyeth, I will none receive. I will not hear you.

What am I the better to hear and know that another man is evil? Much hurt and jeopardy of soul may come thereof, but never any virtue nor goodness. Speak unto the self person charitably, if he would amend him. Let us speak of our own matters. Let us remember what account we must make for our own sins, we shall not answer for his. Let us not therefore search the sins of other persons, but our own. For what excuse may we make unto our lord if we be curious and ready to spy and find the faults of other persons and nothing remember our own? None, surely. Is it not a rebuke for a stranger to look in every corner of another man's house where he hath [Y4] nought to do? Yes surely, sir. And more rebuke is it to search another person's life or acts. Notwithstanding here you must know that masters, sovereigns, and such persons as have charge of people by any office may (according unto the same) search the acts of other persons, and they be also bound thereto. But not to backbite them, but rather to reform them.

Well sir, say you, it is a pleasure to the backbiter to tell his tale and a pleasure for me to hear it, what shall I then do? Be not deceived, man. For all that is gay is not gold; sin seemeth sweet, but it is not so. For commonly, these backbiters when they have said evil they be weary of their own saying and oftimes they wish they had not so said. For the fear it should come out that they said and they be rebuked thereof, and make themselves (as often they do) of their friend a foe, and so is it also of the hearer that often wisheth he had not come in that company that day. It is not therefore pleasure that so fretteth a person and putteth him to pain. The wise man sayth, hast thou (sayth he) heard a tale? Keep it within thyself then, and let it die in thee. For believe me, it will not burst nor break thy belly. What is that to say? Let it die within thee, that is (sayth Chrysostom) quench thou it, bury it, let it never come forth, nor yet be moved nor signified by any mean of thee, but rather blame thou the backbiter and forget thou what thou heard. Put clean of thy mind what he said as if thou [Y4v] had never heard speak thereof. And so shall thou live in great peace and surety of conscience.

And if thou use to blame the backbiters and to threaten them that thou will tell the parties, thou may peradventure unto thy great merit bring them from that custom, or at the least thou shalt make them afraid to backbite in thy presence. For as well saying, laud and praise is a beginning and nourishing of amity, friendship and love, so evil saying is a beginning of hatred, discord, and debate. Bid therefore the backbiter look upon himself, it is an evil thing for any manner of persons to be curious and busy about other men's deeds and to search their lives and be negligent of themselves. But the backbiter hath no leisure to examine himself nor to search his own life, for looking upon other men's. For while he giveth so great diligence unto the curiosity of knowing upon other men's deeds, he must needs be negligent of his own. And that is a great folly. Since all the time a man may have is little enough and too little to search his own life, to recount his own sins. And if he ever be occupied with other men's matters, when shall he have leisure to cure and heal his own?

Beware now therefore Christians, of this breath. Beware of this pestilence that infecteth both parties: for doubtless it is the very assault of the devil, that we by the negligence of our own sins should be the more in his danger and our sins ever more grievous and more inexcusable. [Y5] For who so readily findeth his neighbor's default shall the more hardly obtain forgiveness for his own. For by the same judgment that we judge our neighbor, shall we of God be judged, and that appeareth by the gospel where our savior sayth: Nolite iudicare et non iudicabimini. That is to say: Have not you will nor consent to judge other persons and then shall not you be judged. For not only the sin of a person shall appear at the judgment as it was, but also it shall both seem and be much more grievous by the judgment that he made upon his neighbor. For as the meek, mild, and gentle heart by compassion of his neighbor in excusing his fault doth diminish and make less his own sin, so doth the cruel, envious stomach in judging and showing his neighbor's sin much multiply and make grievous his own sin.

Let us therefore, Christians, avoid and eschew all detraction and backbiting. And surely know that no penance nor good deeds may in this life avail us except we abstain from backbiting. For after the gospel those things that enter by the mouth do not defoul the person, but those things that do issue and pass out by the mouth do defoul and blemish the soul. If a person in thy presence should stir in dirt or any stinking matter, wouldst thou not blame and rebuke him? Yes, verily. So then do thou the backbiter. For I assure thee, no stink can so move and grieve thy [Y5v] smelling as detraction doth hurt the souls of the hearers. Avoid therefore and beware of backbiting. For the backbiting of thy neighbor is also the backbiting of God, his master and maker. And many backbiters have been so mad that from the backbiting of the neighbor they have fallen unto the blaspheming of God. Forsake therefore and flee this backbiting in any wise if you will flee sin and please God.

Bibliography

Aerts, Dirk, *Leuven in Books, Books in Leuven: The Oldest University of the Low Countries and Its Library* (Leuven, 1999)

Ampe, Albert (ed.), *Dictionnaire de Spiritualité Ascetique et Mystique* ... (Paris, 1960)

Andersson, Roger and Stephen Borgehammar, "The Preaching of the Bridgettine Friars at Vadstena Abbey (ca. 1380–1515)," *Revue Mabillon* n.s. 8 (1997), 209–36

Anstruther, Godfrey, *A Hundred Homeless Years: English Dominicans 1558–1658* (London, 1958)

Archer, Ian, "John Stow, Citizen and Historian," in Gadd and Gillespie (eds.), *John Stow* (London, 2004), pp. 13–26

Bale, John, *Select Works of John Bale*, edited by Henry Christmas, Parker Society (Cambridge, 1849)

Yet a Course at the Romish Fox (Zurich, 1543)

Barratt, Alexandra, *Anne Bulkeley and Her Book: Fashioning Female Piety in Early Tudor England – A Study of London, British Library, MS Harley 494* (Turnhout, 2009)

Barron, Caroline M., *London in the Later Middle Ages: Government and People 1200–1500* (Oxford, 2004)

"The Parish Fraternities of Medieval London," in C. M. Barron and C. Harper-Bill (eds.), *The Church in Pre-Reformation Society* (Woodbridge, 1985), pp. 13–37

Barron, Caroline M. and Matthew Davies (eds.), *The Religious Houses of London and Middlesex*, Centre for Metropolitan History (London, 2007)

Baskerville, G., "A Sister of Archbishop Cranmer," *English Historical Review* 51 (1936), 287–89

Bateson, Mary (ed.), "A Collection of Original Letters from the Bishops to the Privy Council, 1564," *Camden Miscellany* 9 (London, 1893)

Beaven, Alfred B., *The Aldermen of the City of London temp. Henry III–1908*, 2 vols. (London, 1911–12)

Bell, David N., *What Nuns Read: Books and Libraries in Medieval English Nunneries* (Kalamazoo, MI, 1995)

Bellenger, Aidan, *English and Welsh Priests, 1558–1800* (Bath, 1984)

Benzing, J., *Die Buchdrucker des 16. und 17. Jahrhunderet in deutschen Sprachgebiet* (Frankfurt, 1963)

Bindoff, S. T., *The House of Commons 1509–1558*, 3 vols. (London, 1982)

Birrell, T. A., *English Monarchs and Their Books from Henry VIII to Charles II: The Panizzi Lectures 1986* (London, 1987)

"The Printed Books of Dame Margaret Nicollson: A Pre-Reformation Collection," in J. Bakker, J. A. Verleun, and J. v. d. Vriesenaerde (eds.), *Essays on English and American Literature and a Sheaf of Poems, Presented to David Wilkinson* (Amsterdam, 1987), pp. 27–33

Blench, J. W., *Preaching in England in the Late Fifteenth and Sixteenth Centuries: A Study of English Sermons 1450–1600* (New York, 1964)

Blosius, Ludovicus, *A Mirror for Monks (Speculum Monachorum) by Ludovicus Blosius* (New York, 1926)

Bobrick, Benson, *Wide as the Waters: The Story of the English Bible and the Revolution It Inspired* (New York, 2001)

Bowers, John M., "*Piers Plowman* and the Police: Notes Toward a History of the Wycliffite Langland," *Yearbook of Langland Studies* 61 (1992), 1–50

Bowker, Margaret, *The Henrician Reformation: The Diocese of Lincoln under John Longland 1521–1547* (Cambridge, 1981)

Brigden, Susan, *London and the Reformation* (Oxford, 1989)

"Thomas Cromwell and the 'Brethren'," in C. Cross, D. Loades, and J. J. Scarisbrick (eds.), *Law and Government under the Tudors: Essays Presented to Sir Geoffrey Elton* (Cambridge, 1988), pp. 31–49

Broadway, Jan, "Unreliable Witness: Sir William Dugdale and the Perils of Autobiography," in Christopher Dyer and Catherine Richardson (eds.), *Wiliam Dugdale, Historian, 1605–1686: His Life, His Writings, and His County* (Woodbridge, 2009), pp. 34–50

Brodrick, James, *The Progress of the Jesuits (1556–79)* (New York, 1947)

St. Peter Canisius SJ 1521–1597 (New York, 1935)

Brou, Alexander, *Ignatian Methods of Prayer* (Milwaukee, 1949)

Brown, Keith, "The Friars Observants in England 1482–1559," PhD dissertation (University of Oxford, 1987)

Brown, Nancy Pollard, "Paperchase: The Dissemination of Catholic Texts in Elizabethan England," *English Manuscript Studies 1100–1700* (1989), 120–43

Calendar of State Papers, Domestic Series 1566–79, Addenda (London, 1871)

Calendar of State Papers, Domestic Series 1581–90, vol. CLXXXVII (London, 1865)

Caraman, P. G. "An English Monastic Reformer of the Sixteenth Century," *Clergy Review* 28.1 (1947), 1–16

Card, Tim, *Eton Established: A History from 1440 to 1860* (London, 2001)

Castin, W. C., *The History of St. John's College Oxford 1598–1860* (Oxford, 1958)

Chaix, Gérard, "Sainte-Barbe, Cologne, et l'empire du xvi° siècle," *Analecta Cartusiana* 83.III, *Die Kartäuser in Österreich* (1980–81)

Chambers, D. S., *Faculty Office Registers 1534–1549* (Oxford, 1966)

Cheetham, Francis, *English Medieval Alabasters* (Oxford, 1984)

Chester, Allen G., *Hugh Latimer, Apostle to the English* (Philadelphia, 1954)

Chibi, Andrew A., *Henry VIII's Conservative Scholar: Bishop John Stokesley and the Divorce, Royal Supremacy and Doctrinal Reform* (Bern, 1997)

Chrysostom, John, "The Homilies on the Statutes," trans. W. R. W. Stephens, in Philip Schaff (ed.), *A Select Library of the Nicene and Post-Nicene Fathers, vol. IX: St. Chrysostom: On the Priesthood; Ascetic Treatises, Select Homilies and Letters, Homilies on the Statutes* (Grand Rapids, MI, 1956)

Clark, John (ed.), *Father Augustine Baker: Directions for Contemplation: Book H* (Salzburg, 2000)

Clark, Peter, *English Provincial Society from the Reformation to the Revolution: Religion, Politics and Society in Kent 1500–1640* (Cranbury, NJ, 1977)

Clay, Rotha Mary, "Further Studies on Medieval Recluses," *Journal of the British Archaeological Association* 3rd ser., 16 (1953), 74–86
    The Hermits and Anchorites of England (London, 1914)

Coates, Alan, *English Medieval Books: The Reading Abbey Collections from Foundation to Dispersal* (Oxford, 1999)

Cognet, Louis, *Post-Reformation Spirituality* (New York, 1959)

Coldicott, Diana, *Hampshire Nunneries* (Chichester, 1989)

Collis, Jennifer Mary, "The Anchorites of London in the Later Middle Ages," MA thesis (University of London, 1992)

Connelly, John Patrick (ed. and trans.), *Year by Year with the Early Jesuits (1532–1556): Selections from the "Chronicon" of Juan de Polanco, S.J.* (St. Louis, 2009)

Cook, G. H. (ed.), *Letters to Cromwell and Others on the Suppression of the Monasteries* (London, 1965)

Coppens, Christian, *Reading in Exile: The Libraries of John Ramridge (d. 1568), Thomas Harding (d. 1572) and Henry Joliffe (d. 1573), Recusants in Louvain*, Libri Pertinentes no. 2 (Cambridge, 1993)

Councer, C. R., "The Dissolution of the Kentish Monasteries," *Archaeologia Cantiana* 47 (1935), 126–43

Crosignani, G., Thomas M. McCoog, and Michael Questier (eds.), *Recusancy and Conformity in Early Modern England: Manuscript and Printed Sources in Translation* (Rome, 2010)

Cross, Claire, "The End of Medieval Monasticism in the North Riding of Yorkshire," *Yorkshire Archaeological Journal* 78 (2006)

Crowley, Robert, *The Select Works of Robert Crowley*, ed. J. M. Cowper, EETS ES 15 (London, 1872)

Cunich, Peter, "The Brothers of Syon, 1420–1695," in Jones and Walsham (eds.), *Syon Abbey* (Woodbridge, 2010), pp. 39–81

Da Costa, Alexandra, "John Fewterer's *Myrrour or Glasse of Christes Passion* and Ulrich Pinder's *Speculum passionis domini nostri*," *Notes and Queries* 56 (2009), 27–29

Darlington, Ida (ed.), *London Consistory Court Wills 1492–1547*, London Record Society 3 (London, 1967)

Davies, Matthew (ed.), *The Merchant Taylors' Company of London: Court Minutes 1486–1493* (Stamford, 2000)

Davis, E. Jeffries, "The Beginning of the Dissolution: Christchurch Aldgate, 1532," *Transactions of the Royal Historical Society* 4th ser., 8 (1925), 127–50

De la Mare, Albinia (ed.), *Catalogue of the Collection of Medieval Manuscripts Bequeathed to the Bodleian Library, Oxford, by James P. R. Lyell* (Oxford, 1971)

De Moreau, E., *Histoire de L'Eglise en Belgique*, 6 vols. (Brussels, 1945–52)

Deneef, Alain and Xavier Dusausoit, *Les Jesuites Belges 1542–1992: 450 ans Le Compagnie de Jesus dans les provinces belgiques* (Brussels, 1992)

De Vocht, Henri, *History of the Foundation and the Rise of the Collegium Trilingue Lovaniense, 1517–1550*, 4 vols. (Louvain, 1955)

"Thomas Harding," *English Historical Review* 35 (1920), 233–44

Dickens, A. G., "The Last Medieval Englishman," in Peter Brooks (ed.), *Christian Spirituality, Essays in Honour of Gordon Rupp* (London, 1975), pp. 143–81

Thomas Cromwell and the English Reformation (New York, 1959)

Tudor Treatises, Yorkshire Record Series 125 (Wakefield, 1959)

Dionysius Carthusiensis, *Dionysii Cartusiensis Opera Selecta.*, ed. Kent Emery, Corpus Christianorum Continuatio Medievalis, vols. CXXI and CXXI(A) (Turnhout, 1991)

Doctoris ecstatic D. Dionysii cartusiana Opera Omnia (Montreuil, 1896–1901; Tournai, 1902–13; Parkminster, 1935)

Doyle, A. I., "Books Connected with the Vere Family and Barking Abbey," *Transactions of the Essex Archaeological Society* n.s. 25 (1958), 222–43

Dugdale, William, *Monasticon Anglicanum*, 8 vols. (London, 1817–30)

Durrant, C. S., *A Link between Flemish Mystics and English Martyrs* (New York, 1925)

Earwacker, J. P., *East Cheshire: Past and Present*, 2 vols. (London, 1877)

Eire, Carlos, "Early Modern Catholic Piety in Translation," in Peter Burke and R. Po-chia Hsia (eds.), *Cultural Translation in Early Modern Europe* (Cambridge, 2007), pp. 83–100

Ellis, Henry, "Account of the Convent of English Nuns Formerly Settled at Louvain, in South Brabant: In a Letter Addressed to the President," *Archaeologia* 36 (1855), 74–77

(ed.), *Original Letters Illustrative of English History*, 4 vols. (London, 1846)

Elton, G. R., *Policy and Police: The Enforcement of the Reformation in the Age of Thomas Cromwell* (Cambridge, 1972)

Reform and Renewal: Thomas Cromwell and the Common Weal (Cambridge, 1973)

Emden, A. B., *A Biographical Register of the University of Oxford AD 1500 to 1540* (Oxford, 1974)

A Survey of Dominicans in England Based on the Ordination Lists in Episcopal Registers (1268–1538), Dissertationes Historicae Fascicules 18 (Rome, 1967)

Erler, Mary C., "The Abbess of Malling's Gift Manuscript (1520)," in Felicity Riddy (ed.), *Prestige, Authority and Power in Late Medieval Manuscripts and Texts* (York, 2000), pp. 147–57

"Bishop Richard Fox's Manuscript Gifts to His Winchester Nuns: A Second Surviving Example," *JEH* 52 (2001), 1–4

"A London Anchorite: Simon Appulby, His *Fruyte of Redempcyon* and Its Milieu," *Viator* 29 (1998), 227–39

"Religious Women after the Dissolution: Continuing Community," in Matthew Davies and Andrew Prescott (eds.), *London and the Kingdom: Essays in Honour of Caroline M. Barron*, Harlaxton Medieval Studies 16 (Donington, 2008), pp. 135–45

Women, Reading, and Piety in Late Medieval England (Cambridge, 2002)

Faulkner, Thomas, *An Historical and Topographical Description of Chelsea and Its Environs*, 2 vols. (Chelsea, 1829)

Fletcher, John Rory, *The Story of the English Bridgettines of Syon Abbey* (South Brent, Devon, 1933)

Fonseca, J. M. R., *Annales Minorum*, ed. L. Wadding, 3rd edn., 17 vols. (Rome, 1931–35)

Foster, Joseph, *Alumni Oxonienses, Vol. III: Early Series (1500–1714)* (Liechtenstein, reprint edn., 1968)

Freeman, Thomas, "'The Good Ministrye of Godlye and Vertuouse Women': The Elizabethan Martyrologists and the Female Supporters of the Marian Martyrs," *Journal of British Studies* 39 (2000), 8–33

Gadd, Ian and Alexandra Gillespie (eds.), *John Stow (1525–1605) and the Making of the English Past: Studies in Early Modern Culture and the History of the Book* (London, 2004)

Gairdner, James, *Lollardy and the Reformation in England: An Historical Survey*, 4 vols. (London, 1908)

Gasquet, Francis Aiden, *Henry VIII and English Monasticism* (London, 1935)

Gee, John Archer (ed.), *The Life and Works of Thomas Lupset* (New Haven, CT, 1928)

Gillespie, Alexandra, "Stow's 'Owlde' Manuscripts of London Chronicles," in Gadd and Gillespie (eds.), *John Stow* (London, 2004), pp. 57–67

Gillespie, Vincent (ed.), *Syon Abbey, with The Libraries of the Carthusians*, ed. A. I. Doyle, Corpus of British Medieval Library Catalogues 9 (London, 2001)

Gillow, Joseph (ed.), *Biographical Dictionary of English Catholics*, 5 vols. (London, 1885)

Goodrich, Margaret, "Westwood, A Rural English Nunnery with Its Local and French Connections," in Joan Greatrex (ed.), *The Vocation of Service to God and Neighbor* (Turnhout, 1993), pp. 43–57

Greatrex, Joan, "On Ministering to 'Certayne Devoute and Religiouse Women': Bishop Fox and the Benedictine Nuns of Winchester Diocese on the Eve of the Dissolution," in W. J. Sheils and Diane Wood (eds.), *Women in the Church* (Oxford, 1990), pp. 223–35

Green, M. A. E. W. (ed.), *Letters of Royal and Illustrious Ladies of Great Britain*, 3 vols. (London, 1846)

Greengrass, Mark, "Two Sixteenth-Century Religious Minorities and Their Scribal Networks," in H. Schilling and I. G. Toth (eds.), *Cultural Exchange in Early Modern Europe, Vol. I: Religious and Cultural Exchange in Europe, 1400–1700* (Cambridge, 2006), pp. 317–37

Haigh, Christopher, *The English Reformation Revised* (Cambridge, 1987)

Hallen, A. W. Cornelius (ed.), *The Registers of St Botolph, Bishopsgate London*, 3 vols. (London, 1889, 1893, 1895)

Hallett, Nicky (ed.), *English Convents in Exile, 1600–1800, Volume 3: Life Writing* (London, 2012)

  Lives of Spirit: English Carmelite Self-Writing of the Early Modern Period (Aldershot, 2007)

Halvorson, Jon Derek, "Religio and Reformation: Johannes Justus Lansperger … and the Sixteenth-Century Religious Question," PhD dissertation (Loyola University, 2008)

Haren, Michael J. (ed.), *Calendar of Entries in the Papal Registers Relating to Great Britain and Ireland: Papal Letters, Vol. XV, 1484–1492* (Dublin, 1978)

Haude, Sigrun, *In the Shadow of "Savage Wolves": Anabaptist Munster and the German Reformation during the 1530s* (Boston, Leiden, Cologne, 2000)

  "The Silent Monks Speak Up: The Changing Identity of the Carthusians in the Fifteenth and Sixteenth Centuries," *Archiv für Reformationgeschichte* 86 (1995), 134–40

Hamilton, Adam, *The Angel of Syon* (Edinburgh, 1905)

  (ed.), *The Chronicle of the English Augustinian Canonesses Regular of the Lateran at St. Monica's in Louvain*, 2 vols. (Edinburgh, 1904–06)

Hamper, William, *The Life, Diary, and Correspondence of Sir William Dugdale* (London, 1828)

Harben, Henry A., *Dictionary of London* (London, 1918)

Harline, Craig, *The Burdens of Sister Margaret: Inside a Seventeenth-Century Convent*, abridged edition (New Haven, CT, 2001)

Harper-Bill, Christopher (ed.), *Register of John Morton, Archbishop of Canterbury 1486–1500*, vol. I, Canterbury and York Society 75 (Leeds, 1987)

Harris, Oliver, "Stow and the Contemporary Antiquarian Network," in Gadd and Gillespie (eds.), *John Stow* (London, 2004), pp. 27–35

Hasler, P. M., *The House of Commons (1558–1603)*, 3 vols. (London, 1981)

Hasted, Edward, *The History and Topographical Survey of the County of Kent*, 12 vols. (London, reprint edn., 1998)

Heale, Martin, "'Not a Thing for a Stranger to Enter Upon': The Selection of Monastic Superiors in Late Medieval and Tudor England," in Janet Burton and Karen Stover (eds.), *Monasteries and Society in the British Isles in the Later Middle Ages* (Woodbridge, 2008), pp. 51–68

Heinze, R. W. (ed.), *Proclamations of the Tudor Kings* (Cambridge, 1976)

Hendricks, L., *The London Charterhouse: Its Monks and Martyrs* (London, 1889)

Hennessy, George, *Novum Repertorium Ecclesiasticum Parochiale Londinense* (London, 1898)

Hitchcock, E. V. (ed.), *The Life and Death of Sir Thomas More*, EETS OS 186 (London and Oxford, 1932)

Hodgett, Gerald A. J. (ed.), *The Cartulary of Holy Trinity, Aldgate*, London Record Society 7 (London, 1971)

  "The Unpensioned Ex-Religious in Tudor England," *JEH* 13 (1962), 195–202

Hogg, James, "Richard Whytford," in James Hogg (ed.), *Studies in Saint Birgitta and the Brigittine Order*, 2 vols. (Salzburg, 1993), II: 254–66

(ed.), *Richard Whitford's The Pype or Tonne of the Lyfe of Perfection*, 5 vols., Salzburg Studies in English Literature: Elizabethan and Renaissance Studies 89 (Salzburg, 1979–89)

Horst, Irwin Buckwalter, *The Radical Brethren, Anabaptism and the English Reformation to 1558* (Nieuwkoop, 1972)

Horstmann, C. (ed), *Yorkshire Writers: Richard Rolle of Hampole, an English Father of the Church, and His Followers*, 2 vols. (London, 1895–96)

Houlbrooke, Ralph, *Church Courts and the People during the English Reformation 1520–1570* (Oxford, 1979)

Howlett, R. (ed.), *Monumenta Franciscana*, 2 vols., Rolls Series (London, 1882)

Hudleston, Roger (ed.), *A Mirror for Monks (Speculum Monachorum) by Ludovicus Blosius* (New York, 1926)

Hughes, Paul L. and James F. Larkin (eds.), *Tudor Royal Proclamations*, 3 vols. (New Haven, CT and London, 1964–69)

Hughes-Edwards, Mari, "Anchoritism: The English Tradition," in Liz Herbert McAvoy (ed.), *Anchoritic Traditions of Medieval Europe* (Woodbridge, 2010), pp. 131–52

Hugo, Thomas, "The Hospital of Le Papey in the City of London," *Transactions of the London and Middlesex Archaeological Society* 5 (1881), 183–221

Hunter, Joseph, "Appendix II – A Catalogue of the Deeds of Surrender…" in *Eighth Report of the Deputy Keeper of the Public Records* (London, 1847)

Hutchison, Ann M., "Syon Abbey Preserved: Some Historians of Syon," in Jones and Walsham (eds.), *Syon Abbey* (Woodbridge, 2010), pp. 228–51

"What the Nuns Read," *Mediaeval Studies* 57 (1995), 205–22

Jack, Sibyl, "Dissolution Dates for Monasteries Dissolved under the Act of 1536," *Bulletin of the Institute for Historical Research* 43 (1970), 161–81

"The Last Days of the Smaller Monasteries in England," *JEH* 21 (1970), 97–124

James, M. R. (ed.), *Catalogue of the Manuscripts of Emmanuel College Cambridge* (Cambridge, 1904)

James, N. W. and V. A. James (eds.), *The Bede Roll of the Fraternity of St. Nicholas*, 2 vols., London Record Society 39 (London, 2004)

Jamison, Catherine, "Notes on Jesus Commons," *Notes and Queries* 173 (1937), 92–93

Jolliffe, P. S., *A Check-List of Middle English Prose Writings of Spiritual Guidance* (Toronto, 1974)

Jones, E. A. and Alexandra Walsham (eds.), *Syon Abbey and Its Books, Reading, Writing and Religion c. 1400–1700* (Woodbridge, 2010)

Jones, Philip E. (ed.), *Calendar of Plea and Memoranda Rolls Preserved among the Archives of the Corporation of the City of London at the Guildhall A.D. 1458–1482*, 6 vols. (Cambridge, 1961)

Jordan, W. K., *Edward VI: The Threshold of Power, The Dominance of the Duke of Northumberland* (London, 1970)

Edward VI, The Young King: The Protectorship of the Duke of Somerset (Cambridge, MA, 1968)

Ker, N. R. *Medieval Manuscripts in British Libraries*, 4 vols. (Oxford, 1969–92)

King, John N., *English Reformation Literature: The Tudor Origins of the Protestant Tradition* (Princeton, NJ, 1982)

King, John N. and Mark Rankin, "Print, Patronage and the Reception of Continental Reform: 1520–1603," *Yearbook of English Studies* 38 (2008), 49–67

Kingsford, C. L., "Additional Material for the History of the Grey Friars, London," *Collectanea Franciscana II*, British Society for Franciscan Studies 10 (Aberdeen, 1922)

  English Historical Literature in the Fifteenth Century (New York, reprint edn., 1972)

  The Grey Friars of London (Aberdeen, 1915)

  John Stow's Survey of London (Oxford, 1971)

Kirby, T. F., *Annals of Winchester College* (London, 1892)

Kirchberger, Claire, *Spiritual Exercises of a Dominican Friar* (New York, 1929)

Kitching, C. J. (ed.), *London and Middlesex Chantry Certificate 1548*, London Record Society 16 (London, 1986)

Knowles, David, "The Case of St. Albans Abbey in 1490," *JEH* 3 (1952), 144–58

  The Religious Orders in England, Vol. III: The Tudor Age (Cambridge, 1961)

Knowles, David and R. Neville Hadcock, *Medieval Religious Houses: England and Wales* (London, 1971)

Kollock, Margaret R., *The Lord Mayor and Aldermen of London during the Tudor Period* (Philadelphia, 1906)

Lang, R. G. (ed.), *Two Tudor Subsidy Assessment Rolls for the City of London: 1541 and 1582*, London Record Society 29 (London, 1993)

Latimer, Hugh, *Sermons and Remains of Hugh Latimer*, ed. George Elwes Corrie, Parker Society, 2 vols. (Cambridge, 1845)

Lawrence, Veronica (ed.), *Richard Whytford: A Looking Glace for the Religious*, vol. I, Salzburg Studies in English Literature: Elizabethan and Renaissance Studies 92.18, 3 vols. (Salzburg, 1979)

  "Syon MS 18 and the Medieval English Mystical Tradition," in Marion Glasscoe (ed.), *The Medieval Mystical Tradition in England, Exeter Symposium V, 1992* (Woodbridge, 1992), pp. 145–62

Lee, Paul, *Nunneries, Learning and Spirituality in Late Medieval English Society: The Dominican Priory of Dartford* (York, 2001)

Lehmberg, Stanford E., *The Reformation Parliament 1529–1536* (Cambridge, 1970)

Lempriere, William (ed.), *John Howes' MS., 1582* (London, 1904)

Brewer, J. S. *et al.* (eds.), *Letters and Papers, Foreign and Domestic, of the Reign of Henry VIII*, 22 vols. (London, 1862–1932)

Lewis, Flora, "'Garnished with Gloryous Tytles': Indulgences in Printed Books of Hours in England," *Transactions of the Cambridge Bibliographical Society* 10 (1995), 577–90

Little, A. G., *The Grey Friars in Oxford* (Oxford, 1892)

Littledale, Willoughby A. (ed.), *The Registers of Christ Church, Newgate, 1538 to 1754*, Harleian Society Registers 21 (London, 1895)

Liveing, H. G., *Records of Romsey Abbey* (Winchester, 1906)

Loades, David M., *The Reign of Mary Tudor* (New York, 1979)

Lobel, M. D., *British Atlas of Historic Towns, Vol. III: The City of London from Prehistoric Times to c.1520* (Oxford, 1989)

London County Council, *Survey of London, Vol. XXVII: Spitalfields* (London, 1957)

Machyn, Henry, *A London Provisioner's Chronicle, 1556–1563 by Henry Machyn*, ed. Richard W. Bailey, Marilyn Miller, and Colette Moore, online: http://quod.lib.umich.edu/m/machyn

McConica, James, "The Catholic Experience in Tudor Oxford," in Thomas M. McCoog (ed.), *The Reckoned Expense: Edmund Campion and the Early English Jesuits* (Turnhout, 1996), pp. 39–63

MacCulloch, Diarmaid, "Protestantism in Mainland Europe: New Directions," *Renaissance Quarterly* 59.3 (2006), 698–706

Thomas Cranmer: A Life (New Haven, 1996)

Tudor Church Militant: Edward VI and the Protestant Reformation (London, 2001)

McCutcheon, Elizabeth, "A Mid-Tudor Owner of More's *Utopia*, Sir William More," *Moreana* 18 (1981), 32–35

McLaren, Colin A., "An Edition of Foxford, A Vicars'-General Book of the Diocese of London 1521–1539, ff. 161–268," M.Phil. thesis (University of London, 1973)

McLaren, Mary-Rose, *The London Chronicles of the Fifteenth Century: A Revolution in English Writing* (Cambridge, 2002)

Manzione, Carol Kazmierczak, *Christ's Hospital of London, 1552–1598* (Selinsgrove, 1995)

Marks, Richard B., *The Medieval Monastic Library of the Charterhouse of St. Barbara in Cologne*, 2 vols., Analecta Carthusiana 21, 22 (Salzburg, 1974)

Marshall, Peter, *Reformation England 1480–1642* (London, 2003)

Religious Identities in Henry VIII's England (Aldershot, 2006)

Mayer, Thomas F. (ed.), *The Correspondence of Reginald Pole*, 4 vols. (Aldershot, 2002–08)

The History of the University of Oxford III: The Collegiate University (Oxford, 1986)

Reginald Pole, Prince and Prophet (Cambridge, 2000)

Mayr-Harting, Henry, "The Functions of a Twelfth-Century Recluse," *History* 60 (1975), 337–52

Meale, Carol M., "The Miracles of Our Lady: Context and Interpretation," in Derek Pearsall (ed.), *Studies in the Vernon Manuscript* (Woodbridge, 1990), pp. 115–36

Mendyk, Stan A. E., *"Speculum Britanniae": Regional Study, Antiquarianism and Science in Britain to 1770* (Toronto, 1989)

Merriman, R. B. (ed.), *The Life and Letters of Thomas Cromwell*, 2 vols. (Oxford, 1968)

Moore, Norman, *The History of St. Bartholomew's Hospital*, 2 vols. (London, 1918)

Moorman, John R. H., *The Grey Friars in Cambridge 1225–1538* (Cambridge, 1952)

Medieval Franciscan Houses, 2 vols. (St. Bonaventure, NY, 1983)

More, John, "Extracts from the Private Account Book of Sir William More, of Loseley, in Surrey, in the Time of Queen Mary and of Queen Elizabeth," *Archaeologia* 36.2 (1855), 284–310

Morris, John (ed.), *The Troubles of Our Catholic Forefathers Related by Themselves*, 1st ser., 2 vols. (London, 1872–75)

Mulder-Bakker, Anneke B., *Lives of the Anchoresses: The Rise of the Urban Recluse in Medieval Europe* (Philadelphia, 2005)

Muller, J. A., *Stephen Gardiner and the Tudor Reaction* (New York, 1926)

Munk, William, *The Roll of the Royal College of Physicians of London*, 2nd edn., 5 vols. (London, 1878)

Neame, Alan, *The Holy Maid of Kent: The Life of Elizabeth Barton, 1506–1534* (London, 1971)

Newcourt, Robert, *Repertorium Ecclesiasticum parochiale Londinense* (London, 1716)

Nichols, J. G. (ed.), *Grey Friars of London Chronicle*, Camden Society 53 (London, 1852)

Nichols, J. G. and John Bruce (eds.), *Wills from Doctors' Commons*, Camden Society 83 (Westminster, 1863)

O'Malley, John W., *The First Jesuits* (Cambridge, MA, 1993)

Overall, W. H. and H. C. Overall, *Analytical Index to the Series of Records Known as the Remembrancia … City of London AD 1579–1664 in the Library of the Guildhall* (London, 1878)

Overell, M. A., "Bernardino Ochino's Books and English Religious Opinion 1547–80," in R. N. Swanson (ed.), *The Church and the Book, Studies in Church History* 38 (Woodbridge, 2004), pp. 201–11

Palmer, C. F. R., "History of the Priory of Dartford, in Kent," *Archaeological Journal* 36 (1879), 241–71

Paul, John, "Dame Elizabeth Shelley, Last Abbess of St. Mary's Abbey, Winchester," *Papers and Proceedings of the Hampshire Field Club and Archaeological Society* 23.2 (1965), 60–71

Paxton, Catherine, "The Nunneries of London and Its Environs in the Later Middle Ages," PhD dissertation (University of Oxford, 1992)

Pelling, Margaret and Charles Webster, "Medical Practitioners," in Charles Webster (ed.), *Health, Medicine and Morality in the Sixteenth Century* (Cambridge, 1979), pp. 165–235

Pelling, Margaret and Frances White, *Physicians and Irregular Medical Practitioners in London 1550–1640* (2004), online: www.british-history.ac.uk

Philpot, John, *The Examinations and Writings of John Philpot, BCL*, ed. Robert Eden, Parker Society 34 (Cambridge, 1842)

Piccope, G. J. (ed.), *Lancashire and Cheshire Wills and Inventories from the Ecclesiastical Court, Chester*, Chetham Society 33 (Manchester, 1851)

Polanco, Juan de, *Year by Year with the Early Jesuits (1532–1556): Selections from the "Chronicle" of Juan de Polanco, S.J.*, trans. John Patrick Donnelly, SJ (St. Louis, 2009)

Pollard, A. F., *Records of the English Bible* (London, 1911)

Power, Eileen, *Medieval English Nunneries c. 1275 to 1535* (Cambridge, 1922)

Powell, Susan, "Preaching at Syon Abbey," *Leeds Studies in English* n.s. 31 (2000), 229–67

Raymo, Robert, "Works of Religious and Philosophical Instruction," in Albert E. Hartung (ed.), *A Manual of the Writings in Middle English 1050–1500, vol. VII* (New Haven, 1986), pp. 2467–582

Reed, A. W., "John Clement and His Books," *The Library* 4th ser., 6 (1926), 320–39

Rex, Richard, "The English Campaign against Luther in the 1520s," *Transactions of the Royal Historical Society* 39 (1989), 85–106

"The Friars in the English Reformation," in Peter Marshall and Alec Ryrie (eds.), *The Beginnings of English Protestantism* (Cambridge, 2002), pp. 38–59

The Theology of John Fisher (Cambridge, 1991)

Rhodes, J. T., "Abbot Blosius and Father Baker," in Geoffrey Scott (ed.), *Dom Augustine Baker 1575–1641* (Leominster, 2012), pp. 133–52

"Dom Augustine Baker's Reading Lists," *Downside Review* 111 (July 1993), 157–73

"Private Devotion in England on the Eve of the Reformation," PhD dissertation (University of Durham, 1975)

"Religious Instruction at Syon in the Early Sixteenth Century," in James Hogg (ed.), *Studies in St. Birgitta and the Brigittine Order*, 2 vols. (Salzburg, 1993), II: 151–69

"Syon Abbey and Its Religious Publications in the Sixteenth Century," *JEH* 44 (1993), 11–25

Riley, H. T. (ed.), *Chronica monasterii St. Albani*, Rolls Ser. 28, pt. 6, vol. II (London, 1873)

Robertson, Mary L. "'The Art of the Possible': Thomas Cromwell's Management of West Country Government," *Historical Journal* 32 (1989), 793–816

Robinson, Hastings (ed.), *Original Letters Relative to the English Reformation*, 2 vols., Parker Society (London, 1847)

Rosenfield, Manuel C., "Holy Trinity, Aldgate, on the Eve of the Dissolution," *Guildhall Miscellany* 3 (1970), 159–73

Rousseau, Marie Hélène, *Saving the Souls of Medieval London: Perpetual Chantries at St. Paul's Cathedral c.1200–1548* (Farnham, 2011)

Ryan, Patrick, "Diocesan Returns of Recusants for England and Wales, 1577," *Miscellanea XII*, Catholic Record Society 22 (London, 1921)

Ryckes, John, *The Image of Love*, in *The Complete Works of St. Thomas More*, vol. VI, pt. 2, Appendix A, ed. E. Ruth Harvey (New York and London, 1981)

Rymer, Thomas, *Foedera, conventiones, literae et cujuscunque generis acta publica inter reges Angliae*, 3rd edn. (1741)

Sander Olsen, Ulla, "De kroniek van Abdis Marie van Oss, Maria Troon, Dendermonde [text edition]," in *Oudheidkundige Kring van het Land van Dendermonde*, Gedenkschriften R. 4:21 (Jaarboek, 2000), pp. 250–332

"The Late Medieval Chronicle of Marie Van Oss, Abbess of the Brigittine Monastery Maria Troon in Dendermonde, 1466–1507," in Erik Kooper (ed.), *The Medieval Chronicle: Proceedings of the 1st International Conference on the Medieval Chronicle, Dreibergen/Utrecht 13–16 July 1996* (Amsterdam, 1999), pp. 240–50

Sargent, Michael (ed.), *Nicholas Love's Mirror of the Blessed life of Jesus Christ: A Critical Edition Based on Cambridge University Library Additional MSS 6578 and 6686* (New York, 1992)

Scarisbrick, J. J., *Henry VIII* (Berkeley, 1968)

Scheepsma, Wybren, *Medieval Religious Women in the Low Countries: The Modern Devotion, the Canonesses of Windesheim, and Their Writings* (Woodbridge, 2004)

Scott, Kathleen L., *Later Gothic Manuscripts 1390–1490*, 2 vols. (London, 1996)

Shagan, Ethan H. (ed.), *Catholics and the "Protestant Nation": Religious Politics and Identity in Early Modern England* (Manchester, 2005)
Popular Politics and the English Reformation (Cambridge, 2003)

Sharpe, Kevin, *Sir Robert Cotton 1586–1630: History and Politics in Early Modern England* (Oxford, 1979)

Sharpe, Reginald R. (ed.), *Calendar of Letter Books … L: temp. Edward IV–Henry VI* (London, 1912)

Shirley, Elizabeth, "Life of Mother Margaret Clement," typescript copy of original manuscript held at Priory of Our Blessed Lady of Nazareth, Bruges

Simons, Walter, *Cities of Ladies: Beguine Communities in the Medieval Low Countries, 1200–1565* (Philadelphia, 2001)

Sisson, C. J., "Grafton and the London Grey Friars," *The Library* 4th ser., 11 (1930), 121–49

Skeat, W. W. (ed.), *The Vision of William Concerning Piers the Plowman*, 2 vols. (Oxford, 1886)

Stephan, John, "The Last Will and Testament of Gabriel Dunne, Abbot of Buckfast," *Buckfast Abbey Chronicle* 27 (1951), 173–82

Stow, John, *Stow's Survey of London*, ed. C. L. Kingsford, 2 vols. (London, 1972)

Strype, John, *Ecclesiastical Memorials Relating Chiefly to Religion, and the Reformation of It, and the Emergencies of the Church of England, under King Henry VIII, King Edward VI and Queen Mary I*, 6 vols. (Oxford, 1822)
Memorials of … Thomas Cranmer, 3 vols. (Oxford, 1812)

Surtz, Edward, *The Works and Days of John Fisher* (Cambridge, MA, 1967)

Sutton, Anne, "Lady Joan Bradbury (d. 1530)," in C. M. Barron and A. F. Sutton (eds.), *Medieval London Widows 1300–1500* (London, 1994), pp. 208–38

Tauler, Johannes, *Johannes Tauler, Sermons*, trans. Maria Shrady (New York, 1985)

Thompson, A. Hamilton (ed.), *Visitations in the Diocese of Lincoln 1517–1531*, 3 vols., Lincoln Record Society 33, 35, 37 (Hereford, 1940, 1944, 1947)

Thompson, E. Margaret, *The Carthusian Order in England* (London, 1930)

Tite, Colin G. C., *The Early Records of Sir Robert Cotton's Library: Formation, Cataloguing, Use* (London, 2003)

Tittler, Robert, "Money-Lending in the West Midlands: The Activities of Jane Jeffries 1638–49," *Bulletin of the Institute for Historical Research* 67 (1944), 249–63

Travitsky, Betty, "Bibliography of English Women Writers 1500–1640," online: www.itergateway.org/mrts/earlywomen/index.cfm?action=showwriter&id=599

Trollope, William, *A History of the Royal Foundation of Christ's Hospital* (London, 1834)

Van Nieuwenhove, Rik, "Hendrik Herp, *A Mirror of Perfection, Part 4*," in Rik van Nieuwenhove, Robert Raeson, SJ, and Helen Rolfson (eds.), *Late Medieval Mysticism of the Low Countries* (New York, 2008), pp. 144–64

Wabuda, Susan, "Bishops and the Provision of Homilies 1520 to 1547," *Sixteenth-Century Journal* 25.3 (1994), 551–66

Preaching during the English Reformation (Cambridge, 2002)

Wainewright, John Bannerman, "Two Lists of Influential Persons Apparently Prepared in the Interests of Mary, Queen of Scots, 1574 and 1582," *Miscellanea VIII*, Catholic Record Society 13 (London, 1913)

Walker, Claire, "Continuity and Isolation: The Bridgettines of Syon in the Sixteenth and Seventeenth Centuries," in Jones and Walsham, *Syon Abbey* (Woodbridge, 2010), pp. 155–76

Walters, H. B., *London Churches at the Reformation* (London, 1939)

Warner, Lawrence, "New Light on Piers Plowman's Ownership ca. 1450–1600," *Journal of the Early Book Society* 12 (2009), 183–94

Warren, Ann K., *Anchorites and Their Patrons in Medieval England* (Berkeley, 1985)

Warren, Nancy Bradley, *The Embodied Word, Female Spirituality, Contested Orthodoxies, and English Religious Cultures, 1350–1700* (Notre Dame, 2010)

Webb, E. A. (ed.), *The Records of St. Bartholomew's Priory and of the Church and Parish of St. Bartholomew the Great, West Smithfield*, 2 vols. (Oxford, 1921)

Welch, Charles (ed.), *The Churchwardens' Accounts of the Parish of All Hallows, London Wall* (London, 1912)

Westlake, H. R., *The Parish Gilds of Mediaeval England* (London, 1919)

Whitfield, Peter, *London, A Life in Maps* (London, 2006)

Wilkins, David, *Concilia Magnae Britanniae et Hiberniae ab Anno MDXLVI ad Annum MDCCXVII*, 4 vols. (London, 1731)

Williams, Franklin B., Jr., *Index of Dedications and Commendatory Verses in English Books before 1641* (London, 1962)

Williams, Glanmore, *Wales and the Reformation* (Cardiff, 1997)

Wizeman, William, *The Theology and Spirituality of Mary Tudor's Church* (Aldershot, 2006)

Wooding, Lucy E. C., *Rethinking Catholicism in Reformation England* (Oxford, 2000)

Woodruff, C. Eveleigh (ed.), *Sede Vacante Wills: A Calendar of Wills Proved before the Commissary of the Prior and Chapter of Christ Church, Canterbury*, vol. III (Canterbury, 1914)

Wright, Thomas (ed.), *Three Chapters of Letters Relating to the Suppression of Monasteries*, Camden Society 26 (London, 1843)

Wriothesley, Charles, *A Chronicle of England during the Reigns of the Tudors, from A.D. 1485 to 1559*, 2 vols., Camden Society (Westminster, 1875–77)

Wunderli, R., "Pre-Reformation London Summoners and the Murder of Richard Hunne," *JEH* 33 (1982), 209–24

Index